fellatio

Philosophy and Friendship

For Rob, Katie and Patrick

Philosophy and Friendship

Sandra Lynch

Edinburgh University Press

© Sandra Lynch, 2005

Edinburgh University Press Ltd
22 George Square, Edinburgh

Typeset in Sabon and Futura
by Servis Filmsetting Ltd, Manchester, and
printed and bound in Great Britain by
The Cromwell Press, Trowbridge, Wilts

A CIP record for this book is available from the British Library

ISBN 0 7486 1727 2 (hardback)

The right of Sandra Lynch
to be identified as author of this work
has been asserted in accordance with
the Copyright, Designs and Patents Act 1988.

Contents

Acknowledgements

Parts of this book were written during a period in which I was teaching in the School of Philosophy at the University of New South Wales in Sydney and in receipt of a Women's Research Award at that university. I am grateful for the assistance I received during the tenure of this award from Emeritus Professor Mary Chan, who encouraged and assisted me in drafting a proposal for this book. I also wish to express my appreciation of the support and encouragement of Emeritus Professor Genevieve Lloyd in getting the book under way and for her role in general as my mentor. In addition, I want to acknowledge my philosophical mentors in the Departments of Philosophy at the University of Illinois and Macquarie University, particularly Associate Professor Ross Poole, who supervised my Master's thesis on the topic of friendship. I thank the University of New South Wales for the access it has allowed me to library facilities there.

Portions of the manuscript have been presented at the Conference of the Australian Society of Continental Philosophy at the University of NSW (Australia) in 2000, and at the UNESCO Conference 'Philosophical Issues in Educating for Democracy', also at the University of NSW in 2002, and at the University of Deusto (Spain) in 2000.

For comments on the manuscript I am grateful to Rob Lynch, Katie Lynch, Anna Roache and two anonymous referees at Edinburgh University Press. But most especially I want to express my gratitude to my friend Dr Christina McWilliam, whose lucid, insightful comments and helpful suggestions on almost the entire manuscript I found invaluable. The book has benefited from her skill as a critical reader, and her support, sense of humour and common sense encouraged me throughout the process.

I am also grateful to family and close friends who have patiently supported me over the period during which the manuscript has been written. They have encouraged and helped me in all manner of ways and I hope they are aware of how much I value that support. Finally, I want to thank Jackie Jones, editorial director at Edinburgh University Press, for her positive and supportive approach to this project; and Fiona Sewell for her work as copy editor of the manuscript.

Preface

Contemporary commentators on friendship have lamented what they identify as a relatively recent period during which the topic of friendship has been neglected within the philosophical tradition. Wayne Booth's comments provide an example.

> The neglect of friendship as a serious subject of inquiry in modern thought is itself a strange and wondrous thing; after millennia during which it was one of the major philosophical topics, the subject of thousands of books and tens of thousands of essays, it has now dwindled to the point that our encyclopedias do not even mention it. The fourth edition of the *Encyclopaedia Britannica* (1810) had twenty long columns on 'friendship' . . . But friendship is not even mentioned, as a general topic or in the index, in *The Encyclopaedia of Philosophy*.[1]

In fact, if we take Michael Pakaluk's anthology of the pre-eminent philosophical texts on friendship in the West, *Other Selves*, as a benchmark, there are significant contributions to the canon in the third century BC, the first century BC, the first century AD, and then in every century since the twelfth century, with the exception of the fourteenth century. Friendship has been neglected in the relatively recent past, but from within the context of contributions over the centuries that neglect seems less striking. Rather the persistence of philosophical regard for friendship is intriguing, especially in the context of the practical limitations that certain features of modern life impose upon friendship. The mobility, urban dislocation, time constraints, transience and heterogeneity that characterise modern life might be expected to disrupt conceptions of friendship constructed within the context of life in more homogeneous societies.

Underlying the heterogeneity that characterises modern society is an appreciation – perhaps even a veneration – of individuality and freedom of choice; and these concerns are reflected in the nature of our relations with friends. Their currency supports Georg Simmel and Ronald Sharp in their view of friendship in modern Western society as generally a privatised relationship; one which is characterised by non-formal and non-prescriptive modes of interaction, by spontaneity and by interaction on the basis of feeling and inclination. This book argues that this lack of prescription, in part due to the voluntary nature of friendship, opens relations between friends to creative construction, to some uncertainty with regard to what friends can expect of one another. At the same time, this creativity and uncertainty within interactions between friends make friendship a vulnerable and potentially fragile relationship. Friends are apt to misunderstand or misinterpret one another. Relations that emphasise individuality and free choice are apt to be confused with or degenerate into relations in which self-interest or self-gratification guide our actions. The book argues that this should not be taken to imply that friendship is necessarily free of self-interest; rather it implies that the pleasure, personal gain or support we enjoy within friendship do not provide us with motives for our engagement with friends. Cynical dismissals of friendship as a relationship of self-interest are simplistic responses to the complex motivations operating in relations among friends.

We are vulnerable to pain and disappointment in friendship, since friends have in common with enemies the capacity to hurt us. This dimension of relations between friends is not generally emphasised within the philosophical tradition on friendship. Among the ancients, the most influential figures within the tradition idealise friendship as a relationship between virtuous men, characterised by a complete union of feeling on all subjects. But it is Montaigne, writing in the sixteenth century, who is unsurpassed in his idealisation of friendship. He describes the friendship he shared with Etienne de La Boétie as 'so entire and so perfect that certainly you will hardly read of the like, and among men of today you see no trace of it in practice. So many coincidences are needed to build up such a friendship that it is a lot if fortune can do it once in three centuries.'[2] This notion of complete union between friends has its appeal for modern and pre-modern audiences alike. However, this book responds to the demands of rational reflection to take a critical eye to this ideal of a rare and perfect friendship. It sees highly idealised treatments of friendship as producing relatively static conceptions, which downplay the significance of friendship as a dynamic relationship between individuals. Such treatments fail to take account of the more familiar and less perfect friendships that we experience to differing degrees and within different contexts in everyday life, or to appreciate the way in which the meaning of friendship emerges through interaction between friends. The heterogeneity of modern life is regarded as making friendship more difficult to sustain for modern individuals than it would have been for the good men of Aristotle's homogeneous Greek polis – at least in Aristotle's version of the polis. Modern friends are required to be alive to the limits of their understanding of one another, able to tolerate difference and perhaps even to weather a storm; and discourse on friend-ship ought to be able to recognise that friendships are often disturbed by misunderstandings, unmet expectations or disagreements.

This book recognises friendship as valuable to us, despite the risk of experiencing pain, distress and disillusionment. This kind of risk might seem to be more characteristic of enmity than friendship, but it is worth remembering that we are put into relation by emotions like hate, as well as by liking and affection. Spinoza has some sensible advice about the nature of sociability in this respect. As Lloyd and Gatens interpret him, he tells us that '[d]ynamic relations between individuals – Spinoza's version of sociability – inevitably involve negative as well as positive emotions; hate as well as love and civic friendship'.[3] If we acknowledge friendship as a dynamic relation between individuals we can apply the force of these comments to relations between friends. We can acknowledge friendship as a relationship that will inevitably involve negative as well as positive emo-tions; and we can recognise the potential of conflict and negative emotion to disrupt or undermine a friendship. Yet, just as enmity can be valuable in that our social engagement with an enemy can lead us to reassess our-selves and our relations with others, this book argues that disruption in our engagement with friends can be similarly valuable. Of course, we can dismiss enemies, faithless friends or friends who disappoint us. But the juxtaposition of liking, care and affection with the recognition of differ-ence or conflict makes that dismissal more complicated in the case of friends. Commitment to the Aristotelian maxim that friends of the best kind like and care for one another as persons in themselves presents modern friends with a dilemma. The maxim prohibits motivation on the basis of self-interest or an ulterior purpose. But as the book argues, it is vague in terms of what it is to like and care for others in themselves, or what kind of behaviour treating friends as ends in themselves might require friends to exhibit.

In its consideration of the extent to which modern preoccupations with friendship mirror ancient and pre-modern conceptions, the book draws out the value, pleasures and (often latent) power of friendship in human life. At the same time, it recognises the tensions, conflicts and darker motivations often inherent in the relationship. In the *Nichomachean Ethics*, for example, Aristotle argues that friendship is necessary for life and that no one would choose to live without friends, since friendship is conducive to happiness. He insists that human beings are naturally inclined to make friends; and Cicero, Kant and Emerson agree with him. This might confirm contemporary views that we value friendship because it satisfies deep-seated human needs and desires. But the book argues that this cannot be the full story, since while friendship might be natural, it is not inevitable or predetermined. Friendship is a voluntary relationship and, as Elizabeth Telfer argues, its development among children can be fostered or inhibited.[4] Acknowledging this, the book draws attention to the way in which the formative experiences of life can affect an individual's capacity to make friends and to the psychological characteristics that underpin that capacity. Our capacity to respond to and comply with ill-defined norms of friendship is seen as affected by early life experience and the understanding of relations with others that we develop in response to that experience. While we might be naturally inclined to form friendships, contemporary commentators can acknowledge that there is much about us, our upbringing, and the society or culture of which we are a part that will affect the nature of the friendships we share with others.

Post-Freudian societies will necessarily take different views of the self and its relations with others from those that might be extracted from ancient texts. Thus relatively recent neglect of friendship may have been a consequence of contemporary reactions to this lack of fit. It may also be explained by the idealisation of friendship evident in the work of Aristotle, Cicero and Montaigne; to the spirituality of the accounts of Aelred of Rievaulx and Aquinas; or perhaps to the sentimentality evident in Emerson's treatment of friendship. Pakaluk suggests an alternative, though not unrelated, reason for the recent neglect of friendship in the philosophical literature. His explanation focuses on the place of friendship in contemporary ethical thought. He argues that this neglect is a function of the difficulty that some contemporary moral theories face in accommodating friendship.[5] Friendship cannot neatly be imbedded within theories that are concerned with universalisability and impartiality, or within theories concerned with human beings in general, rather than those we choose as friends. Hence friendship becomes ethically problematic for those theories. Ethical theories that focus on the individual and the idea of living well can accommodate relations between friends. But they face the difficulty of balancing an individual's concern for a friend with appropriate concern for herself within those relations; issues of sincerity and authenticity arise in this regard.

What seems most problematic for ethical theories is the difficulty of providing an analysis of friendship that can account for two features simultaneously. The first of these is the personal significance of our social engagement with our friends, despite tensions or misunderstandings that may arise between friends. The second feature is the morally significant dimensions of our engagement with friends. The fact that friendship is not only possible, but actual in a world that in many ways militates against it, suggests the force of friendship's significance in human life. It indicates both the depth of our need for friendship and our capacity to move beyond our own immediate concerns to respond to the needs and concerns of others. That we engage with friends out of both need and desire paints a sanguine picture of our natures.

This book attempts to address the difficulty of accounting for both the personal and the ethical significance of friendship. It does so via a consideration of notions of similarity and difference between friends and an exploration of the concepts of duty and respect in friendship. Friendship is seen as predicated upon a tension between similarity and difference, and the relationship's personal significance for us is seen as dependent upon the way in which we respond to that tension. The ethical significance of friendship is discussed within the context of a reinterpretation of Aristotle's distinction between civic friendship and his more personal form of friendship, and an analogous reinterpretation of Kant's distinction between practical and pathological love. This work of reinterpretation offers a way of appreciating friendship's personal significance without denying its ethical significance or the role of duty in friendship; it also draws attention to friendship's relationship to theories of morality that emphasise universalisability and impartiality.

My philosophical interest in friendship was first explored in research towards a Master's degree undertaken fifteen years ago. That interest in friendship became entwined with doctoral research towards a thesis on the process of self-constitution. The doctoral thesis took David Hume as the starting point for an analysis of the interaction of reason, imagination and emotion in the process of self-constitution. The structure of this book reflects the history of these academic interests. Part I examines the way in which the term 'friend' is used colloquially and in the philosophical literature. It considers the difficulties that emerge from that usage and compares different models or principles that have been adopted in the literature as accounts of friendship. Part II considers the ethical significance of friendship and the role of duty in friendship, including the question of whether the principle upon which friendship is founded might be duty. Part III argues for the contribution that friendship can make to self-understanding and explores the particular view of the process of self-constitution that makes such an argument possible and reasonable. This final part includes a comparison between ancient and modern conceptions of friendship. The book argues that the possibility of friendship is founded on a particular kind of motivation and on particular understandings of relations with others. But equally it sees the possibility of friendship as coinciding with its creativity. Friendship demands a capacity differentially distributed within society – the capacity to create and appreciate forms of interaction that embody those motivations and understandings.

Notes

1. Booth, *The Company We Keep*, pp. 170–1.
2. Montaigne, 'Of Friendship', p. 136.
3. Gatens and Lloyd, *Collective Imaginings*, p. 68.
4. Telfer, 'Friendship', p. 266
5. Pakaluk, *Other Selves*, pp. vii–xi.

Part I

Identity and Difference in Philosophical Conceptions of Friendship

Chapter 1

Approaching the Kaleidoscope of Friendship

Friendship: the Fluidity of the Concept

Friendship, Cicero tells us, 'is a kaleidoscope and complicated thing'.[1] We might add a fascinating thing; a kind of love perhaps and an enigma to us. Unlike love, which, on some accounts, is regarded as involuntary, friendship maintains an element of freedom of choice. In common with love, it involves a relationship between two beings and so draws us into the mystery of the difficult notion of the individual in himself or herself. The history of the philosophical literature on friendship reveals a changing semantic paradigm in relation to this notion. We are curious about friendship because as social creatures we are born into relation with others and, as Aristotle argues, are naturally constituted to live in company. Aristotle refines his comments to claim that 'man is by nature a pairing rather than a social creature'.[2] The particular kind of pairing that we find in friendship is intriguing, since unlike familial relationships the bond between the partners to a friendship is not determined by circumstance, but must be created. A case could be made to suggest that friendship relations are a triumphant achievement of our species. When romantic love tempers, it often transforms itself into what Plato would have seen as a higher form of love: that of friendship. Today in modern cities the phenomenon of the 'urban tribe' has emerged; the term refers to groups of friends who join forces to provide for each other the support, affection, company and sense of connection that were previously found in familial or marital relations.

This chapter examines some facets of the kaleidoscope that is friendship. It considers the etymological history of the term, its various uses and misuses, drawing examples from the poetry and philosophy of the ancient Greeks as well as from current usage. The taxonomies of friendship constructed by Aristotle and Kant are examined as stimulating instances of the struggle to come to grips with this difficult phenomenon. Aristotle in particular provides a set of standards to which many of the ideas throughout the book respond. While this chapter begins with an attempt to discover what friendship is or what it is that is typical of relations between friends, it concludes with a reorientation of the question – one suggested by Jacques Derrida. Derrida tells us that all searches for the origins and ends of meaning, all definitions, can only fall short. Meaning is always 'under erasure', endlessly deferred and fluid; so that 'all the categories and axioms which have constituted the concept of friendship in its history have let themselves be threatened with ruin'.[3] Consequently, Derrida argues that we can no longer ask: 'What is friendship?' Rather our query must be: 'Who is the friend?' In this respect I concur with Derrida. Our experience of the actual friend will inform, transform and enrich what we receive from the philosophical heritage. It is via our enquiry into the nature of the friend, our understanding and expectations of the other and of ourselves as friends, that we will come to any understanding of our relations with friends. Finally, my analysis prompts the observation that Wittgenstein's notion of the 'family resemblance' concept might be useful in trying to understand friendship. The concept refers to a fluid linguistic paradigm that is derived from practical contexts.

The word 'friend' is derived from the Old English words *freon* – which meant 'free' – and *freo* – which meant 'love'. It is also derived from the Old Teutonic *frijôjan* and the Dutch *vriend* – both of which originally meant 'love'. (Cicero also draws attention to the similarity between *amor* (love) and *amicitia* (friendship).)[4] These denotations capture two important aspects of the modern English term. First, friendship involves an emotional bond: a friend is one for whom we have a depth of feeling. The emotional attachment between friends is a mutual and reciprocal one: friends feel deeply towards each other and know that this feeling is reciprocated. A friend is probably aware that her friend also recognises this. Thus friendship involves not just feeling, but knowledge. This knowledge is not simply of each other's liking, but also of character, personality and general affairs. Friends have – or at least aspire to – an intimate knowledge of one another. The depth of feeling between friends and the intimacy of their knowledge puts them in a potentially vulnerable position in relation to one another. This vulnerability draws attention to the role of trust between friends. As Cicero argues, trust is 'the foundation of that steadfastness and loyalty for which we are looking in friendship'.[5] The kind of confident expectation that explains trust implies a commitment that cannot be adequately characterised in terms of its purposes – at least not in a narrowly instrumental way. As such it is a commitment that delivers participants in a friendship both rewards and challenges.

The second aspect that the etymology of the word 'friend' reveals is that friendship is a voluntary relationship: it is freely entered into and can be freely given up. This element of choice is crucial in friendship. We cannot make a friend of someone simply on the grounds that we find that person appealing. I might enjoy someone's sense of humour, admire her talents or her character, but her appeal to me does not guarantee that I can make her my friend. Similarly, I cannot be forced to become a friend. However, volition also brings a certain vulnerability and fragility to the relationship. From an etymological perspective, the emotional bond between friends and the voluntary nature of the relationship are central characteristics of friendship, but they are not sufficient to explain the genesis and cultivation of friendship. However, these characteristics are sufficient to permit a contrast with what might be seen as deviant or at least debased uses of the term 'friend'. Some of these are so depersonalised as to be empty formalities. Take for example the barrister's customary and ironic mode of address to a colleague, 'my learned friend'. Others indicate a relationship that is basically instrumental in nature. For example, among members of the Mafia in modern Sicily, friendship is viewed as a relationship of equal exchange. Jeremy Boissevain quotes his informant, a *professore*, offering an explanation of a favour done for him by one mafioso:

> 'He helped me for *amiticizia*, for friendship. Because of our father we have friends all over Sicily. They are not criminals. They are men who make themselves respected. They will help you when you need it, but . . . when they turn to you for help, you give it or . . .' and he made the chopping motion that means the application of violence.[6]

Whatever the social importance of friendship in the mafioso's sense of the word, it is clearly unlike the relationship of freely entered and affectionate reciprocity that the etymology of the word leads us to expect. There is a bond between the mafiosi; they exhibit commitment to a shared relationship, but not the passion or freedom of choice which are the desiderata of the etymological account.

This example reveals that the etymological analysis of the word 'friend' does not take account of the kind of activity that friends engage in and which is requisite to the bond created between them. We could measure the mafioso's view of friendship against a modern account of friendship given by Elizabeth Telfer. Telfer identifies a set of necessary conditions which she argues are jointly sufficient as an analysis of friendship. She argues that what she identifies as the 'shared activity' condition and the *'passions'* of friendship are two features that constitute necessary conditions of friendship.[7] Shared activity takes the form of reciprocal services, mutual contact and joint pursuits, which are necessary to relations between friends, but on their own are not sufficient to identify the relationship as one of friendship. The relations between members of the Mafia could easily satisfy the shared activity condition, but they cannot be regarded as friends simply on the strength of that kind of activity. Neighbours, business associates and members of sporting teams can be involved in such activity without regarding themselves as friends or being regarded as friends by others. Telfer argues that friends must also display the passions of friendship, that is, they must have affection for, be fond of and like one another; they must have 'a desire for another's welfare distinguished both from a sense of duty and from benevolence'.[8] Duty and benevolence are motives that lead us to display concern for others in general; whereas affection differs in that it is an attitude in which we wish the best for a particular person, take that person seriously, engage with her and desire her company as a particular individual. The relationships between the mafiosi as presented by Boissevain do not appear to meet this condition.

The mafiosi are engaged in what could be called alliances. Their relationships are not valued in themselves but serve as a means for satisfying other ends. Seneca would dismiss these kinds of relationships as 'bargains', arguing that '[o]ne who seeks friendship for favourable occasions, strips it of all its nobility'. Cicero expresses similar sentiments: 'we do not exercise kindness and generosity in order that we may put in a claim for gratitude; we do not make our feelings of affection into a business proposition . . . we are not led to friendship by the hope of material gain'.[9] Those who form friendships for the sake of utility or advantage destroy goodwill, which is the link in friendship that is most productive of affection on Cicero's view. 'It is not so much what we gain from our friend as the very love of the friend itself that gives us joy, and what we get from a friend gives us joy since it comes to us with love . . . No, truly: friendship does not follow upon advantage, but advantage upon friendship.'[10]

However, to give the passions of friendship, affection and liking, the status of necessary conditions, as Telfer does, might appear to be incompatible with the other elements that emerged from my etymological analysis: the fact that it involves choice and commitment. If we claim that we can choose our friends, but we hold that we cannot choose our feelings, then we might want to say that affection and liking are reasons for friendship, rather than necessary conditions. Telfer answers this objection by explaining that friendship is not like marriage, in the sense that we normally enter into marriage on the basis of certain feelings but that a marriage has a formal or legal status whether or not the feelings obtain. Her argument is that affection and liking as necessary conditions are compatible with choice in friendship, since the right passions are necessary in friendship, but they are not by themselves sufficient; the friends must exercise choice in acting on their feelings. Of course, there is more to it than this and Telfer acknowledges that the process by which a friendship develops between two people must be a mutual one and may well be gradual.[11] Friendship, unlike marriage, may develop over time or just spring up, so that it might be difficult to identify a formal beginning. For Telfer, the two features she identifies as shared activity and the passions of friendship, along with the friends' acknowledgement of these two conditions, constitute three conditions that when satisfied are jointly sufficient for friendship.

While the Sicilian *professore*'s relationship with the mafioso appears to satisfy Telfer's shared activity condition, it fails with regard to the passions of friendship. What appears to motivate the mafioso's activity is a sense of duty and the fear of retribution, rather than affection. The *professore* has inherited the relationship and he is bound not by any depth of feeling, but by the acceptance of an obligation that fear of retribution induces him to honour; the notion of choice becomes a mute point. In the face of this perhaps deviant, or at least debased, usage of the term 'friend', as well as the barrister's ironic usage, we are left to consider how we are to think of friendship. In fact these usages of the semantic cluster that surrounds friendship are enlightening in their confusion. They highlight – in a negative dialectic – those features that lead us to question the designation of a relationship as friendship. At the same time, the etymological analysis of this semantic cluster reveals several recurring characteristics: the notions of freedom of choice, passion, commitment and mutual recognition. These notions all appear in various guises in some of the earliest writing on friendship in ancient Greek literature and philosophy. But, as we shall see, the mafioso's understanding of friendship also has some important parallels with earlier conceptions of friendship and earlier usages of the term 'friend'.

Ancient Notions of Friendship

From Homer we receive a relatively unquestioning depiction of friendship as a formal relationship. The complexities in his and other ancient Greek accounts lie in the links made between unusual protagonists. Treaties between states as allies, between the warrior and his anthropomorphised weapons, and between the warriors themselves are all referred to as friendly relations. However, in the work of Plato and Aristotle, friendship is problematised in analyses that both appreciate the multifaceted nature of relations between those we call friends, and reveal the nuanced emotional, ethical and functional aspects of those relations.

In heroic society friendship was closely connected with virtue, which in turn was displayed in the fulfilment of socially allotted roles. The good or just man displayed the virtues appropriate to his social role. Thus in the Homeric epic, justice requires that one defend one's friends and harm one's enemies. This standard reflects a pragmatic idea of friendship, one that is explained by the precarious nature of Homeric life. Friendship is portrayed as a relation of last resort in times of extreme need. As such it is a structure of support that resonates with the modern-day mafioso's views on friendship, but like those views it militates against the idea of loyalty or love freely given. Homer's protagonists perceive the world as essentially hostile and indifferent. Each warrior-chieftain in Homer's Ithaca led a virtually autonomous household.[12] As leaders, these warriors could meet to discuss concerns of mutual interest, but in fact they did so very rarely. For example, during the twenty years of Odysseus' absence only one meeting took place, and Odysseus's son Telemachus summoned that just prior to his father's homecoming, ten years after the fall of Troy. The rarity of such meetings allowed each warrior-chieftain his autonomy but meant that each faced possible or actual competition with equally autonomous households for the produce of a relatively infertile land. The concept of kinship or tribe, which figures predominantly in other early societies, is muted in Homer's Greece. Without such an overarching concept, essentially combative relations came to the fore in the Homeric epics. Although the virtue of the warrior-chieftain was strength, strength alone did not guarantee survival; it was crucial that he be able to rely on others. In the first instance he relied on family, servants and possessions. But since these were often insufficient to ensure security and wellbeing, there was also a need for an institutional framework of co-operation and mutual aid.

Such co-operative relationships were referred to as guest-friendships and, as Suzanne Stern-Gillet points out, they are ideally and famously exemplified in the encounter between Oedipus and Theseus in Sophocles' *Oedipus at Colonus*.[13] The individual who built up a network of others outside his own household, upon whom he could rely in times of hardship or when in danger, increased the chances of survival for himself and his family. Warrior-chieftains were therefore primarily interested in the actions that a guest-friend would reliably undertake to prevent him from harm. The virtues admired in such a friend were courage, fidelity and sacrifice. The relations between warrior-chieftains were based on the shared activity of martial struggle; and there was a formal acknowledgement between allies that resonates with the elements of the preceding discussion. Yet to these warriors, actions and results were paramount. Emotions and intentions were understated, if not repressed or irrelevant. Utility, rather than passion, comes to the fore in guest-friendship.

For Homer's protagonists reciprocal action and co-operation were crucial to the relationship between guest-friends. When an individual travelled away from his household, the only rights of which he was assured were those guaranteed by a well-disposed member of the community he had entered. The traveller was a 'comer' or 'suppliant' and had to rely upon being accepted by a sufficiently powerful member of that community in order to enjoy food, shelter and protection. He was not, however, regarded as a guest-friend unless he enjoyed a status equal to that of his benefactor, so that he was in a position to return the favours bestowed upon him, at some future date. This is not to say that the Homeric warrior-chieftain only befriended strangers from entirely utilitarian motives – the stranger was after all the immediate beneficiary – but nor was the action entirely altruistic, given the obligation it imposed.

While commitment to a guest friend might imply a certain degree of warmth, relations between warrior-chieftains did not involve ties of an emotional kind, and hence were more like bonds of social obligation than friendships in the more modern sense. It was not even necessary for guest-friends to know one another, since descendants of those who established the relationship could inherit it. In the *Iliad* the Greek Diomedes fights valiantly in battle until he encounters among the enemy Glaucos, a Lycian, a guest-friend of his own family. The two had never met, but by virtue of a compact of guest-friendship between their grandfathers, they do not engage in battle. In token of the friendship they exchange armour and agree to avoid each other.[14] Diomedes and Glaucos had never seen one another prior to their meeting on the battlefield. Their intentions and actions derive from the social relationship they discover themselves to share and the obligations that relationship imposes upon them, rather than those intentions and actions being the origin of their relationship. The trans-generational nature of their treaty brings an interesting complication to contemporary attempts to understand this kind of relationship as friendship.

The expectations and obligations imposed by social roles appear to play a crucial role in the lives of the protagonists of Homer's epics. E. R. Dodds argues that respect for public opinion (*aidōs*) is the strongest moral force that Homeric man knows, and that the enjoyment of public esteem is his highest good.[15] Achilles is not enticed to fight by the promise of the spoils of war, and in fact he notes that staking his life in war has not brought him any great portion of such treasures. He who fights and he who remains behind both receive a portion; the brave man and the coward are held 'in one estimation' as regards the spoils of war. Thus Achilles suggests that there is no reason to fight other than the kudos one receives in victory, since it is this public esteem that bestows upon Achilles his status as warrior and his place in society.[16] The pressure of social conformity generally evident in the Homeric epics can be explained by the fact that conformity to social expectations provides the Homeric individual with the major source of unity that he is likely to experience. Peter Jackson has argued that the *Iliad* is characterised by 'the absence of a central, co-ordinating centre of consciousness, volition and emotion in the self – a subject'.[17] Jackson's point is that the Homeric individual derives his sense of himself from his place in society and from his achievements and relations within that society. From a contemporary perspective we might say that the subjectivity of the Homeric individual was 'decentred' or culturally derived. Dodds's view that 'Homeric man has no unified concept of what we call "soul" or "personality"' would seem to support such an assessment.[18] As a consequence of this feature of Homeric life, objective conformity to the expectations of friendship is more significant than action in conformity with feeling for the Homeric individual. Stern-Gillet acknowledges these features of Homeric life when she notes that pre-classical Greek friendship is 'a social institution which has little to do with the inner lives of individuals'.[19]

My discussion of guest-friendship is not intended to indicate that Homer's characterisation of friendship lacks any reference at all to passion or feeling. *Philos* is used by Homer to refer to a number of different kinds of bond. Stern-Gillet explains that it is used as a possessive reflexive, for example to indicate one's relationship to one's own body parts (*phila gounata* – one's knees); it is also used as an adjective which designates those one loves or members of one's household; and finally it is used as we have indicated to designate those connected by the bond of guest-friendship.[20] Not surprisingly, the English word cannot accurately capture the extent of the Greek usage. Adkins uses a slightly different categorisation in an attempt to clarify ancient Greek usage, distinguishing an emotive and a descriptive aspect of the word.[21] However, what he calls the emotive aspect does not signify the kind of feeling that contemporary readers would associate with friendship; rather it signifies possession and is always passive in sense. While it can be translated as 'one's own', 'dear' or 'beloved' in English, the translation must capture the feeling that the Homeric individual – almost invariably a male – feels for what belongs to him, for what is his own. The object of his affection may be an inanimate object or another person, but it is dear to him primarily because of the contribution it makes to his own survival. This possessive aspect of the word 'friend' might suggest that Homeric usage was egocentric, a desire for friends simply reflecting a concern for one's own survival. This is a possible interpretation, but the emotive-possessive aspect can simply be taken as a reflection of the functional view of friendship that is typical of the Homeric poems. The descriptive aspect of the term that Adkins distinguishes differs from the emotive in that it is active in sense. It refers to the act of befriending that created and maintained a co-operative relationship between two guest-friends; one that then survived within their respective communities and was inherited by their descendants, thus becoming property in a different sense.

Although guest-friendship was certainly the most important kind of friendship Homer recognised, it is clear that there are in both the *Iliad* and the *Odyssey* indications of the existence of a more intimate notion of friendship. It is one that spills over the rigid contours of the code of friendship and heroic duty and becomes something closer to modern expectations of friendship. For example, Achilles' guiding principle was his thirst for personal honour. This prompted not only his disrespect towards Agamemnon, but also his neglect of the plight of his fellow warriors. However, when his friend Patroclus was killed in battle, Achilles realised that his stubbornness and resentment at being slighted had outweighed his affection and concern for his friend and had brought their own punishment. His grief made him anxious to avenge Patroclus' death, despite the prophecy of his own death:

> the black cloud of sorrow covered Achilles: and with both hands he took the grimy dust, and cast it on his head, and disfigured his fair face; and the black ashes clung to his celestial garment. And flung at all his length he lay in the dust, and tore his hair, and marred it with his hands . . . And over against them Antilochus wept and wailed, holding Achilles by the hands, who groaned within his noble heart – for he feared lest he should lay the iron to his throat.

Achilles himself lamented:

> since my dear friend is dead, Patroclus, whom I honoured above all my friends, and cherished as myself. Him have I lost . . . Let me die at once, since it was not mine to help my friend in death; far from his fatherland he fell, and found not me beside him, to ward off woe. And now, – since I return not to my country dear, and succoured not Patroclus, nor many more my friends, who died before divine Hector, but sit unprofitable beside my ships, a cumberer of the ground, – I, who am such in war as is none other of the bronzen-coated Achaeans.[22]

The relationship between Achilles and Patroclus reached levels of intensity inconceivable by the standards of guest-friendship. By comparison with the pragmatic nature of guest-friendship, it had a selfless quality that moved Achilles beyond a concern for his own honour. Even a modern sensibility, unaccustomed to the formality of many of the Homeric social relations, must be moved by Homer's portrayal of the tragic devotion between the two friends. This more intimate and altruistic notion of friendship is also evident in the relationship between Orestes and Pylades. Pylades' father disowned Pylades for his part in aiding Orestes and his sister, Electra, to avenge the murder of their father by in turn murdering their mother and her lover. Pylades refused to abandon Orestes or Electra and accompanied them into exile, gaining nothing by his loyalty except to share in his friends' fate.

Relations among Greek hetairoi constituted another friendship grouping that allowed for a more intimate relationship than that consistent with guest-friendship. It was generally made up of a group of men of similar status, although there were female hetairai in both Sparta and Mytilene.[23] Each of the heroes of the *Iliad* and the *Odyssey* is described as supported by a group of hetairoi, and friendship groups of this type became the basis of military organisation in both Crete and Thebes. These groups must have made some contribution to the limited reliability of Homeric life and politics. However Plato, in the *Laws*, recognised that such relationships had as much potential for creating division as they did for engendering solidarity. Within his dialogues he explores a tension between love (*eros*) and friendship (*philia*), juxtaposing the two terms with one another in his discussions. For example, in the *Lysis*, when Socrates and Menexus try to establish how one man becomes the friend of another, one translation has Socrates asking whether 'the lover is the friend, but not the loved . . . [or whether] the object of the love . . . is the friend to the lover'.[24] The juxtaposition of friend and lover is not surprising since both *eros* and *philia* are equated with desire of some kind and both involve relations primarily between men. At least in the early stages of the kind of relationship being discussed here, one of the protagonists is said to experience or aim to practise *philia*, while the other was permitted, perhaps even condemned, to endure *eros*. There seems little question over which was the more desirable form of attachment; rather the debate raised questions of protocol and temperateness in regard to the expression of *eros*.

Like Plato, Plutarch also recognised the unifying force of relationships among the hetairoi. But Plato's concern was with their potential to become divisive, fostering competition, jealousy and enslavement to one person. Whether *eros* unified or divided was dependent in part on the extent to which a man was able to control or sublimate his erotic desire. Socrates argued that love must not be guided by an innate desire for pleasure, for enslavement to pleasure is a sickness. Rather love ought to be guided by 'an acquired judgment that aims at what is best'.[25] For Plato the impulse to seek what is highest, 'the beyond' in his terms, is initiated by the process of falling in love with visible physical beauty. Socrates presented love as a gift from the gods; and the lover who followed the noble and philosophic life, forsaking irrational desire and wanton pleasure, was seen as destined to experience celestial bliss after death.

The *Symposium* presents a similar argument, in which love is a longing for the Good, for the eternal, and training in love is regarded as development. Love of an individual body leads to an appreciation of the beauty of all bodies; this brings passion for the individual into due proportion.[26] Love involves a process of going beyond ourselves to an appreciation of universal beauty. Plato's strategy was to construct an overtly metaphysical concept of *eros* as love of the Good and thereby to diminish the significance of non-erotic friendship. However, as noted above, he was well aware that erotic friendship was not without its problems; and in fact in the *Laws* he went so far as to recommend that sexual relations between men be legally prohibited and emphasised the 'injurious consequences' that accompany some hetairic practices, among them devotion to certain physical exercises.[27] The homo-erotic bond between hetairoi of different age and status was a privileged but precarious relationship. It was pedagogical in that the older man was intended to act as tutor to the youth, and yet it was also romanticised. Its precarious nature was due in part to the fact that it was not considered proper to love a youth beyond a certain age, although the boundaries of that age were apt to shift; the fact that boys inevitably grew older and lost their adolescent charms also made the bond unstable.

The specificity of Athenian law regarding the restrictions and prohibi-tions on homosexual love (*paidikon eros*) confirms that the homoerotic bond was problematical for the early Greeks, if not highly susceptible to perversion. During the trial of Timarchus in 345 BC on charges of pederasty, Aeschines discussed the many laws that dealt with the relationship between Greek males. The laws ranged from those restricting the operation of the gymnasium to those that specified penalties for various criminal acts, including fines, imprisonment and execution.[28] The precariousness of the homoerotic bond could be transcended if the relationship developed into one of *philia* or civic friendship, a relation that, as Michel Foucault puts it, 'was lasting, having no other limit than life itself; and . . . [which] obliter-ated the dissymmetries that were implied in the erotic relation between man and adolescent'.[29] Thus for the ancient Greeks it was desirable that *philia* develop from within *eros*, creating, as Foucault goes on to put it, 'an affin-ity of character and mode of life, a sharing of thoughts and existence, mutual benevolence' between the two. The erotic element of the pedagogi-cal relationship was played out; the complementarity of tutor and pupil was transcended and broken by the state as both accepted their responsibility as separate citizens of the polis. They are drawn into a civic commitment, a public friendship. An explicit distinction emerges here between friendship as an erotic bond – what I will call erotic friendship – and friendship as a public relationship – or what I will civic friendship.

A model of friendship as romantic, pedagogical and open to manipula-tion is juxtaposed to a model of friendship as likeness and confirmation of the existing order. *Eros* is sublimated by noble citizens in the service of love of the Good, or it is redefined in a broader sense as 'that Love [which] longs for the good to be his own forever'. The latter is the approach Diotima takes in the *Symposium*, where she distinguishes between a narrow sense of *eros*, which refers to 'only one of Love's many activities', and the broader sense associated with the possession of the Good forever.[30] The model of friend-ship that emerges most forcefully is one akin to Aristotle's view of friend-ship as a bond that unites the virtuous and exclusively male citizens of the polis in a shared conception of the Good. Aristotle defines politics as the business of friends. The Greek polis is presented as an arena of like-minded citizens, who 'agree about their interests, adopt the same policy, and put their common resolves into effect'.[31] The idea that the entire citizenry of the polis was made up of friends demanded that the equality of rights that existed between hetairoi be extended to include all those who share the same political and cultural organisation. This public conception of civic friendship necessarily involves a devaluing of erotic friendship, which 'is for the most part swayed by the feelings and based on pleasure'.[32] The potential for conflict between groups of hetairoi located within a wider democratic organisation, but which had normalised erotic friendships, is resolved and friendship remains a public relationship. Chapter 2 includes discussion of the way in which the ideal of the polis as a community of friends was in fact undermined by practices of exclusion.

This chapter has moved from a consideration of the etymology of the word 'friend' to a discussion of a set of conditions which are jointly regarded as sufficient to reflect contemporary understandings of the relationship in which friends participate. We have examined questionable uses of the term from widely different historical periods, such as that employed by the mafiosi and the guest-friendships depicted in ancient Greek literature. Although these uses seem at odds with the idea of friendship as a relationship of emotional reciprocity, they do exhibit some of the features we commonly associate with friendship. They are reciprocal arrangements that delineate a special – if not an emotional – attachment between the participants; and commitment and trust are evident in the interactions between the participants – even if that commitment is held in place by tradition and fear of retribution. We have seen that ancient Greek philosophy and literature do provide examples of intimate relations of emotional attachment between male friends. But as powerful as these are, they are presented as either incidental to guest-friendships – as in the Homeric epics – or apt to develop into homoerotic relationships. In his treatment of homoerotic love Plato presents a model in which the beloved sets the lover on an epistemological and ethical quest. So Plato leaves us with a conviction that the relationship between the lovers or friends is not the main game for him. By comparison, Aristotle develops a closer connection between friendship of the best kind and the pursuit of goodness. The next section of this chapter examines the taxonomies of friendship that Aristotle and Kant offer, to establish what these taxonomies might contribute to attempts to define friendship. My argument is that analysis of friendship in its various guises undermines efforts to provide one essential or overarching definition of the concept. This is partly because the boundaries of the taxonomies fracture under close inspection from a contemporary perspective; and partly because the analysis reveals a complicated network of similar and also dissimilar features within the various uses of the term 'friend'. These considerations lead me to argue that friendship is best understood as a 'family resemblance' concept.

The Aristotelian Taxonomy

Early in his discussion of friendship in the *Nichomachean Ethics* Aristotle distinguishes three kinds of friendship, arguing that we love or like our friends for three different kinds of reasons or on the basis of three different kinds of motivation. Like the reasons provided by the mafiosi and Homer's guest-friends, Aristotle's reasons can appear to be instrumental. This might be evidence of deviant or debased usage of the term 'friend', since Aristotle himself tells us that only one of the three kinds of friendship identifies the participants as friends in an unqualified sense. However, the difficulty of identifying appropriate motivation can also be taken as an indication of the problems we face in trying to offer an unqualified definition of the term 'friendship'.

Aristotle was undoubtedly correct to insist on the need to distinguish between different reasons or motivations in friendship and to appreciate that we do not aim at the same kind of thing in all instances of friendship. The three kinds of friendship he identifies are friendship of utility or advantage, friendship of pleasure and friendship of the good, which is sometimes referred to as primary friendship. He argues that

> there is in each case a kind of mutual affection known to both parties; and those who love each other wish for each other's good in respect of the quality for which they love them. So those who love each other on the ground of utility do not love each other for their personal qualities, but only in so far as they derive some benefit from each other. Similarly with those who love one another on the ground of pleasure; because it is not for being a certain character that witty people are liked, but because we find them pleasant. So when people love each other on the ground of utility their affection is motivated by their own good, and when they love on the ground of pleasure it is motivated by their own pleasure.[33]

Aristotle offers relationships between foreigners as an example of friendships of utility, while purely erotic or sexual relationships illustrate friendships of pleasure.[34] But unlike these lesser kinds of friendship, friendship of the good 'is permanent, reasonably enough; because in it are united all the attributes that friends ought to possess'.[35] These comments suggest that, at least from an Aristotelian point of view, friendship of the good will be able to provide us with the basis of an overarching definition of friendship. Within such a friendship, the friend desires the good for his friend for the friend's own sake and not for the sake of anything else; 'a man's best friend is the one who not only wishes him well but wishes it for his own sake (even though nobody will ever know it)'.[36] Aristotle presents friendship of the good as 'friendship in the primary and proper sense [since it] is between good men in virtue of their goodness, whereas the rest are friendships only by analogy'.[37] Cicero adopts a similar view, going so far as to suggest that friendship can only exist between good men. However, he does note that he is talking about true and perfect friendship, not the friendships of everyday folk or ordinary people. The latter are a source of pleasure and profit but, unlike true friendships, are not based on virtue, and on his view 'it is hard to keep up a friendship, if one has deserted virtue's camp'.[38]

Thus while Aristotle and Cicero recognise different kinds of friendship, the significance of that recognition is obscured by their emphasis on the ideal or perfect kind. Their approach reflects an inclination to search for best instances, but it also creates a tension between actual friendships and the ideal form. This tension is exacerbated by Aristotle when he goes on to argue that the similarity between those who engage in friendships of utility and pleasure is that they are persons of low character by comparison with friends of the good; their friendships are only incidental to the utility or pleasure they find in the relationship and they are friendships only by analogy with friendship of the good.[39] But Aristotle also states that 'since people describe as friends those who are attracted to one another only for reasons of utility . . . or of pleasure . . . presumably we too should call such people friends'. Aristotle appears reluctant to describe these relationships as friendships, but does so in acknowledgement of common usage.

However, Aristotle's definition of friendships of utility leaves us with a difficulty not unlike the one that friendships among the mafiosi create. We have no way to differentiate between these utilitarian relationships and relationships in which parties agree to co-operate for specific purposes, but may have no feelings of liking or affection for one another. Aristotle argues in the *Nichomachean Ethics* that friends must have affection for one another on one of his three grounds and that their affection must be mutual. But he tells us that in friendships of utility and pleasure the requisite affection will be insufficient to survive the demise of a friend's usefulness or his pleasant qualities.[40] This is because my affection in such friendships is motivated by the friend's usefulness or pleasure to me, rather than by concern for the friend's good. But if this affection cannot survive the demise of the friend's usefulness or pleasure, then it will be difficult to distinguish between friendships of utility and alliances or purely commercial relationships. The distinction will only be clear in particular circumstances: that is, in cases in which people form alliances or partnerships for the advantage they gain from their association, although they do not actually like or feel any affection for each other. John Cooper points out that in the *Politics* Aristotle emphasises that mere mutual commerce does not involve any interest in one another as persons, any concern for the kind of people the participants are, whereas civic friendship does,[41] and we will look at the implications of this in following chapters.

However, from a contemporary perspective it seems counterintuitive to conclude that relationships of mutual commerce are open to being identified as friendships, as long as the participants feel some degree of mutual affection – and even though that affection is not expected to outlast the utility of the relationship to its participants. Modern individuals might feel a degree of affection for business associates or work colleagues and yet not regard them as friends. Aristotle might argue that affection does not necessarily imply any interest in the kind of person the object of our affection might be; but it is not clear that these two sentiments would be easy to disentangle in the context of interpersonal interaction. The clear distinction Aristotle makes between the motivations typical of the different kinds of friendship may not be appropriate to modern friendship. Modern intuitions about friendship presume that some degree of affection and concern for the friend in himself or herself is required by friends; and that this affection and concern are seen as distinct from the friend's utility, pleasure or goodness. Aristotle's advice is that we should go along with common usage. So, from a modern perspective, it is not unreasonable to conclude that liking in friendships of utility or pleasure cannot be liking purely in respect of a particular quality.

Aristotle's taxonomy would lead us to conclude that Homeric guest-friends and friends among the mafiosi are engaged in friendships of utility and as such in inferior kinds of friendship. But if we apply modern intuitions to these cases, we are left with a dilemma. As noted above, these cases satisfy our intuitions about friendship in some respects, but not in others. The tension between modern-day uses of the term 'friend' and Aristotle's taxonomy might be due in part to Aristotle's scant and opaque analysis of the lesser kinds of friendship.[42] But it is certainly also due to differing understandings of what it is to love and care for a friend in himself or for his own sake. Aristotle's understanding of this notion is addressed through his discussion of primary friendship in the next chapter, after a brief comparison between Aristotle and Kant on the taxonomy of friendship.

The Kantian Taxonomy

Kant discusses friendship in both the *Doctrine of Virtue* and his 'Lecture on Friendship'. In his 'Lecture' he identifies three kinds of friendship that bear some resemblance to Aristotle's triad; they are based respectively on need, taste and disposition. Of the first kind of friendship Kant says, '[t]he friend-ship of need comes about when men can trust one another in the mutual provision for the needs of life. It was the original form of friendship amongst men, and is encountered mostly in the crudest social conditions'.[43] Kant claims that this kind of relationship, like Aristotle's friendship of utility, does not survive changes in the friends' circumstances; the friendship will break up if its ground – mutual advantage or mutual need – disappears. Kant's perspective is slightly different from Aristotle's, since Kant sees this kind of friendship as a reflection of a crude or primitive social structure, rather than poor character. His view is that this kind of friendship is only relevant where the needs of the friends are simple: 'in proportion as their needs increase the frequency of such friendship diminishes'.[44] In the lap of luxury, man is so absorbed in satisfying the multiplicity of needs definitive of that stage that he has little time for or interest in attending to the affairs of others.

Thus, unlike Aristotle, Kant places emphasis on the effect that socio-economic conditions have on the development of friendships within a society – an emphasis that data from modern anthropology supports. This point is discussed in more detail in Chapter 3. The similarities between Kant and Aristotle lie in their attitude to reciprocity within this kind of friend-ship. In Kantian associations of need or exchange, just as in Aristotelian utility friendships, proportional reciprocity creates the bond between the friends;[45] such friendships might survive some failure of reciprocity, but the friendship will eventually collapse if the mutual advantage of the relation-ship disappears.

Kant interrupts and problematises his taxonomy by going on to argue that a friendship of need is in fact presupposed in every friendship. He has in mind not material need or pleasure, but the need for confidence. Kant's view is that in every friendship we need to have confidence that a friend would be competent to care for our affairs and to further our necessities. He qualifies this requirement by arguing that 'no true man would impor-tune a friend with his troubles'. So we need to trust that a friend would help us, but nevertheless a good man must strive not to impose upon a friend: 'I must have confidence only; rather than make demands, I ought to bear my own troubles; he again must have the same confidence in me, but must also refrain from demanding proof . . . The finest sweets of friend-ship are its dispositions of good-will; and on these we must avoid encroach-ing.'[46] We must be benevolently disposed to our friend, but the friend must ensure that he is never in need of our benevolence, since any demonstra-tion will disturb the equality that Kant sees as crucial to the relation.[47] In the context of identifying kinds of friendship, the notion of a friendship of need underlying all friendship is curious if good men can never be aware that their need would be satisfied. This might suggest that the focus of friendship between good men is as much the individual's concern to achieve self-sufficiency, in order to avoid imposing on his friend, as it is his concern for his friend. Lesser men will be concerned with proportional reciprocity and hence their goodwill must presumably be constrained by their concern for their own advantage. Perhaps this notion of a friendship of need underlying all friendship is an attempt to ground friendship in a natural disposition to friendly relations of some type with our fellow beings. Aristotle and Cicero would certainly agree that we are, in general, naturally inclined to make friends.

The second kind of friendship Kant identifies is the friendship of taste. It has echoes of Aristotle's friendship of pleasure, and like Aristotle, Kant provides only scant analysis of this kind of friendship. Curiously, he refers to it as a pseudo-friendship and argues that is more likely to occur between persons of different station and occupation. Kant's argument is that variety and not uniformity is the source of this kind of friendship, so that 'a scholar can form such a friendship with a business-man or a soldier . . . [p]rovided the scholar is not a pedant and the businessman not a blockhead'.[48] Each entertains the other, supplementing something in which the other is lacking. The pinnacle of friendship for Kant is the friendship of disposition or sentiment. This is friendship in the absolute sense in which we achieve complete communion with our friend and in which we are in agreement with regard to intellectual and moral principles. It is a disposition of feeling, rather than a disposition to actual service, and is typified by the confidence such friends have to reveal themselves to one another unreservedly. Thus for Kant friends of the best kind must be similar, at least with respect to the intellectual and moral principles they adopt. By comparison, friends of taste – such as the businessman and the scholar – are presumably those whose differences in thought extend to differences in their intellectual and moral principles. Friendship of taste presents us with a model of friendship predicated on difference rather than similarity. But since Kant identifies this kind of friendship as pseudo-friendship, he alerts us to the tension between similarity and difference in friendship.

The Aristotelian and Kantian analyses of friendship take as their starting point one of the features that the etymology of the English word 'friend' highlighted – the fact that friends have affection or a depth of feeling for one another. Kant and Aristotle both offer an explanation of the genesis of affection between friends in terms of a taxonomy of friendship. Kant's taxonomy resembles Aristotle's: the friendship of 'crude' or basic need is akin to that of utility; the friendship of taste could be interpreted in terms of pleasure; and the friendship of disposition shares features with primary friendship. Of the different kinds of friendship each identifies, one kind emerges as the best or the perfect form of friendship – although Aristotle notes that such friendships are rare and Kant thinks they are unachievable. But rather than helping to provide an essential or general definition of friendship, their accounts demonstrate tensions in the way in which the word is used in each of the kinds of friendship identified.

From the perspective of a modern reader, both the Kantian and the Aristotelian analyses of friendship struggle with the nature of the connection between friends and what that connection implies about or demands of friends. The accounts appear to agree that the lesser kinds of friendship demand proportional reciprocity with regard to utility or pleasure. But neither account explains how or whether friendships of need or utility differ from commercial or strategic relationships; nor do they show what the relationship between liking and pleasure is in friendships of pleasure. Both Aristotle's and Kant's accounts of friendship of the best kind leave us with similar queries about the relationship between love or liking and goodness.

This whistle-stop tour through the historical discourse on friendship has been intended to indicate the difficulty of distilling essential criteria definitive of friendship from considerations of relations between those regarded as friends. In fact consideration of etymology and the philosophical literature only indicates the complexity of the concept. Cicero's reference to friendship as a 'kaleidoscope' captures the fluidity and complexity of the cluster of characteristics that emerge in analyses of friendships. Liking, affection, love, intimacy, freedom, choice, utility, pleasure, goodness, equality, reciprocity and mutuality, shared activity, goodwill, trust, care and concern, loyalty, steadfastness, similarity, difference, vulnerability and fragility have all been addressed as features associated with understandings of friendship. The etymological analysis identified two basic features of friendship: love and freedom. Some of our list of features can be categorised under these two features; love can be taken to imply care and concern, intimacy and affection. Freedom can be taken to imply choice and equality, as well as vulnerability and fragility, since friendship is a voluntary relationship, not circumscribed by any formal obligation. But in the context of relations between individuals who refer to themselves as friends, various of these features are present in different degrees and different combinations. Some of them are absent altogether from certain relationships, while others are not always present. For example, in the friendships Boissevain discusses among members of the Mafia, freedom of choice is a problematic feature and intimacy may be absent; in Aristotelian friendship of utility, intimacy and similarity may well be missing; in Ralph Waldo Emerson's spiritual and emotional friendships, utility (in any narrow practical sense of the word) and shared activity may well be absent.[49] Creating a taxonomy of friendship does not impose order on this variety of features. Within their taxonomies, Aristotle and Kant consider the process of how and why we select our friends; but in each of the kinds of friendship they identify, the cluster of features associated with friendship appear in overlapping and flexible combinations.

Thus while we may think of the concept as a coherent idea within certain contexts, the variation in the use of the term 'friend' makes the attempt at definition an unwieldy activity. Nuances attached to particular uses are at odds with some uses, but not others. The concept is exposed as a web or network of semantic subtleties. It is for this reason that I suggest that friendship might best be regarded as a 'family resemblance' concept. Wittgenstein uses the idea of family resemblance in the context of a discussion of language games. Within that discussion he examines the complicated network of similar and dissimilar features which make up the concept of what we call 'games'. He advises us not to conclude that there must be something common to all games, simply on the basis of the fact that they are all called 'games'. Rather he suggests instead that we '*look and see* whether there is anything common to all'. He argues that if we do so, we will find correspondences between some games. This might lead us to conclude that we have found a common feature or features, but these correspondences will disappear when we make comparisons with other games. Similarities will 'crop up and disappear' so that we will not find anything that is common to all games; rather we will find 'similarities, relationships, and a whole series of them at that'. Wittgenstein characterises these similarities as 'family resemblances'.[50] Understanding a 'family resemblance' concept depends upon seeing how it functions in practical contexts, since its usage reveals 'a complicated network of similarities overlapping and criss-crossing'.[51] The analysis of friendship reveals just this kind of network of correspondence and lack of correspondence. We find a network of features, which, while similar, are not present in the same degree or in the same combination in all instances of friendship. Grasping the concept is – as Derrida might put it – endlessly deferred. There is always more to be said about friendship, since as we discuss it we have only one plane of the structure of overlapping and criss-crossing features in our gaze. As we shift our gaze to consider it from another angle, we are obliged to move the previous foreground to our peripheral vision.

Like the concept 'game', the concept 'friendship' is consequently blurred or indistinct, as Wittgenstein might put it.[52] On this view 'friendship' is a term that is used in different senses; its meaning evolves as it is applied to different contexts, and consequently we may not be able to identify a central sense of the term. John Davis explains Wittgenstein's idea of 'a family resemblance' concept by suggesting that such concepts 'are like equilibria that contain discordant elements'. He argues that:

[F]or Wittgenstein, generality is a product of family resemblance – the generality of a concept is produced out of the myriad overlapping and criss-crossing senses in which that concept is used. This means, however, that since there is no single – therefore essential – meaning shared by all of the ways in which an expression is used, we accordingly have no way of specifying concepts apart from describing their actual uses and conditions of application.[53]

Given the lack of an essential or central notion of friendship, the strategy Derrida recommends seems wise. Rather than asking what friendship is, we can aim to shift our focus to ask: 'Who is the friend?' Stern-Gillet's comment that '[f]riendship is too multi-sided a phenomenon to be assimilated either to an activity or to a process' reinforces the wisdom of the proposal to focus on the friend.[54] Chapter 2 turns to consider the nature of our identification with and attachment to the other in friendship.

Notes

1. Cicero, 'On Friendship', p. 111.
2. Aristotle, *Nichomachean Ethics*, 1169b11–35 and 1162a1–26.
3. Derrida, *Politics of Friendship*, p. 295.
4. Cicero, 'On Friendship', pp. 90 and 115.
5. Ibid., p. 103.
6. Boissevain, *Friends of Friends*, p. 26.
7. Telfer, 'Friendship', p. 251.
8. Ibid.
9. Seneca, 'On Philosophy and Friendship Epistle IX', p. 121; and Cicero, 'On Friendship', p. 91.
10. Cicero, 'On Friendship', pp. 98–9.
11. Telfer, 'Friendship', p. 257.
12. Adkins, 'Friendship and "Self-Sufficiency" in Homer and Aristotle', pp. 32–3.
13. Stern-Gillet, *Aristotle's Philosophy of Friendship*, p. 6.
14. Homer, *Iliad*, VI, 215–36.
15. Dodds, *The Greeks and the Irrational*, p. 18.
16. Homer, *Iliad*, IX, 315–32, 402 and 410–16.
17. Jackson, *Relativism and the Character of Subjectivity in Homer's Iliad*, p. 92.
18. Dodds, *The Greeks and the Irrational*, p. 15.
19. Stern-Gillet, *Aristotle's Philosophy of Friendship*, p. 6.
20. Ibid.
21. Adkins, 'Friendship and "Self-Sufficiency" in Homer and Aristotle', pp. 33–5.
22. Homer, *Iliad*, XVIII, 70–106.
23. Hutter, *Politics as Friendship*, pp. 26–7 and 59.
24. Plato, *Lysis*, 213b–c.
25. Plato, *Phaedrus*, 237d8–9.
26. Plato, *Symposium*, 210b–c.
27. Plato, *Laws*, 636a7–9 and 836a 3–7.
28. Aeschines, 'Against Timarchus', pp. 11–23.
29. Foucault, *The Uses of Pleasure*, p. 201.

30. *Symposium* 206a11. However, as Price points out, Diotima, after redefining *eros*, at times loses sight of *eros* in any familiar sense (*Love and Friendship in Plato and Aristotle*, p. 25).

31. Aristotle, *Nichomachean Ethics*, 1167a18–b64.

32. Ibid., 1156b2–23.

33. Ibid., 1155b29–1156a16.

34. Ibid., 1156a16–b10.

35. Ibid., 1156b2–23.

36. Ibid., 1168a18–b7.

37. Ibid., 1157a10–34.

38. Cicero, 'On Friendship', p. 94; see also pp. 86–8 and 116.

39. Aristotle, *Nichomachean Ethics*, 1157a34–b20.

40. This implies that liking between friends of the good will be able to survive the demise of a friend's goodness, perhaps because a friend of the good is concerned for his friend for that friend's own sake. On the other hand, it might imply that the goodness of such friends will not simply evaporate; good people will not just turn bad. This suggests that a man's virtue is not a contingent fact about him. But as Telfer points out ('Friendship', p. 255), even Aristotle himself acknowledges later that it is (*Nichomachean Ethics*, 1165b12–22).

41. Cooper, 'Political Animals and Civic Friendship', p. 319.

42. See Mulgan, 'The Role of Friendship in Aristotle's Political Theory', pp. 15–16, for comments on Aristotle's obscure and controversial consideration of friendship as a political bond and its derivative types.

43. Kant, 'Lecture on Friendship', p. 212.

44. Ibid., pp. 212–13.

45. Aristotle, *Nichomachean Ethics*, 1132b28–1133a13.

46. Kant, 'Lecture on Friendship', p. 213.

47. Ibid.

48. Ibid., p. 214.

49. Emerson is most interested in the spiritual and emotional understanding present between friends. In his essay on friendship he writes: 'To my friend I write a letter and from him I receive a letter. That seems little to you. It suffices me. It is a spiritual gift . . . In these warm lines the heart will trust itself, as it will not to the tongue, and pour out the prophecy of a godlier existence than all the annals of heroism have yet made good' ('Friendship', pp. 229–30).

50. Wittgenstein, *Philosophical Investigations*, part I, S 66.

51. Ibid., S 66.

52. Ibid., S 70–1.

53. Davis, 'A Marxist Influence on Wittgenstein via Sraffa', pp. 139–40.

54. Stern-Gillet, *Aristotle's Philosophy of Friendship*, p. 43.

Chapter 2

The Friend as Another Self

Friendship and Identification with the Other

The taxonomies of friendship examined in Chapter 1 explain the development of relations between friends on the basis of their mutual need, advantage, tastes and pleasures, commitment to notions of the good or commitment to moral and intellectual principles. This chapter examines how we perceive the other as friend; the nature of the attraction between us; what we see ourselves as having in common. It considers the nature of the choice we make in befriending another person: whether we are helpless before the force of our desires and affinities; whether likes or opposites attract; and whether friendship is a form of self-love. The chapter does this via an exploration of the philosophical literature on these topics. To commence, it is worth clarifying what it means to postulate that the passions aroused in friendship might occur in response to a process of identification with the other. When we identify a friend as a particular kind of person we pick out characteristics or features that establish her identity for us as an individual distinct from others. However, to identify with a friend is to associate or feel sympathy with her in terms of her feelings, interests, values, principles or actions; it refers to an association of like-mindedness.

As we have seen, Aristotle presents the Greek polis as an arena of like-minded citizens who agree about their interests, adopt the same policy and act on their common resolutions. This is a model of friendship or *philia* based on likeness and confirmation of the existing order. The idea that all citizens were friends demanded an equality of rights, a harmony of interests, ideas and activities, which we today would regard as impossible, but which was instantiated for Aristotle in the relations among the citizens of the Athenian polis. Aristotle depicts friendship as the public bond that unites the virtuous and exclusively male citizens of the polis in a shared conception of the good and in shared practices. Thus friendship is a kind of 'socio-political cement' and the goal of politics is its development. Civic friendship becomes a political relationship, since it creates unity among virtuous men of like mind and interests who share a conception of the good. Thus these friends identify with one another on the basis of their joint citizenship, their virtue and a shared conception of the good.

This view of friendship is one that commentators find problematic. Given contemporary concerns with distinctions between the private and the public spheres of life and between self and other, Aristotle's definition of friendship can appear foreign to modern sensibilities. There is debate in the philosophical literature about the extent to which Aristotle's ideas are relevant to contemporary notions of political community; and yet his ideas are not without appeal.[1] The title of Jacques Derrida's book, *Politics of Friendship*, suggests an affinity with the Aristotelian ideal of politics as the business of friends, and indeed, Derrida sees in modern friendship something of what Aristotle saw in the fourth century BC.[2] In typical fashion, though, Derrida is more concerned with politics than with friendship. For him the future of the political lies in the formation of new relationships between citizens viewed as friends. It is the political potential of the word 'friend' that interests Derrida: the possibility that we can think beyond the 'homo-fraternity and phallogocentricity' of the Greek model, beyond our philosophical and religious heritage to open out to new possibilities. The anticipated impact of this new form of friendship is that it might underpin a political relation that keeps the old name 'democracy', but is deeper and more inclusive than its predecessor.

By comparison, Aristotle, in his ethical works, is deeply interested in both the political and the private dimensions of relations between friends, in the moral aspects of those relationships and in the contribution of friendship to the good life. For Aristotle the political and the ethical intersect; the sociopolitical structures of the polis are aligned with its ethical prescriptions so that the raison d'être of the polis is living well.[3] Aristotle's account appears to shift uneasily between a public and a private conception of friendship. At points he distinguishes between the sense in which fellow citizens are friends and a more intimate sense of friendship;[4] but from a contemporary perspective his treatment raises questions about the role of feeling or emotion in relations between friends. At the same time it reveals a contrast between Aristotle's ethical theory and theories such as Kant's, which are reluctant to include relations between friends within the sphere of morality. These questions are addressed in Chapters 4 and 5 of this book.

An analysis of Aristotelian civic friendship indicates a second slippage in his account of friendship. Of the three types of friendship Aristotle distinguishes, friendships of utility and friendships of pleasure are less intense than the primary or best form of friendship – friendship of the good. Primary friendships are formed between good men in virtue of their goodness; they are forged in mutual esteem and in the practice of the moral and intellectual virtues. However, as John Cooper points out, Aristotle implies in the *Politics* that civic relations among citizens of a city involve moral concerns for the behaviour of fellow citizens; and that cities deserving of the name must concern themselves with virtue.[5] Citizens are good men, concerned with virtue and united in a shared conception of the good. Aristotle makes the good man's concern with virtue explicit in his commentary on the relations between friends in the best type of friendship. Again, the distinctions Aristotle draws blur, when we see that civic friendship can be regarded as a form of utility friendship. It is a relationship of mutual advantage to the citizens of the polis, but at the same time it is a friendship that unites virtuous men in a shared conception of the good and hence might be regarded as a form of primary friendship.[6]

Cooper notes that what Aristotle means by the good is not entirely clear; but that it is clear that the good is available to human beings living in cities in which virtuous citizens are united by friendship. This is partly explained by the fact that for Aristotle friendship is itself a form of justice.[7] As we shall see later, a conception of the good life for man is related to what Aristotle sees as man's proper function and its relation to happiness. In his discussion of happiness, Aristotle distinguishes three types of "goods": external goods such as honour, wealth and power; goods of the soul, such as happiness, which for Aristotle is activity of the soul in accordance with virtue; and goods of the body, such as physical advantages. At one point in the *Nichomachean Ethics* he claims that friends are the greatest of external goods.[8] But primary friendship between one's close associates is clearly also important for its contribution to the goods of the soul and thus its role in the virtuous man's life.[9] Thus the relationship between friendship, happiness and virtue is not clear enough to be able to decide where to accommodate civic friendship within Aristotle's taxonomy. Civic friendship seems to be caught somewhat uneasily between friendship of utility and friendship of goodness. Aristotle does acknowledge that primary friendships have something in common with friendships of pleasure and the least enduring of friendships (those of utility), since they are pleasurable and useful to virtuous friends. But he argues that primary friends do not engage with one another for the sake of that utility or pleasure; their focus is on goodness. However, the tension in civic friendship between identification with friends on the basis of shared citizenship and identification with them on the basis of their goodness remains.

Aristotle says most about identification with the friend in relation to primary friendship. His insistence that only a good man can love his friend for the friend's own sake and not for any incidental quality is intended to distinguish primary friendship from friendships of utility and pleasure. The latter are accidental friendships on Aristotle's view, in that they are based on a non-essential ground; these friends happen to share particular needs and interests that the relationship satisfies. They may not think past the satisfaction of the shared needs and interests, which are the focus of the relationship. Primary friendships differ in that they are based 'on the ground of [the other's] actual nature';[10] and they demand a particular attitude and a degree of awareness: those who have the desire to be friends (of the good) 'are not [friends] unless they are worthy of love and know it'.[11] Primary friends are aware of their own goodness and the goodness of the other. They share this awareness and so identify with one another on the basis of their goodness. From the perspective of the modern reader it seems that in Aristotle's highest form of friendship we like our friend for the sake of his goodness – rather than for himself. The claim that 'friendship in the primary and proper sense is between good men in virtue of their goodness' indicates a conflation between goodness, as the object of the friendship, and the friend himself, as its object. Aristotle is even more explicit about this conflation when he states that 'friends must be well-disposed toward each other, and recognized as wishing each other's good, for one of the three reasons stated above';[12] that is, on the grounds of either goodness, pleasure or utility.

The implication that even in the highest form of friendship, we like our friend for the sake of something else – for the sake of his goodness rather than for himself – is problematic for a modern reader. We can see a clash between the notion of liking a person for her own sake and liking her for her goodness. If we are not prepared to identify the friend with her goodness and cannot feel an affinity with her on that basis, then we need to consider what we mean when we say that we like or love a person for herself. However, as it turns out, it is far easier to state what does not constitute liking or loving a friend for her own sake than to say what does. In fact the very attempt to state why one likes a friend necessarily suggests liking for the sake of something else, unless the chosen attribute can be identified with the friend in some essential way; this, as we shall see, is precisely the strategy that Aristotle adopts. Yet while I might describe a friend as the possessor of certain attributes, a modern friend is not usually thought of as being defined by those attributes.

Suzanne Stern-Gillet notes that the modern view that friendship involves loving one's friends in and for themselves makes both a fairly straightforward normative claim and a more problematic descriptive claim. The normative claim is that to love someone for their own sake is to love the person for herself, rather than for what she possesses or what she could do for us.[13] Aristotle's understanding of loving or liking a friend for the friend's own sake makes two similar claims. His normative claim is that a friend of the best kind loves the essence of his friend's being, rather than any accidental characteristics or

qualities – such as wealth or musical ability – which might be useful or pleasant in a friend. Stern-Gillet points out that in both the *Nichomachean Ethics*
and the *Eudemian Ethics*, Aristotle distinguishes between 'the love which
responds to the very being of another person and that which remains content-
edly at the periphery of his personality'.[14] Aristotle also makes a descriptive
claim in regard to the notion of loving a friend for his own sake. But, as Stern-
Gillet argues and as we will see below, in Aristotle's ethics this descriptive claim
is interwoven with his normative claim.

The descriptive claim made by the modern view is that friends are loved
for what it is that makes them unique. Stern-Gillet argues that this gives
pride of place to the uniqueness – what she refers to as the unicity – of
friends, and thus to their individual irreplaceability.[15] But the concept of
unicity is vague in modern conceptions of friendship. The vagueness lies in
the fact that we want to be able to say that friends are loved uniquely, but
also that they are loved for their good qualities. These two requirements are
not easily combined. When we attempt to characterise a friend's uniqueness,
we are torn between a focus on a set of features, qualities or traits possessed
by the friend and a conception of the friend as a unique instantiation of that
set. In articulating that uniqueness we have no choice but to attempt to enu-
merate her particular qualities or traits or to abandon ourselves to expressions of sentiment. These considerations lead Stern-Gillet to suggest that
modern friendship is fundamentally non-rational and perhaps not a fit
matter for close analytical scrutiny.[16] Elizabeth Telfer acknowledges that
liking in friendship is a difficult phenomenon to analyse and that the degree
of rationality it involves is limited. She argues that liking seems 'to be "a
quasi-aesthetic attitude", roughly specifiable as "finding someone to one's
taste", and depends partly on such things as his physical appearance, man-
nerisms, voice and speech, and style of life; partly on his traits of character,
moral and other'.[17] The relative importance of these features as a basis for
liking depends on the liker, on Telfer's view. She draws an analogy between
friendship and art, arguing that our reaction to a friend is to the whole personality as a unified thing, much like our reaction to a work of art. None the
less, the difficulties to which Stern-Gillet's comments draw attention remain.

Her comments bring to mind Jean-Paul Sartre's view of love, which is discussed in the next chapter. Sartre refers to love as a conflict, a contradictory
effort and even a useless passion. On his view, the beloved wants to be found
irresistible to the beloved but at the same time he demands free and voluntary engagement. He wants to be freely chosen as beloved; and we could
perhaps think of this choice as made on the basis of qualities that his lover
finds appealing. But it cannot be the qualities themselves that are crucial –
since they might well be possessed by others. Rather he wants these qualities to be found somehow uniquely instantiated in himself as a being the

lover cannot resist. And yet the other's love would be cheapened if it were thought to be the result of some form of psychological determinism. Sartre is describing a contradictory pair of desires in erotic love, but they are ones which might easily be applied to Stern-Gillet's view of modern friendship. The focus on wanting to be liked by friends for our uniqueness is in conflict with the attempt to articulate just what that uniqueness might consist in. The contradictory nature of these desires confirms Stern-Gillet's claim that 'modern friendships are fundamentally non-rational';[18] and hence we might also see it as unsurprising that modern friends do not attempt to analyse their relationships. However, while these competing desires are contradictory and hence make it difficult to explain our love or liking in friendship, the desires themselves are not irrational. We can – and Sartre does – offer good reasons for the appeal of both desires. None the less they leave us with considerable difficulties in regard to the descriptive claim associated with modern friendship's emphasis on uniqueness.

Aristotle does warn us repeatedly that 'discussions about feelings and conduct admit of no more precision than their subject-matter does';[19] so we should no doubt be wary of demands for precision in terms of what friendship entails, given we are within this realm. However, the imprecision in Aristotle's case refers to the difficulty of establishing whether liking a friend for his own sake differs from liking a friend in virtue of his goodness. The difficulty amounts to a problem of interpretation regarding the notion of liking another self for that other person's own sake. In book IX of the *Nichomachean Ethics* Aristotle associates the self with the intellectual part of a man. He says of the good man:

> he is completely integrated and desires the same things with every part of his soul. Also he wishes and effects the things that are or seem to be good for him (for it is the mark of a good man to direct his energies to what is good) and he does it for his own sake (for he does it on account of the intellectual part of him, which is held to be the self of the individual).[20]

Later in book IX he says that 'a person is called continent or incontinent according as his reason is or is not in control, which implies that this part *is* the individual'.[21] So for Aristotle to like a person for his own sake is to like him for his intellect or reason; and since it is reason's function to control and integrate a man's desires and energies in the service of the good, then to like a person consists precisely in liking him for his connection with goodness.[22] Aristotle so closely associates man's essence with the exercise of his rational faculties, with the practice of the virtues and ultimately with contemplation, that to be concerned for the other for the other's own sake is precisely to be concerned for him in respect of these matters. Given Aristotle's definition of the self or person, the two motives we were attempting to distinguish – liking for the friend in himself and liking him for his goodness – amount to the same thing. Stern-Gillet argues that, for Aristotle, to be a self is to be psychically unified; and thus she claims Aristotle does not regard weak-willed and vicious people as selves, since their passions and appetites pull in different directions and they rebel against and weaken the part of themselves that ought to direct them.

> Aristotle views psychic unity as the result of a slow process of integration which is broadly co-extensive with the acquisition of moral virtue. Practical reason, in his outlook, constitutes the hub around which the self is formed, since it alone can effect the integration of the various psychic elements into a whole. Whenever it fails to do so, either through *akrasia* [weakness of will] or vice, the individual remains unfree, a mere bunch of unstable elements and discordant parts. [23]

But if we adopt Aristotle's strategy and identify the friend on the basis of his goodness, then liking a friend for his goodness and identifying with him on that basis has the same structure as the other, lesser forms of friendship – those of utility and pleasure.[24] At one point in book IX of the *Nichomachean Ethics* Aristotle expresses himself in a way that might imply that he sees a distinction between loving a friend for himself and loving him for his goodness. He is discussing how many friends one ought to have and he says that 'it is not possible to have many friends whom we love for their own sake and for their goodness'.[25] This may indicate an appreciation of what I have presented as a more modern distinction between friends in themselves and the goodness of those friends; but Aristotle's account privileges a view that equates loving a friend for himself with loving him for his goodness. The object of primary friendship most often appears as the agent's perception of the friend's goodness and hence its connection with the agent's own conception of goodness. This suggests that in some sense it is for the agent's own sake that he likes his friend. We are understandably suspicious about such a suggestion, since we assume that in examples of the best kind of friendship the participants are genuinely concerned for one another; that each is prepared to put the other's interests before his own, at least on occasion; and that their engagement with one another is not contingent upon or qualified by each one's own individual concerns. Modern concerns with uniqueness as well as Judaeo-Christian misgivings about self-love may reinforce a contemporary reader's discomfort with the suggestion that self-interest or egoism can motivate friendship. The anxiety is related to tension between connotations of stasis and uni-directionality inherent in narcissism, on the one hand; and beliefs that self-respect, self-concern and self-understanding play crucial roles in relations between friends, on the other. These notions are topics of discussion in Chapter 5.

For Aristotle, liking or loving a friend for the friend's own sake is equivalent to identifying with him on the basis of his goodness, and only good

men will be capable of this. Aristotle's recommendation of this form of association is an attempt to ensure that the good men of the polis will like one
another and hence engage in a form of relation *(philia)* that can serve to
ground the communal life of the polis. Thus civic friendship straddles the
distinction between utility and goodness. But from a contemporary perspective, the public nature of aspects of Aristotle's conception of primary friendship determines, first, that the relationship is tainted by instrumentalism;
and second, that Aristotle's schema does not sufficiently recognise crucial
structural features constitutive of friendship: affection, enjoyment as a by-
product rather than an end of friendship, the role of choice, and friendship's
contribution to self-knowledge come to mind here.

With regard to the question of enjoyment in friendship, for example,
modern friends do not necessarily develop friendships with those whose
goodness they admire or esteem. Such admiration and esteem are not sufficient on their own to ensure the development of a friendship. We enjoy our
friends' company in the sense of feeling at ease with them, but we are left
with the question of what it is that explains our ease. We do identify with
friends in that we share and appreciate their interests, sense of humour,
qualities of mind and attitude to life, but – as we have seen – the relationship between these features and our concern for a friend for her own sake
is problematic for modern friends. Modern friends do not necessarily
equate one another's essence with their goodness and relate to one another
on the basis of that goodness. We may well engage with a friend motivated
by what we see as love and concern for the friend for the friend's own sake.
But what that engagement entails will be difficult to predict, since it will
depend on a variety of factors that influence our interaction with the friend.
It is understandable that Aristotle introduced the notion of the friend as
another self, because it reinforces the connection between virtuous friends.
It also provides an explanation of the attraction between friends, their
mutual concern for and enjoyment of one another, that does not appear to
resort to utilitarian motives.

The Friend as a Second Self

On the Aristotelian model, it is in the case of one's own self that one is most
truly a friend. A man's best friend is one who wishes him well for his own
sake; 'and this condition is best fulfilled by his attitude to himself . . . [since]
all friendly feelings for others are extensions of a man's feelings for
himself'.[26] Thus the first of the five characteristics that Aristotle claims are
definitive of a best friend and apply to the good man in relation to himself
is that a friend wishes and effects the good, or apparent good, of another

for the sake of that other. As we have seen, given Aristotle's conception of the person, this turns out to be for the sake of the other's intellect or reason. A friend also wishes the existence and preservation of his friend for the friend's own sake; he spends all his time with his friend; he chooses the same things as his friend; and he shares his friend's joys and sorrows.[27]

The assertion that these characteristics apply to one's self and are extended to the friend in the best friendships again raises the question of the relationship between friendship and self-love. In his discussion of the characteristics definitive of a friend, Aristotle twice compares one's attitude to a friend to that of a mother towards her child.[28] This puts aside the demand for equality between friends. But given that comparison, his claims about the characteristics of primary friendship might be more usefully interpreted as an admonition to give our friends the love, care and understanding that we might hope for from a loving mother. Aristotle says earlier in book VIII of the *Nichomachean Ethics* that parents 'love their children as themselves (for one's offspring is a sort of other self in virtue of a separate existence)'.[29] The translator suggests that Aristotle means that the child is 'other' to the parent only in virtue of a separate existence, like the offshoot of a plant. This clarification does not dispel concerns about tensions between self-love, self-interest and friendship. However, these concerns will be left aside at present.

Aristotle refers to the friend as another self in the *Nichomachean Ethics* and he makes similar references in both the *Eudemian Ethics* and the *Magna Moralia*. However, in the *Eudemian Ethics* he specifies the sense in which such an apparently contradictory claim might have meaning, noting that 'nonetheless a friend means, as it were, a separate self'.[30] Cicero, Aquinas and Montaigne also refer to the friend as another self, although with more caution than Aristotle's comments exhibit. In criticising those who 'recognise nothing as good in the human sphere unless it be something profitable', Cicero maintains that such people know nothing of friendship in its finest and most natural guise – friendship that is desirable and significant for its own sake. He goes on to argue that:

> a man loves himself not in order to exact from himself some pay for his affection, but simply because every man is by his very nature dear to himself. Unless this same principle is transferred to friendship, a man will never find a true friend, for the true friend is, so to speak, a second self . . . [Man] is ever on the search for that companion, whose heart's blood he may so mingle with his own that they become virtually one person instead of two.[31]

Cicero explains close identification between friends as based on love that is explained as a transference of natural feelings for themselves to the other. Although he does not attempt to explain this in any detail, he does emphasise that the existence of friends as separate from one another is predicated on respect: 'take respect out of friendship and you deprive it of its noblest

crown'. Lasting friendships are built up between men who are good themselves, who only demand of one another what is honourable and right, who
love, cherish and show mutual respect to one another.[32] Cicero's emphasis
on respect is a recognition of the separateness of friends and hints at a necessary balance between notions of identity and difference in friendship.

Aquinas also wrote approvingly of Aristotle's reference to the friend as
'a man's *other self*' and of St Augustine's comment: '*Well did one say to his
friend: Thou half of my soul.*' Aquinas noted that when a man loves
another with the love of friendship he apprehends him as his other self in
that he wills good to his friend, just as – or to the extent that – he wills
good to himself.[33] For Aquinas, unity is the principle of union, so like
Cicero he takes our relationship to ourselves as the model for our union
with others and makes love the principle of that union. He draws a distinction between the substantial union which causes love – a union based on
'the love with which one loves oneself – and the union of likeness based on
'the love wherewith one loves other things'. The sense of unity that characterises our relationship to self is prior to and stronger than the sense of
unity we experience in friendship.[34] Writing in a theological context,
Aquinas regards friendship as a form of charity; charity is in turn defined
as 'love of God'. His approach is Aristotelian – to 'know ourselves aright'
we must know that our sensitive and corporeal nature, the outward man,
is secondary to our rational nature or the inward man. Only if we 'know
ourselves aright' can we 'love ourselves aright'. The good have this knowledge and therefore love themselves truly and have the capacity to love
others in the same way.[35]

The good man loves his friend as his other self in the sense that he recognises and loves in the other his inward man. Lesser men experience the love
of 'concupiscence', which is possessive and self-interested, while the love of
friendship becomes an overarching principle for the organisation of one's
life based on love. The friend as another self is subsumed, as we ourselves
are, within our love of God and 'all the things of God, among which things
is man himself'. We love God because His substance is goodness and we
love ourselves and others as God's creatures. But this leaves us with a
concern similar to that addressed in the discussion of Aristotle: loving a
friend for the friend's own sake turns out to be dependent upon how we
view the nature of man in himself and how we interpret the good for man.
Aquinas is offering us what he takes to be a good reason for loving friends.
This might be seen to be at odds with the notion of loving a friend for that
person's own sake, since we could think of that notion as equivalent to
loving the other for no good reason. This is precisely what Stern-Gillet
seems to think modern friends do and why she thinks modern friendship is
fundamentally non-rational. The unconditional love of a parent for a child

provides an illustration of this kind of love. A parent's unfailing love for a child – despite what might be seen as good reasons for withdrawing love – provides the child with a sense that she is loved for her own sake.

Montaigne is another philosopher of friendship who identifies the friend as another self. His essay on friendship takes himself and his friendship with Etienne de La Boétie as its focus. In fact the essay is primarily a panegyric to the friendship they shared for the four years preceding La Boétie's death in 1563. Montaigne describes the friendship as 'so entire and perfect that certainly you will hardly read of the like, and among men of today you see no trace of it in practice. So many coincidences are needed to build up such a friendship that it is a lot if fortune can do it once in three centuries.'[36]

His essay on friendship is of interest for its use of the language of religious ecstasy to describe the friendship: 'our souls mingle and blend with each other so completely that they efface the seam that joined them, and cannot find it again'; 'our souls pulled together with such union'. His description of his first meeting with La Boétie includes these comments: 'we found ourselves so taken with each other, so well acquainted, so bound together, that from that time on nothing was so close to us as each other'. Expressing his grief on La Boétie's death, he wrote: 'I was already so formed and accustomed to being a second self everywhere that only half of me seems alive now.'[37]

Like Aristotle and Cicero, Montaigne gave priority to the friendships of virtuous men, but his conception of true or perfect friendship was narrower, more elitist and exclusive than those of the ancients. He referred to his friendship with La Boétie as 'sovereign and masterful', indivisible and unique by comparison with the more common friendships of ordinary and less virtuous men. Aristotle and Cicero did not hold the lesser forms of friendship in the contempt that Montaigne appears to have reserved for ordinary or customary friendship; indeed Montaigne criticised the ancients, complaining that 'the very discourses that antiquity has left us on this subject seem to me weak compared with the feeling I have'.[38] His feeling for La Boétie was one of complete union but, like Cicero, Montaigne does not attempt to analyse his feeling of being and having a second self. He comments – perhaps over-dramatically – that if pressed to tell the reader why he loved La Boétie: 'I feel that this cannot be expressed, except by answering: Because it was he, because it was I.'[39] Aristotle, Cicero, Aquinas and Montaigne attempt to avoid utilitarian explanations of the love and attraction between friends by emphasising a view, of the friend as another or a second self. However, it is difficult to dispel misgivings about such a view since its treatment leads us to suspect that the love or attraction does not fully take account of the separateness of the friends; or that it is underpinned by moral or religious concerns, rather than a concern with the friend for the friend's own sake. The love between friends appears as a phenomenon that need not or cannot be explained.

The notion of the friend as another self is not without its critics in the philosophical literature. Seneca dismissed the idea out of hand, commenting that 'he who has been unable to love more than one, has had none too much love even for that one'.[40] His argument is that friendship is essentially a social virtue, and is not confined to one object. Thus the 'pretended' friendship for one and only one is dismissed as a form of self-love, rather than unselfish love. Kierkegaard is similarly dismissive of any recommendation that in perfect friendship we extend our friendly feelings for ourselves towards our friend, again arguing that the idea amounts to nothing more than self-love. Kierkegaard opposes friendship or 'poetic love' to 'love of neighbour'. He does so because he sees human beings faced with an exclusive choice between love of one and only one other and love of all others. Since friendship is preferential, it is by definition selfish, on this view. This characterisation of friendship, along with Kant's approach to friendship, will be addressed in detail in Chapter 3.

In general the philosophers discussed above place more emphasis on similarity and equality between friends – shared concerns, shared character traits, even complete fusion on all matters – than on taking account of the otherness of the friend. In the opening pages of book VIII of the *Nichomachean Ethics*, Aristotle considers whether friendship is founded on similarity or difference. He supports each possibility with proverbs and literary quotations: Empedocles' view that 'Like is drawn to like' is juxtaposed to Heraclitus' claim that 'Opposition unites.'[41] But given the three kinds of friendship he identifies, friends – despite any apparent differences – must at least share a similar concern for utility, pleasure or goodness, since Aristotle says they love each other for one of these reasons. His view of civic friendship as a political bond also implies a similar focus on the prosperity of the polis, as does Cicero's definition of friendship as 'complete sympathy in all matters of importance, plus goodwill and affection'.[42] Thus, despite whatever reservations we might have about the notion of the friend as another self, these philosophers see friendship as predicated on similarity: similar virtue, similar beliefs and values, similar status and similar tastes. This is the case whether the particular philosopher emphasises friendship as a public relationship – as Aristotle does – or whether he is most concerned with friendship as a private relationship – as is the case with Cicero and Montaigne.

The etymological analysis of friendship in Chapter 1 indicated that freedom of choice was a significant feature of the dynamic of friendship. But when we consider the emphasis that Aristotle, Cicero, Aquinas and Montaigne place on similarity and on the notion of the friend as another self, we might well wonder about the nature of our choice in friendship. Do we make a choice in friendship or are we destined to fall into friendship – attracted, compelled or mesmerised by the forces of our own character, it strengths and flaws? If we do not choose freely and with a level head, then attraction in friendship would appear to have a similar structure to attraction in romantic relationships. If this is the case, then it might disqualify freedom of choice as a necessary criterion of friendship. There are commentators whose approach to the explanation of attraction between friends is more enigmatic and esoteric than that of Aristotle. To some extent Montaigne's discourse on friendship spills over into this kind of view, when he uses the language of religious ecstasy to describe his friendship with La Boétie. But this approach is more clearly demonstrated in the work of the philosophical essayist Ralph Waldo Emerson and in the literature of Johann Wolfgang von Goethe.

Elective Affinity

Emerson claims that conversation 'is the practice and consummation of friendship' and that great conversation 'requires an absolute running of two souls into one . . . Yet it is affinity that determines *which* two shall converse.'[43] The attraction between two individuals who become friends is explained on the basis of an affinity between the 'two souls'. The notion of affinity between individuals was one that Goethe had explored in his novella *Wahlverwandtschaft*, which was translated into English as *Elective Affinities* and published thirty years before Emerson's essay on friendship. R. J. Hollingdale, the English translator of *Elective Affinities*, tells us that the emotional and romantic connotations the term *Wahlverwandtschaft* eventually acquired derived from Goethe's novella. But at the time of the novella's publication the German term *Wahlverwandtschaft* was a technical one used exclusively in eighteenth-century chemistry. The Swedish chemist Torburg Bergmann had written a treatise on chemical attractions in 1775, *De attractionibus electives*, which was translated into German in 1782 by Hein Tabor as *Die Wahlverwnadtschaften* (*The Elective Affinities*). During convalescence from an illness in 1768–9, Goethe read about alchemy and became fascinated with chemistry. This fascination is evident in his work, especially in *Faust* and *Elective Affinities*, where he fastens upon the organic structure of a chemical reaction to depict his thesis.

In an 1809 advertisement for his book, Goethe wrote that 'this strange title' was one suggested to him 'by his continuing work in the field of physics', that it was a 'metaphor in chemistry' whose 'spiritual origin' is demonstrated in the novella. The almost universal view of the book at the time was that 'it was intended to demonstrate the chemical origin of love', and as such it was generally charged with being immoral.[44] Goethe himself reportedly said in conversation with his secretary, Riemer, that 'his idea with the new novel, *Elective Affinities*, was: to represent social relationships and the conflicts of the same, symbolically understood'.[45] In a letter to Schiller (23 October 1799) Goethe criticises the work of the French author Crébillon in terms that make his fascination with chemical relationships as an analogy for social relationships explicit: 'there is no trace of the delicate chemical relationship (*chemische Verwandtschaft*) through which they (his characters) attract and repel, neutralize each other and again separate and re-establish themselves'.[46] It is just this delicate economy of forces that Goethe explicitly addresses in chapter 4 of his novella via discussion of an article on chemical attraction and repulsion. Eduard reads aloud to his wife, Charlotte, and another main character, the Captain. Charlotte expresses some confusion about the use of the term 'affinity' in the context of what appears to be a discussion of inanimate things, and her husband explains that he is using the term as a metaphor: '"It is a metaphor which has misled and confused you", said Eduard. "Here, to be sure, it is only a question of soil and minerals; but man is a true Narcissus: he makes the whole world his mirror"'.[47]

The Captain agrees, claiming that man treats everything he discovers outside himself in this way, that he sees his attributes reflected in the outside world, 'his wisdom and his folly, his will and his caprices, he lends to the beasts, the plants, the elements and the gods'.[48] Literary theorists would argue that man is engaged in 'the pathetic fallacy' as he projects the affinities he discovers in himself upon relationship in nature, so that the elements of nature are personified. Eduard uses friendship as a metaphor for these natural processes:

> Sometimes they will meet as friends and old acquaintances who hasten together and unite without changing one another in any way, as wine mixes with water. On the other hand, there are others who will remain obdurate strangers to one another and refuse to unite in any way through mechanical mixing and grinding, as oil and water shaken together will a moment later separate again.[49]

Charlotte sees the force of the metaphor quickly. She recognises in these elementary forms of nature, and in the way in which they interact, people she has known and even contemporary social circles. But the Captain continues to explore the concept of affinity in relation to natural elements, focusing on the attraction of opposites and the creation of new substances.

> This affinity is sufficiently striking in the case of alkalis and acids which, although they are mutually antithetical, and perhaps precisely because they are so, most decidedly seek and embrace one another, modify one another, and together form a new substance. Think only of lime, which evidences a great inclination, a decided desire for union with acids of every kind.[50]

It is Eduard who provides the catalyst to develop Goethe's metaphor, when he comments that 'the affinities become interesting only when they bring about divorce'.[51] He goes on to explain that limestone immersed in dilute sulphuric acid will form calcium sulphate or gypsum, and give off a thin gaseous acid. Eduard argues that 'there has occurred a separation and a new combination, and one then feels justified even in employing the term "elective affinity" because it really does look as if one relationship was preferred to another and chosen instead of it'.[52] In this connection, A. G. Steer notes that the German term *Wahlverwandtschaft* might be literally translated as 'choice relationship'.[53] But Charlotte immediately retorts that this is hardly a choice, but rather a matter of natural necessity or opportunity. She comments that 'where your natural substances are concerned, the choice seems to me to lie entirely in the hands of the chemist who brings these substances together'.

For Eduard, his wife's remarks have a double meaning and he makes the metaphor between chemical elements and the novel's protagonists explicit: 'Confess it now! When all is said, I am in your eyes the lime which the Captain, as a sulphuric acid, has seized on, withdrawn from your charming company, and transformed into a stubborn gypsum.'[54] Charlotte's tacit agreement implies that she compares herself to the gaseous acid given off; but she notes that while playing with analogies is amusing, man must consider what validity the words 'choice' and 'elective affinity' possess in this context. Her concern is with the consequences of accepting the metaphor: 'I know, alas, of all too many cases in which an intimate and apparently indissoluble union between two beings has been broken up by a chance association with a third and one of the couple at first so fairly united driven out into the unknown.'[55]

The text implies that we can look on attraction and repulsion between individuals as necessary or inevitable, given the chemical analogy of the interaction between limestone and diluted sulphuric acid. On the same grounds we can employ the term 'elective affinity' to describe the chemical interaction, since it looks 'as if' one relationship was preferred to another and chosen instead of it. As the Captain puts it, 'one credits such entities with a species of will and choice'. But the nature of the species of will and choice that we bestow on these entities is precisely the point for Goethe. He moves subtly between a fascination with chemical relationships – treated sometimes as a metaphor and at other times as an analogy for social relationships – and a personification of chemical entities. Social relationships are credited with the necessity and inevitability usually reserved for relationships between elements of nature; while simultaneously, the elements of nature are accorded a species of will and choice usually taken as characteristic of human beings.

The moral dimension of the question of choice becomes significant here. If chemical relationships between substances are presented as necessary or inevitable, then any reference to choice would seem to be illusory. Substances necessarily attract and repulse one another and this can only be seen as providing us with the appearance, rather than the reality, of preference. If social interaction is governed by the same mechanisms of necessary and inevitable attraction and repulsion, then choice is just as illusory for human beings. On the other hand, if chemical entities are accorded a species of will and choice on the basis of man's narcissism, then are we to assume that they have a species of responsibility in their dealings with one another? Charlotte rejects this possibility, arguing that where natural substances are concerned, choice lies entirely in the hands of the chemist who brings these substances together. For her, any new chemical combinations brought about by the attraction and repulsion of substances should be seen as a consequence of opportunity. It is the chemist who creates an opportunity by choosing to bring the substances together. If Goethe's analogy is to have any force then Charlotte's comments imply that we must ask who or what fulfils the role of the chemist in the 'chemical' interactions between human beings. Charlotte is exploring the metaphor and discovering its limits.

Goethe's own comment about the novella suggests impending doom: 'that it must end in evil hauses, one sees right at the beginning'.[56] His comment also raises the moral dimension of the preferences our choices reveal – at least in terms of the utility of a view which reduces human activity to the activity of chemical bonds created by affined entities. However, Goethe raises the moral question more explicitly in the novel itself. Eduard comments to Charlotte that just as the social circles in which they live 'can be unified through laws and customs, so in our chemical world too there exist intermediaries for combining together those things which repulse one another'.[57] The example given in the text is the combination of oil and water by means of alkaline salt. If laws and customs can unify people and groups who might otherwise find one another repellent, Goethe leaves the reader to ponder the potential of laws and customs to interfere with attractions that are doomed to end in 'evil hauses'.

The search for a role in human interaction analogous to that of the chemist in chemical interactions or for the locus of the 'species of will and choice' relevant to human beings yields only ourselves – in the sense of our own mental capacities. Goethe's novella leaves us with an unresolved tension between blind fate on the one hand and ideas of rational freedom of action on the other. Steer regards the question of its resolution as the underlying problem of the novella. The apparent contradiction between Goethe's two alternatives evokes a Kantian epistemological framework according to which we act under the presupposition of our own freedom, despite a conviction that our actions may well be determined by a force outside of ourselves. Kant recognises that we know objects only as they affect us. This recognition gives rise to a distinction between appearances or the phenomena of the sensible world, and things-in-themselves or the noumena of the intelligible world. On the basis of this distinction, we see ourselves as belonging to the world of sense and as subject to the laws of nature. But we also conceive of ourselves as belonging to the intelligible world, conceiving of our will as free from determination by the causal influences of the world of sense; and obedient to laws that are grounded in reason alone.

Kant's two standpoints are the basis for his resolution of the contradiction between seeing ourselves as both free and yet determined. We see ourselves as free as members of the intelligible world; but as members of the sensible world, the laws of nature – which do not apply in the intelligible world – determine us. As members of the sensible world we do not consider ourselves free from our desires and inclinations. But as members of the intelligible world and in virtue of our freedom we conceive of ourselves as responsible for action on the basis of those desires and inclinations.[58] If, as rational beings, we thought of our will as determined by some external force, our wills would not be our own. But if we thought in this way, it would none the less be impossible to establish how the conviction that some external force controlled us would affect our action. We might believe that every action we undertake has been determined by this external force, but it would make no difference to us at the point at which we had to make decisions about our actions. Thus Kant concludes that we have no choice but to think of ourselves as free: 'we must attribute to every being endowed with reason and a will this property of determining himself to action under the Idea of his own freedom'.[59] His argument is that on the basis of our rationality, freedom is a necessary presumption of all thought and action, so that when we make a choice we must act 'under the idea of freedom'. As Christine Korsgaard puts it, '[t]he point is not that you must *believe* that you are free, but that you must choose *as if* you were free. It is important to see that this is quite consistent with believing yourself to be fully determined.'[60]

Thomas Nagel, in a discussion of moral luck in his book *Mortal Questions*, supports this apparently paradoxical view when he states that although the presence of determinism appears to obliterate responsibility, its absence is no more hospitable to the concept of an individual's responsibility. His point is that either way our actions are viewed externally, as part of the course of events. We are forced to recognise that, despite the fact that significant aspects of our existence, our nature, our experience and our choices are beyond our control, we are responsible for our actions; 'our acts remain ours and we remain ourselves, despite the pervasiveness of the reasons that seem to argue us out of existence'.[61] We are forced to act *as if* we have choice, since to adopt the opposing view that we cannot be held morally responsible for our actions leaves us, in Nagel's opinion, 'with no one to be'.[62]

In the context of Goethe's analogy between chemical and social relationships, Charlotte's reference to the chemist as the locus of choice in the interaction between chemical elements raises a number of questions. What is the relation between the chemist's choice or creation of opportunity and human choice or free will? Where does responsibility for the consequences of the inevitable attractions and repulsions generated by these choices lie? Eduard suggests that attraction and repulsion are simply serendipitous or a matter of blind fate. Some elements naturally attract one another, while others naturally repel one another; just as some human beings find each other naturally attractive, while others remain obdurate strangers. Affined entities 'choose' or determine their union. These processes of attraction are explained in terms of degrees of affinity: from the close and strong to the distant and weak.

Those natural elements that repulse one another can be combined via the intercession of an intermediary, just as laws and customs can unify strangers in certain circumstances. But what is truly interesting – at least to Eduard – is the process by which the affinities themselves bring about divorces: where the introduction of new elements causes an existing affinity to break down and a new, novel and unexpected one emerges. A pun, which is lost in translation, emphasises this interest: the German word for analytical chemist is 'scheidekünstler' and the word for divorce is 'scheidung'. Goethe's view of affinity is associated with a view of emotional attraction as powerful, urgent and non-rational and with ourselves as passive and powerless in the face of such emotion. Martha Nussbaum points out that this view makes for a problematic relationship between emotion and our sense of self.[63] Her comments reinforce Nagel's opinion that removing ourselves from the realm of morally responsible action leaves us 'with no one to be', since we are at the mercy of chemical affinities.

If the affinities Goethe explores are simply serendipitous and we are powerless before them, then a tragic outcome may be inevitable. But Charlotte seems to suggest that the situation is more complex than the chemical analogy indicates. She challenges the physicality of the analogy and, in response to the Captain, extends its anthropomorphism. In doing so she adopts a position that underscores the juxtaposition of Kant's two standpoints. The Captain comments that chemical affinity is 'striking in the case of alkalis and acid which, although they are mutually antithetical, and perhaps precisely because they are so, most decidedly seek and embrace one another, modify one another, and together form a new substance'. Charlotte replies expressing her scepticism:

> [W]hen you call all these curious entities of yours affined, they appear to me to possess not so much an affinity of blood as an affinity of mind and soul. It is in just this way that truly meaningful friendships can arise among human beings: for antithetical qualities make possible a closer and more intimate union.[64]

Perhaps Charlotte has in mind the role that the resolution of conflict can have in developing intimacy. For her the crucial affinity is one of mind, rather than blood. Mapping her comments on to a Kantian perspective, it is one established by the intelligible rather than the sensible world. Charlotte accepts the serendipitous chemical analogy at a physical or sensible level: affinity at the physical level might be evident between elements that are not antithetical, such as water and wine, or between mutually antithetical elements such as acids and alkalis. But her concern is with the restriction of the concept of affinity to the physical when it is applied to human nature. Charlotte's exploration of the metaphor reveals its limitations. She is concretising it and finding it inadequate. Like most extended metaphors it begins to break down under close scrutiny, and in this case we see that the metaphor has slipped to become an actual description. When we talk about relations between friends, we often speak of 'the chemistry' between the friends, as if there is some genuine flesh and blood reaction to the presence of a friend. Here Charlotte is talking about actual relationships, rather than employing the metaphor. Affinity at the physical level is juxtaposed to affinity of the mind: affinity at the mental level might be evident between human beings whose qualities are not antithetical, but it is antithetical qualities at the mental level that interest Charlotte, since she believes that these can give rise to meaningful friendships.

Charlotte is insisting that Eduard and the Captain recognise the difference between physical and mental qualities and that they acknowledge in human beings a role analogous to that of the chemist in chemical interactions. From a Kantian perspective, she is insisting that they not deny man as a rational cause. Kant acknowledged that 'the concept of the intelligible world is only *a point of view* which reason finds itself constrained to adopt outside appearances *in order to conceive of itself as practical*'.[65] But he none the less argued that man as a rational cause is active by means of practical reason. Thus from the perspective of our membership of the intelligible world, the will is free and we must choose on the basis of a reason that it generates. But given our capacity to see ourselves from two standpoints simultaneously – as thoroughly determined in our behaviour, but also as free to choose – our view of ourselves is inherently unstable. That instability impacts on our relationships, since the juxtaposition of these standpoints has ethical consequences. Recognition of our freedom to choose and the acceptance of our natures as rational causes imply that human beings, such as Goethe's protagonists, have some capacity to avoid the 'evil hauses' the novella prefigures. Fate may well have determined the eruption of the attraction between the four main protagonists (Eduard and the Captain, Eduard and Ottilie, Charlotte and Ottilie, and Charlotte and the Captain), which Goethe's novel goes on to explore. But recognition of the protagonists' natures as rational causes demands that they make a choice in relation to that determination. This is necessary if they are to do anything or – as Nagel might express it – if they are to 'be' anyone – whether that be friend, lover or foe.

On Goethe's rendition, affinity is indeed serendipitous, and in this opinion he echoes Montaigne, who implies that there is some luck in the discovery of affinities. Montaigne tells us that his affinity with La Boétie was a matter of such good fortune that we couldn't expect to witness so close a union more than once every three hundred years. But unlike Montaigne, who does not recognise any destructive potential within the concept of such a union, Goethe does not idealise affinity. But then, nor does Goethe restrict discussion of friendship and attraction to relations between virtuous men. His concept of elective affinity encompasses repulsion as well as attraction; separation and 'divorces' as well the creation of new combinations. It implies that relationships are vulnerable to change, given those forces of attraction and repulsion. What is unique in Goethe's use of the concept of elective affinity is that it offers an account of attraction between friends that implies a degree of determinism. It is in the nature of affined entities to show preferences for some entities – perhaps even against their better judgement – and to be repulsed by others. Affined entities appear to be attracted to one another by their very natures, or we might say *for no good reason*; or at least for no reason that philosophers of friendship such as Aristotle or Cicero entertain. But Goethe has Charlotte remind us that the existence of attraction or affinity can lead to 'evil hauses'; affinity does not determine behaviour or relieve us of responsibility for our actions in relation to others. We cannot simply give ourselves up to an affinity completely, allowing our actions to be fully determined by our sensible nature. We must recognise our status as members of the intelligible world who must conceive of themselves as responsible for action, and so take account of the impact or the ethical import of our elected affinity on others. This is a requirement that appears to have more force in conceptions of friendship than it has in conceptions of romantic and erotic love.

Notions of the friend as another self and of friendship as a fusion of souls are problematic with regard to explaining the ground upon which a friendship is based. They appear to overcome concerns that friends love one another for some ulterior motive. But given the claim that genuine friends love one another for themselves, we suspect that such notions could simply disguise a concern with self, rather than a focus on others for themselves. Friendship could be seen as merely a form of self-love if we take the friend to be another self. Still, the idea of friendship as a form of elective affinity has its advantages. Attraction and affection between friends is explained by an affinity which determines their special regard for one another. They are quite simply irresistibly concerned with one another. But this resort to the 'chemistry' between individuals opens up questions relating to choice in friendship, since one feature that is taken to distinguish friendship from formal or blood relations is that friends are freely chosen. As suggested above, if we are prepared to view ourselves from Kant's two standpoints, then we can explain the chemical attraction at the sensible level and our choices in relation to that attraction at the intelligible level of our experience. But this implies that the similarity or affinity between friends is not the crucial constitutive factor in friendship – it may be necessary, but on its own it is not sufficient to explain the relationship.

Emerson's comments in his essay on friendship concur with this view that the emphasis in friendship should not be on similarity, affinity or identity; rather, the foundation of the best friendships is the friends' recognition of their separateness from one another. As he puts it, '[t]he condition which high friendship demands is the ability to do without it . . . there must be very two, before there can be very one . . . The least defect in self-possession, in my judgment, vitiates the entire relation.'[66]

Friendship and Self-Sufficiency

The concept of self-possession is discussed in Chapter 5 in relation to contemporary understandings of self-constitution. It includes discussion of the balance of dependence on and independence from others required for healthy social development; the relationship between self-love, self-interest and self-concern; and it assumes an awareness of the genesis of the self in social interaction with significant others. This brings a specifically modern focus to the debate on the nature of friendship, and of course we cannot expect to find in older or ancient texts intimations of conceptions of the self embraced by contemporary readers. Post-Cartesian and post-Freudian societies will necessarily have very different conceptions of self from those that can be extracted from the exegesis of ancient texts. Some of the difficulties apparent to modern readers in Aristotle's account of friendship and its role in our lives are clearly related to differing conceptions of selfhood or subjectivity; others are related to a different understanding of the notion of self-love; while others again are related to a failure to take difference seriously.

Aristotle's account of the friend as another self would have been less likely to arouse concerns about egoism had he been able to address the 'otherness' of the friend. Aristotle does this to some extent via the juxtaposition of his commendation of the good man's attitude to his friend as a second self with a demand for self-sufficiency. But Julia Annas suggests that the notion of loving a friend as our second self for his own sake can be interpreted in a way that minimises concerns about egoism. Annas argues that 'the prime case of liking X for X's sake is precisely that which *does* have reference to the agent, but an agent who can in fact come to regard another's desires, etc. as his own'. Thus liking someone for their own sake is explained as derivative; but Annas insists that what matters in friendship 'is not whether the desire does or does not have some reference to the agent, but whether it is a desire for the person's welfare for his own sake or not'.[67] Suspicions about egoism in Aristotle's account might have been undermined had he addressed the process by which an individual might come to regard another and different person as another self. What happens when I attempt to understand and accept my friend's behaviour does not involve thinking herself to be me, but rather imagining myself in her position as far as I am able.

Emerson's approach to this question of the friend as a second self is both more circumspect and less problematic than the approaches of Aristotle, Cicero or Kierkegaard. Like Aristotle and Cicero he argues that we are by nature social beings, but revealingly says of the source of our characteristic delight in our relationship with a close friend that '[t]he only joy I have in his being mine, is that the *not mine* is *mine*'.[68] Emerson idealises close interpersonal interaction in friendship. He recommends that we open ourselves to the possibility of intimacy, that we indulge the affection he believes we will find in others, and enjoy the increase in our intellectual and active powers that will come with the increase in our affection.[69] But despite his idealism he recognises our remoteness from one another and the tension implicit in a view of the friend as another self:

> Friendship, like the immortality of the soul, is too good to be believed. The lover, beholding his maiden, half knows that she is not verily that which he worships; and in the golden hour of friendship we are surprised with shades of suspicion and unbelief. We doubt that we bestow on our hero the virtues in which he shines, and afterwards worship the form to which we have ascribed this divine inhabitation. In strictness, the soul does not respect men as it respects itself. In strict science all persons underlie the same condition of infinite remoteness.[70]

Emerson sees ebb and flow as characteristic of the human condition: 'If the good is there, so is the evil; if the affinity, so the repulsion.' This characteristic has an explosive and a pedagogical function in friendship: at the most intense point of our feelings of union, we are surprised to discover our remoteness from one another. We become clearly aware of the distance that separates us, and Emerson seems to imply that the self-possessed individual will find this less of a surprise. Emerson follows Aristotle and Cicero in emphasising that friendship of the best kind is dependent upon the self-possession or the self-sufficiency of each of the friends. Cicero tells us that friendship is not the child of insufficiency and poverty, arguing that if this were the case, the less confidence a man had in himself, the better suited he would be for friendship. He argues, on the contrary, that 'the more confidence a man has in himself, the more he finds himself so fortified by virtue and wisdom that he is completely self-sufficient and believes that his destiny is in his own hands, so much the better will he be both at making and at keeping friends'.[71] Aristotle sees self-sufficiency as a characteristic of good men who 'have no need of friends, because they have their good things'.[72] He goes on to explain that it is more characteristic of a friend to confer than to receive a benefit and that the self-sufficient man is in the best position to do this. We are left to conclude that the self-sufficient man is likely to make a good friend, despite the fact that he has no need of friends. But precisely what does self-sufficiency entail?

Agnes Heller criticises the notion of self-sufficiency (autarky), arguing that it is like the state of death in the sense that 'an autarkic person dies for all human relationships'.[73] In a discussion of Plato she points to the close association of *philia* with *eros* especially in the *Lysis*, and to the eroticisation of *philia* in the Platonic Dialogues generally. Her argument is that for Plato our whole life 'is just a single strenuous effort to find the object of our desire, to possess something which cannot be possessed, to achieve autarky – self-sufficiency – the only state where we can finally find peace'. Perhaps this is our fantasy, and the view that a completely autarkic person dies to all human relationships is thoroughly logical from a semantic perspective; but it is none the less jaundiced if we apply it to Aristotle's position. The reason that Aristotle emphasises self-sufficiency in friendship of the good is related to a concern that the good man cannot be said to need friends in any narrowly instrumental way.[74]

Aristotle tells us that the self-sufficient man exercises and cultivates his intellect; he engages in contemplation, the only activity that is appreciated for its own sake; he will show more interest in what is beautiful and unprofitable than in what is useful and profitable. Profit is not his chief interest, since he is of independent means and has an adequate, although not superfluous, supply of the necessaries of life.[75] Thus the self-sufficient man will not need friends of utility, since he can supply what is needed by his own efforts; nor will he need friends of pleasure, since he has no need of imported pleasure. But he will have friends, since friends 'are considered to be the greatest of external goods' and it would seem paradoxical to deprive the good and self-sufficient man of such goods, especially given man's nature as a social creature constituted to live in company.[76] But in the same discussion Aristotle leaves us with this explanation of the self-sufficient man's friendships: the self-sufficient man needs friends to receive his benefits and to provide him with external examples of virtuous and pleasurable activity that he can contemplate, since human beings are better able to observe neighbours than themselves. Again Aristotle's explanation portrays friendship as complicated by motives of self-interest. The focus of the self-sufficient man's activity in friendship appears to be on himself, rather than his friend.

The difficulty of assimilating the concept of self-sufficiency to that of friendship is due to the association between self-sufficiency and independence. Thomson's translation of Aristotle's *Nichomachean Ethics* indicates that the ancient Greek word *autarkēs* (self-sufficient) normally carried the sense of independence.[77] Aristotle's definitions of man's proper function and of happiness highlight that sense of independence. As we have seen, man's proper function is activity of the soul in accordance with a rational principle, while perfect happiness is found in contemplative activity – that activity in accordance with the highest virtue. Thus perfect happiness is associated with an activity – contemplation – which the wise man can practise 'by himself and the wiser he is, the more he can do it'.[78] Aristotle explains that the help of 'fellow-workers' may improve his contemplative activity, but the focus here is on the quality of contemplation, rather than on the relationship between fellows engaged in contemplation.

In book I of the *Ethics* Aristotle departs from normal usage and specifies a particular usage of the word *autarkēs* in relation to human beings. He states that by self-sufficient 'we do not mean what is sufficient for oneself alone living a solitary life, but something that includes parents, wife and children, friends and fellow-citizens in general; for man is a social being'.[79] He then qualifies this view, telling the reader that we cannot extend the application of the social bonds requisite to the self-sufficient man so far as to include all those with whom he interacts, since this 'will proceed to infinity'. He addresses this problem in relation to friends in book IX, chapter 9, of the *Nichomachean Ethics*, where he tells us that there must be a limit to the number of one's friends and that this limit is determined by the chief factor in friendship: the possibility of intimacy. Aristotle is drawing attention to a very practical problem. We simply cannot be intimate with a large number of people and it is probably 'as well to aim at having not as many friends as possible, but only as many as are enough to form an intimate circle'. Strong friendship 'is felt only towards a few'; and we must understand our limits with respect to the number of people we 'can love for their own sake and for their goodness', and be content to find even a few of this quality.[80]

So the self-sufficient man does not lead a solitary life and Aristotle's concept of self-sufficiency does take account of the fact that man is a social being, constituted to live in the company of family, friends and acquaintances. But the association between self-sufficiency and independence means that we have a particular image of the self-sufficient man. He is one who supplies what he needs by his own efforts in those spheres of life concerned with useful and pleasurable things. He is also capable of exercising and cultivating his intellect by his own efforts, although he can benefit from the input of good friends within this sphere. So he has friends, as he must if he is to participate fully in the social life available to human beings, but he does not need them in the sense that he is dependent on them for physical, financial, emotional or intellectual sustenance. Yet this conclusion seems to trivialise a relationship that, Aristotle argues, acts as a social cement; provides us with what 'is considered to be the greatest of all goods'; and is a source of understanding, in that through intimacy good men 'come to appreciate each other's characters as being like their own'.[81]

Aristotle addresses the apparent incongruity between self-sufficiency and friendship by explaining, first, that although the good and self-sufficient man has no need of friends, in virtue of his goodness we would not wish to deny him the good of friendship. And second, in virtue of man's nature as a social being, we recognise that self-sufficiency does not exclude social relations. However, to the modern reader, the term 'self-sufficiency' does seem an inappropriate and incongruous recommendation in the context of friendship. If what is crucial in friendship is the care a friend has for his or her friend for that friend's own sake, then it is the quality of care that distinguishes a good friend. Care in friendship is related to the intimacy of the relationship, as Chapter 4 will argue. Aristotle's focus on the good man's self-sufficiency in terms of the necessaries of life restricts our appreciation of the role of intimacy in friendship. This is so despite Aristotle's recognition of man's social nature, his reference to the crucial role of intimacy in developing an appreciation of the character of others, and his recognition that intimacy places a practical limitation on the number of friendships we can develop. Aristotle's treatment of friendship and other relational goods occurs within the context of his focus on virtuous conduct and contemplation as the supreme good and the end to which man aims. Consequently, his discussion of self-sufficiency is subsumed within this context.

Martha Nussbaum, in her book *The Fragility of Goodness*, argues that appropriate human self-sufficiency involves relational good and notes that Aristotle recognises this. However, she goes on to argue that relational good entails vulnerability. Thus she alerts us to the pleasure and fulfilment – as well as to the risks – inherent in intimacy: '[A] completely invulnerable life is likely to prove impoverished . . . [since] vulnerability is a necessary background condition of certain human goods: thus, anyone who loves a child makes herself vulnerable, and the love of children is a genuine good.'[82]

Nussbaum argues that while much human vulnerability can be explained as a consequence of our own ignorance or moral deficiency, vulnerability also comes with the territory within close interpersonal relationships. She endorses Aristotle's claim that the best forms of vulnerable goods (political action, love and friendship) are themselves the relatively stable, rather than the relatively transient, forms of good. But her point is that opening ourselves to intimate relations with others as friends, parents or lovers is risky. It makes us vulnerable to suffering. Caring for another for that person's own sake implies making her concerns to some extent my concerns, so that we become vulnerable in the face of a friend's suffering, her difficulties and disappointments. Nussbaum argues that this puts us at the mercy of luck, at least to some extent.[83] Our emotional investment in the relationship also makes us vulnerable to the possibility of rejection by the friend. As Nussbaum points out, philosophers seek to limit the risk and vulnerability we face in friendship. Aristotle's elevation of friendship based on character over other less stable forms is an example of this focus on stability. An honourable character and virtuous action are seen as less transient than goods associated with utility or pleasure, such as money or appearance.

It is clear that Aristotle recognised that appropriate human self-sufficiency does involve relational good. His discussion in book I, chapter 7, of the *Nichomachean Ethics* indicates that he saw self-sufficiency as a characteristic that humans display within the community of which they are a part. But the association between independence and self-sufficiency later in the *Ethics* undermines any detailed consideration of the nature and consequences of the intimacy requisite to communal relations, such as friendship. Given our nature as social beings, acceptance of the vulnerability we face within intimate relationships must temper any view of the good friend as self-sufficient.

Like Aristotle, Emerson also emphasises the importance of independence between friends of the best kind. But he characterises friends of the best kind as self-possessed rather than self-sufficient. Rather than emphasising the fact that the good and self-sufficient man has no need of friends, Emerson argues that friends of the best kind must have the ability to do without friendship – irrespective of their pleasure in or need for friendship. Aristotle's claim that despite the good man's self-sufficiency we would not wish to deny him friends is less curious when interpreted from Emerson's perspective. Emerson equates the ability to do without friends – self-possession – with the state in which we are 'our own', which for him is the foundation of friendship of the best kind. And as we saw, he argues that the least defect in self-possession will contaminate friendship.[84] Cicero and Seneca seem to exaggerate this demand. Seneca takes the call to self-possession so far as to see mourning the death of a friend, especially excessive mourning, as a sign of weakness and moral failure, since he is in agreement with the view that friendship is not borne out of need.[85] Cicero claims that in the face of the death of a friend, 'to be crushed by grief at one's own misfortunes is the act not of a man who loves his friend, but of one who loves himself'.[86] These views are open to the criticism that they may not sufficiently appreciate the value of friendship to human life, since they appear to suggest that we maintain an emotional distance from even our closest friends.

Yet the call to self-possession need not make this demand and it is less likely to do so if the model of friendship we adopt is one that recognises, even expects, the expression of some degree of difference among friends. Models of friendship associated with ideals of similarity and fusion illustrate varying degrees of blindness to difference, and Aristotle's account of friendship provides a good example of such a model. However, if we accept Aristotle's definition of a friend as someone who cares for his or her friend for that friend's own sake – but do not accept the normative view of the self that accompanies his definition – then we must entertain the possibility that friends may not always find themselves in agreement. The notion of absolute harmony between friends is at odds with empirical reality; the attitudes and actions of friends can surprise us and may cause friction. If harmony is achieved through the suppression of all dissension, then the authenticity of the relationship would be suspect. The trust, care and liking which are definitive of friendship ought to preclude friends from continually disguising their thoughts and feelings. Lack of conflict is not necessarily a sign of deep affection or strength of commitment. It can just as easily indicate lack of commitment or fear of rejection. In fact some degree of conflict can have constructive effects within a relationship, while completely avoiding conflict can limit the degree of intimacy between friends. Given Aristotle's own recognition in the *Eudemian Ethics* that the friend must be a separate self, we might expect some disagreement or conflict between friends.[87] Modern notions of friendship take difference more seriously than Aristotle did; however, as we shall see in the next chapter, among the ancients, Cicero was well aware of the challenges that conflict poses to friendship.

Notes

1. For indications of this debate see MacIntyre, *After Virtue*; Mulgan, 'The Role of Friendship in Aristotle's Political Theory'.
2. Derrida, *Politics of Friendship*.

3. Aristotle, *Politics*, 1252b29–30 and 1280b5–12.

4. Aristotle, *Nichomachean Ethics*, 1171a3–25.

5. Cooper, 'Political Animals and Civic Friendship', p. 304.

6. Cooper ('Political Animals and Civic Friendship', p. 319) and MacIntyre (*After Virtue*, p. 147) disagree on this point. Cooper regards civic friendship as a form of advantage friendship, while MacIntyre sees it as a form of primary friendship or friendship of the good.

7. Cooper discusses this point about the relationship between the good and city life in 'Political Animals and Civic Friendship', pp. 304 and 321.

8. Aristotle, *Nichomachean Ethics*, 1098b12 and 1169a23–b11. Aristotle's position on this is contradictory, since at another point he claims that honour is the greatest external good (*Nichomachean Ethics*, 1123b13–35).

9. Ibid., 1170b15.

10. Ibid., 1156a16–b2.

11. Ibid., 156b23–1157a9.

12. Ibid., 1157a10–34 and 1155b29–1156a16.

13. Stern-Gillet, *Aristotle's Philosophy of Friendship*, p. 61.

14. Ibid., pp. 66–7.

15. Ibid., p. 75.

16. Ibid., pp. 8 and 75.

17. Telfer, 'Friendship', p. 253.

18. Stern-Gillet, *Aristotle's Philosophy of Friendship*, p. 8.

19. Aristotle, *Nichomachean Ethics*, 1164b28–1165a19.

20. Ibid., 1166a13–17.

21. Ibid., 1168b34–35.

22. In book I of *Nichomachean Ethics,* Aristotle explains man's function in this way: '[I]f we assume that the function of man is a kind of life, viz., an activity or series of actions of the soul, implying a rational principle; and if the function of a good man is to perform these well and rightly; and if every function is performed well when performed in accordance with its proper excellence; if all this is so, the conclusion is that the good for man is an activity of the soul in accordance with virtue' (ibid., 1098a12–17).

23. Stern-Gillet, *Aristotle's Philosophy of Friendship*, pp. 29, 26–7.

24. Richard Mulgan notes that Aristotle first describes friendship of the good as 'friendship on account of virtue' but that he also refers to it as 'friendship on account of character' (*Nichomachean Ethics,* 1164a12). Mulgan claims that the second phrase is the one that 'more accurately captures its meaning in the context of Aristotle's general social theory' (Mulgan, 'The Role of Friendship in Aristotle's Political Theory', p. 17). However, on my interpretation as supported by Stern-Gillet, Aristotle's uses of the two phrases are different ways of expressing the same concept.

25. Aristotle, *Nichomachean Ethics*, 1171a3–25.

26. Ibid., 1168a18–b7.

27. Ibid., 1165b30–1166a15.

28. Ibid.

29. Ibid., 1161b15–1162a1.

30. Aristotle, *Nichomachean Ethics*, 1166a32, 1169b6–7, 1170b6–7; *Eudemian Ethics*, 1245a34–35.

31. Cicero, 'On Friendship', p. 108.

32. Ibid., p. 108.
33. Aquinas, 'Questions on Love and Charity', p. 162.
34. Ibid., p. 163.
35. Ibid., pp. 164 and 180.
36. Montaigne, 'Of Friendship', p. 136.
37. Ibid., pp. 139–40.
38. Ibid., p. 143.
39. Ibid., p. 139.
40. Seneca, 'On Philosophy and Friendship', p. 127.
41. Plato in the *Lysis* also explores the idea that the basis of all friendship is the attraction of opposites. But Price in *Love and Friendship in Plato and Aristotle* (p. 11) points out that this assumes that all friendship has the same nature, a thesis that comes to grief over cases where dissimilarity makes for enmity. Price argues that in fact this model of friendship based on the attraction of opposites is best applied to cases of utility friendship and – despite his view of utility friendship as paradoxical from a contemporary perspective – he quotes Aristotle for support: 'Friendship because of utility seems especially to arise from contraries, e.g. between poor and rich, ignorant and learned' (*Nichomachean Ethics*, 1159b12–14).
42. Cicero, 'On Friendship', p. 91.
43. Emerson, 'Friendship', p. 228.
44. These comments are made by Hollingdale in the introduction to Goethe, *Elective Affinities*, p. 14.
45. Steer, *Goethe's Elective Affinities*, p. 291.
46. Ibid., p. 37.
47. Goethe, *Elective Affinities*, p. 50.
48. Ibid.
49. Ibid., p. 52.
50. Ibid., pp. 52–3.
51. Eduard goes on to say that, '[i]t even used to be a title of honour to chemists to call them artists in divorcing one thing from another'. Goethe, *Elective Affinities*, p. 53.
52. Ibid., p. 54.
53. Steer, *Goethe's Elective Affinities*, p. 38.
54. Goethe, *Elective Affinities*, pp. 54–5.
55. Ibid., p. 55.
56. The phrase 'evil hauses' was apparently borrowed from astrology and means simply that the eventual tragic outcome is obvious (Steer, *Goethe's Elective Affinities*, p. 291).
57. Goethe, *Elective Affinities*, p. 52.
58. Since we cannot *know* the intelligible world, we can only say that we *conceive of* our will as free. The intelligible world is 'something of which it [practical reason] has no knowledge' (Kant, *The Moral Law*, p. 118).
59. Kant, *The Moral Law*, p. 109.
60. Korsgaard, *Creating the Kingdom of Ends*, p. 163.
61. Nagel, 'Moral Luck', p. 38.
62. Ibid., p. 37.
63. Nussbaum, *Upheavals of Thought*, pp. 24–6. Nussbaum supports her analysis of the 'unthinking movements' view of emotion with reference to the Stoic phi-

losopher Seneca, who compared emotions to fire, to currents of the sea, to fierce gales and to intruding explosive forces, despite his commitment to a cognitive view of emotion. She also asserts that it is not only the Western tradition that treats emotions as forces of nature, since analogous metaphors are found in Indian and Chinese poetry and in the African novel (p. 26, fn.10).

64. Goethe, *Elective Affinities*, p. 53.
65. Kant, *The Moral Law*, p. 118.
66. Emerson, 'Friendship', pp. 229–30.
67. Annas, 'Plato and Aristotle on Friendship and Altruism', p. 542.
68. Emerson, 'Friendship', p. 219.
69. Ibid., p. 221.
70. Ibid., p. 222.
71. Cicero, 'On Friendship', p. 91.
72. Aristotle, *Nichomachean Ethics*, 1169b5.
73. Heller, 'The Beauty of Friendship', pp. 6–7.
74. Heller does recognise this. When she refers to the friendship between Brutus and Cassius in Shakespeare's *Julius Caesar* she describes Brutus as 'an altogether morally motivated man – "self-sufficient" in the Aristotelian sense'. But she none the less refers to the men as two 'best friends' (ibid., p. 13).
75. Aristotle, *Nichomachean Ethics*, 1125a5–27, 1177a25–b13 and 1179a20–b7.
76. Ibid., 1169a23–b35.
77. Ibid., p. 74, fn.2.
78. Ibid., 1177a25–b13.
79. Ibid., 1098b12–1099a7.
80. Ibid., 1171a3–25.
81. Ibid., 1175a10–34.
82. Nussbaum, *The Fragility of Goodness*, p. xxx.
83. Ibid., p. xxix.
84. Emerson, 'Friendship', pp. 229–30.
85. Seneca, 'On Philosophy and Friendship', p. 123.
86. Cicero, 'On Friendship', p. 83.
87. Aristotle, *Eudemian Ethics*, 1245a34–35.

Chapter 3

The Other Self as Friend

Difference: Threats and Challenges

> [I]f we do find some individuals who would think it shameful to put money ahead of friendship, where shall we find those who would not put honours, public office, military command, civil authority, or wealth ahead of friendship – the sort who, if these things were placed on one side of the scales and the laws of friendship on the other, would show a definite leaning toward the latter?[1]

Cicero believed that human beings find it hard to make light of power and will cast friendship aside in the interests of attaining power and influence. His most scathing commentary on this tendency is that those who engage in this kind of defection from the duties of friendship assume that their behaviour will not be open to serious criticism; such men take it that others will assume that only an extremely important reason could have led them to cast friendship aside. Cicero presents power, influence, manipulation and weakness as factors both intimately related and antithetical to the practice of friendship. So while Aristotle located civic friendship within the public sphere as a bond that constituted and sustained the life of the Greek polis, Cicero was sceptical about the possibility of true friendships among men who are engaged in politics and affairs of state. Despite the many similarities in their accounts of friendships of the best kind, Cicero recognised, as Aristotle did not, that friendship has as much potential for creating conflict within the political sphere as it does for fostering harmony. In this respect, Cicero's view of friendship or *amicitia* is similar to that of the Epicureans, who also saw friendship as inimical to politics.

Given the fierce political strife that characterised the Roman Republic, particularly during the last twenty years of free Roman institutions prior to the age of Caesar (70–50 BC), *amicitia* could not serve as a civic bond. Horst Hutter explains that the foundation of the state during the time of the Roman Republic had been *concordia*, a harmony that represented the legal resolution of stalemated conflict between rival noble households and their supporters.[2] These rival groups were known as *patriae potestates*, and *concordia* entailed their acknowledgement of equality before Roman laws and institutions. Political power (*potestas*) was wielded by political parties or factions (*patriae potestates*), the two main parties in the Roman Republic being the *populares* and the *optimates*. The *populares*, as the name suggests, were the popular party, agitating for change and the extension of citizens' rights, while the *optimates* were the senatorial party, representing the status quo, the maintenance of tradition, and the preservation of the extensive power enjoyed by Rome's magistrates and consuls.[3] *Concordia* enabled men of dissimilar character and virtue to share citizenship based on a similarity of rights; and as such it created a fragile harmony in the context of political dissension. The law became the social bond underlying the state. Cicero's long experience in the Roman criminal courts, particularly in his defence of the victims of politically motivated prosecutions, undoubtedly encouraged him in this view. The system of authority predicated on the institution of *patria potestas* produced what Hutter refers to as 'an uneasy equilibrium of ever-shifting alliances'.[4] When the conflict between rival *patriae potestates* developed into civil war in the late Roman Republic, *concordia* collapsed and *amicitia* assumed the conspiratorial character that Cicero chronicled. Victory of one group of conspirators over another was often preceded by violence and followed by bloody recrimination.

The events that preceded Cicero's own death illustrate the instability of friendship within the political sphere and the fierceness of the reprisals of enemies. After Cicero had helped Octavian (Caesar Octavianus, the greatnephew of Julius Caesar) to win the consulship, Octavian abandoned him in order to form an alliance with Marc Antony (Marcus Antonius) and Lepidus (Marcus Aemilius Lepidus) in 43 BC. The deliberations of this Second Triumvirate upon the elimination of their republican enemies are recorded by Plutarch:

> It is said that for the first two days Caesar (Octavius) kept up his struggle to save Cicero, but yielded on the third and gave him up. The terms of their mutual concessions were as follows: Caesar was to abandon Cicero, Lepidus his brother Paulus, and Antony, Lucius Caesar, who was his uncle on his mother's side.[5]

The competitive nature of the *patriae potestates* produced the military imperium that effected their downfall and the downfall of the Roman Republic. In principle, *amicitia* might well have acted as a civic bond, but in the context of the fierce political partisanship of the late Roman Republic it became a fragile and pragmatic relationship. It came to consist in the rendering of services and protection between *amici* in pursuit of power, public office and the spoils associated with the expansion of the Roman Empire. The word *amicitia* was once used interchangeably with *factio* to refer to a band of friends; however, *factio* gradually acquired a pejorative connotation. By the time of the late Roman Republic *amicitia* had largely degenerated into *factio*, so that the language of friendship was employed as a disguise for political conspiracy. As Taylor puts it: 'It [*factio*] came to be used for a clique, generally of men of high position, who had common designs for their own advantage in the state. Unanimity of purpose, according to a speech which Sallust puts into the mouth of a tribune, is *amicitia* among good men and *factio* among bad men.'[6]

However, as an ideal, *amicitia* was a relationship that served to regulate and preserve the authority of the *patriae potestates* by providing linkages between households. To be effective it had to involve an equivalent degree of reciprocity between the friends, so that every act of friendship was regarded by the recipient as a debt incurred to be balanced by an appropriate response in the future. There is a parallel here between the pragmatism of Homeric guest-friendship discussed in Chapter 1 and the structure of *amicitia*. The role of guest-friendship in providing limited stability between competing households in Homer's Ithaca was not unlike the role that *amicitia* might have played in regulating conflict between rival *patriae potestates*. Both guest-friendship and *amicitia* could be inherited by descendants of those who had entered into the relationships; and in both relationships, the actions a friend was prepared to undertake on one's behalf and the loyalty of his support were more significant than his intentions and feelings.

The parallel between guest-friendship and *amicitia* can be extended further, into recent times, to include the attitudes to friendship that Jeremy Boissevain records among members of the Mafia in modern Sicily.[7] In that context, modern *amicitia* also demands a rigid and explicit reciprocity; and, as with Homeric guest-friendship and *amicitia* in Cicero's Rome, it is mutual service that is crucial to the relationship; the primary motive, although not necessarily the only motive, being the satisfaction of needs for protection, support and even retribution. However, *amicitia*'s potential to satisfy such needs, so as to regulate and maintain the authority and linkages between the *patriae potestates*, came under strain during the period of the late Roman Republic. Cicero's suspicion of friendship within the public realm is a response to this strain.

Cicero had been responsible for the exposition in Latin of the doctrines of the major schools of Hellenistic philosophy, so that his contemporaries were familiar with the Stoic doctrine that the wise man loves his friend as much as himself, and with the view the Stoics shared with Aristotle that friendship could serve as the basis of political community. As Hutter points out, for those raised on such ideas, a friend's failure to fulfil one's expectations of support within the political arena, or his disloyalty towards the state, must have produced a sense of betrayal and bitterness that increased the intensity with which political struggles were conducted.[8] But as Cicero explains, 'if we put friendship together through the expectation of advantage, a change in our expectations would also rend it apart'.[9] Since it often happens that the interests of both parties do not agree or that they have a difference of opinion on political matters, friendships founded on advantage are likely to collapse. Expediency can both cement and dissolve friendships.

Given that *amicitia* in Cicero's Rome failed as a mechanism for regulating conflict between rival *patriae potestates* and hence as a civic bond, Cicero concluded that true friendship was unlikely to survive in the political sphere. A true friend ought to offer support in adversity, but most men are interested in their own advantage, in Cicero's estimation: when they are prospering they drop their friends, or when their friends are in trouble they abandon them.[10] True friendship would only be compatible with political life if the needs of the friend and the requirements of the state did not conflict. Like Aristotle, Cicero claimed that such compatibility would only occur among the virtuous, given that virtue demanded loyalty to the state. But Cicero could hardly ignore the scarcity of such virtue in Rome's turbulent political climate, or the potential for individual citizens supported by their friends to conspire against the state for their own advantage. In his Rome, the ideal of *amicitia* could too easily become *factio* for it to function as civic friendship in the Aristotelian mode. Consequently, he warned that good men, who unwittingly found themselves among friends who engage in wrongful conduct, 'must never consider themselves so bound [by friendship] that they may not abandon their friends when they go wrong in matters of state'.[11]

The contrary positions of Aristotle and Cicero on civic friendship may be due, in part, to the difference in the size of the Greek polis and the Roman state. In his discussion of the polis, Hutter suggests that friendship can only be considered a primarily political phenomenon in a world in which two conditions apply: political experience must be confined in terms of its scale; and political life must be conducted in a public space where individuals can meet regularly. The growth of the population of Rome in the late Republic and the expansion of its empire had made the distance between public policy and individual choice substantial.[12] The size and complexity of the Republic meant that the relationship of friendship could not bridge that distance. However, the question of whether conflict might threaten stability even within relatively small political units remains open; serious differences can develop within small communities and might come to threaten the body politic.

Some of Cicero's comments suggest that the form of political organisation is as relevant as size might be. He warns of the superficiality of *amicitia* under corrupt regimes, specifically under the tyranny of Tarquin; and he

saw the tyrant as incapable of true friendship. The character traits definitive of a tyrant preclude him both from liking or caring for a friend for that
person's own sake and also from being liked in the same manner. The tyrant
could maintain a friendship only as long as no conflict occurred between
the friendship and the maintenance of his power; that is, only as long as the
friend was not opposed to the tyrant's despotic abuse of power, and to that
extent shared in the tyrant's vice. Thus pursuit of power at any cost, its arbitrary exercise and the fear such corruption engenders, make a pretence of
friendship on Cicero's view.[13] *Amicitia* lapses into *factio*; it is characterised
by hypocrisy born of fear and resentment so that it becomes opportunistic,
capricious and shallow. Hutter refers to the way that Republican constitutional forms were reduced to theatrical farce by some Roman emperors,
notably Caligula and Nero. In the late Empire, for example, the debasement
of rational ethical values and forms is strikingly visible when gladiatorial
combat is substituted for argument and deliberation. The analogy with
theatre also applies to the counterfeit of friendship, which, Cicero pre-
sciently argued, appeared under tyranny. Roman political friendship ceased
to be part of a code of legitimate bonds between members of the nobility
and became a farce, even a spectacle:

> In the case of tyranny the power of the tyrant transcends all tradition, law, and
> virtue. It frustrates all expectations of justice and equity, and by its very arbitrari-
> ness hinders the application and development of friendship. The tyrant is sur-
> rounded by sycophants and flatterers who . . . give public life the characteristics
> of a theatrical performance.[14]

Cicero's commentary on friendship and his exclusion of friendship from
the tyrannical order suggest that some form of egalitarian political organisation and some degree of political stability may be necessary if friendship
is to endure, in either the public or the private sphere. The fear and resentment that characterise tyranny will necessarily undermine the trust that is
essential, at least to some degree, to all friendship. This in turn suggests –
contrary to Aristotle's view – that friendship is not, and cannot be, the foundation of the kind of stable and egalitarian political life that Aristotle considered the citizens of the polis to share. Rather, some measure of stability
and equity in the socio-political order of a community or state may be a necessary pre-condition of friendship. Colin Turnbull's 1973 study of the Ik,
which is discussed below, offers contemporary corroboration of the suggestion that stable political and social conditions might be prerequisites of
enduring friendship.

In writing *De Amicitia*, Cicero attempted to reconcile the realities of
Roman political life with the ideals of friendship inherited from the
Hellenistic tradition. His commentary leads us to conclude that the ideal of
friendship could only be maintained if it were insulated from the divisive

realities of political life. When translated into the public world, friendship became a threat to political authority and stability and was itself undermined; friends showed themselves to be unreliable and mercurial. Cicero recommended the steadfast, reliable, well-adjusted and loyal person as a friend, arguing that friendship is unlikely to endure in the private sphere if friends show themselves to be inconstant, unreliable or changeable; just as it was unable to survive in the public sphere where friends displayed these traits in an effort to secure political power and influence. Yet if, as Aristotle claimed, friends 'seem even to become better men by exercising their friendship and improving each other', then an emphasis on stability and constancy must be balanced by openness to change.[15] Boyd Tonkin criticises the passivity and complacency of what he refers to as 'steady-state' models of human affection; and Michael Oakeshott argues that according to such models, 'Friends are not concerned with what might be made of one another, but only with the enjoyment of one another; and the condition of this enjoyment is a ready acceptance of what is, an absence of any desire to change and improve.'[16]

If friendships are to endure they require not only an acceptance and tolerance of the friend as he or she is, but also some degree of acceptance and tolerance of change in the friend. Although friends who are concerned for one another in themselves will hope to see friends make the best of their abilities and talents, the change we see in friends may not necessarily amount to the kind of improvement Aristotle envisages. Aristotle's and Cicero's insistence that virtuous friends will always agree – at least in matters of consequence – fails to take account of the possibility of change that might not be regarded as improving. At the same time it obscures any need to attend to questions about the place of difference in friendship.

Michel de Montaigne went beyond both Aristotle and Cicero in eulogising the personal friendship of virtuous men. Like Cicero, Montaigne lived during a period of social and political upheaval, and the notion of friendship as a civic or political bond seems to have been even less acceptable for him than it had been for Cicero. Before Montaigne was thirty, the religious civil wars between French Protestants and Roman Catholics had broken out. As a Catholic mayor of Bordeaux between 1581 and 1585, Montaigne acted as advisor to Henry of Navarre and helped keep communication open between Protestant Navarre and Catholic France. His experiences would only have confirmed the distinctions he drew between noble friends and citizens; and – as we saw in the previous chapter – between the sovereign friendships of virtuous men and the more common and often pragmatic friendship of ordinary men. He recommended caution in relation to the latter:

> I advise you not to confuse the rules of the two [types of friendship]; you would make a mistake. You must walk in those other friendships bridle in hand, with prudence and precaution; the knot is not so well tied that there is no cause to mistrust

it. 'Love him,' Chilo used to say, 'as if you are to hate him some day; hate him as if you are to love him.' This precept which is so abominable in sovereign and masterful friendship is healthy in the practice of ordinary and customary friendships in regard to which we must use the remark that Aristotle often repeated: 'O my friends, there is no friend.'[17]

The cynical precept that Montaigne quoted was taken from Sophocles' play *Ajax*, and had been criticised by Cicero as hostile to friendship. Cicero drew attention to the illogicality of attempting to be the friend of a person one anticipates will some day be one's enemy. A relationship built on that kind of cynicism would imply that one ought to conceal vulnerability and withhold any communication that could later be used vindictively by the 'friend-turned-enemy'. It is completely at odds with the notion that a friend is one whom we trust and with whom we have no need of pretence; and it suggests that we might find a friend's wrongful conduct to our advantage, since we will be on the lookout for handles of reproach that may be useful in the future. The precept Montaigne recommends could only be a barrier to intimacy and hence destructive of friendship. With regard to sovereign friendships between virtuous men, Montaigne simply dismisses the possibility of disagreement and difference, insulating these friendships from disintegration. At the same time he warns ordinary men to build their common and pragmatic friendships on the anticipation of difference and the possibility of the disintegration of friendship.

Montaigne's idealisation of the relationship between sovereign friends makes it impossible for him to recognise that such friendships are subject to the vulnerability that Martha Nussbaum has identified as inherent to relational goods like love and friendship.[18] His exaggeration of the vulnerability that ordinary friends face in common friendships leads him to recommend an attitude between friends that would undermine their friendship. The degree of caution he recommends is more appropriate to the maintenance of civil relations between individuals who have been estranged from one another; or between those who are necessarily engaged with one another, but are essentially indifferent or even antagonistic towards one another. Montaigne advises his readers to protect themselves against the insecurity he sees as inherent to common friendships, even though doing so would destroy the trust and intimacy we think of as characteristic of friendship. At the same time he idealises and rarefies sovereign friendship so that his sovereign friends are artificially secure in their relationship with one another. But in fact opening ourselves to intimate relations with others is an inherently insecure enterprise, since it brings us both the pleasures of engagement and the risk of disappointment, suffering and rejection.

Jean-Paul Sartre would explain this insecurity as a feature of human existence; for him, insecurity is a consequence of the ontology of human being.

On the Sartrean schema, we are responsible for what we make of ourselves and we are free to break away from what we have made of ourselves; but there is always a tension between our facticity (the facts and circumstances of our lives that restrict our possibilities) and our freedom and responsibility. This is complicated by Sartre's identification of our being-for-others, which ensures that we are not wholly constituted by our own self-determination with regard to the facts and circumstances of our lives. We have a being-for-others that defines us and puts us at the mercy of the judgements and reactions of others. I am incapable of apprehending for myself the self that I am for the other, just as I am incapable of apprehending what the other is for himself. The other as a subject necessarily relates to me as an object; so if the other surprises me engaged in an activity that is shameful, I discover my shame through the other's 'look' (*le regard*). I do not appear to myself as I am 'for-the-other' and I have no access or control over his apprehension of me, although I may try to resist the definition of myself that emerges from the other's perception of me. Interpersonal conflict and friction are inevitable and unsurpassable on this schema. As Sartre puts it, 'conflict is the original meaning of being-for-others . . . the Other's freedom is the foundation of my being. But precisely because I exist by means of the Other's freedom, I have no security.'[19]

Some accounts of human psychology offer an analysis of friendship that implies an alternative explanation of the insecurity inherent in relations between friends. Such accounts appear to interpret all human action as at bottom a matter of self-interest, and hence friendship within that context – given that it is contingent on self-interest – is likely to be inconstant and insecure. Steve Duck, for example, explains that: 'the more we can find out about our own friendships, the better we can surround ourselves with the human medical insurance and the social support that act as important safeguards against occupational stress, psychological illness, negative life events and the like'.[20]

The idea that the genesis of friendship lies in securing one's own advantage or satisfying one's own needs flies in the face of Cicero's stipulation that the exchange of services is the result of friendship, rather than its origin.[21] Duck presents friendship as a skill dependent on a set of further skills, such as the ability to assess others accurately and the ability to adopt appropriate styles of communication and bodily posture. Such skills are no doubt valuable in developing and maintaining friendships, but they are in fact skills that serve a particular conception of friendship. From Duck's perspective, friendship is a form of interaction which is valuable for its ability to satisfy what might well be changing human needs and desires.

We might want to question Sartre's conclusion in *Being and Nothingness* that the structure of human consciousness imposes alienation, insularity and friction on human beings; and the implication that interpersonal relations will inevitably be marked by interpersonal conflict. Equally, just as the ancients did, we might want to reject the idea that friendship is fundamentally a matter of self-interest. However, the sanguine view that friendship is an ever-present human possibility is problematic. I want to explore this view by way of an anthropological example, that of the Ik, a tribe of some 5,000 people who live mainly in a mountainous area of north-eastern Uganda.

The anthropologist Colin Turnbull in his 1973 book on the Ik, *The Mountain People*, argues that friendship in the sense of care and liking for another for the other's own sake seemed to be largely absent among the Ik. Turnbull comments that as a result of rapid and disastrous changes in the social and economic life of the Ik, friendship had been dismissed as 'idiotic and dangerous'.[22] The Ik's first contact with the British occurred in the 1920s, but it was not until just prior to World War II that the Ik were encouraged to settle in the north-eastern corner of Uganda, bordered by Kenya to the east and Sudan to the north. The advent of nationhood gave these boundaries a significance they had not had before. Formerly a nomadic people, the Ik were confined to an area of marginal land that was once only a temporary resting place in their annual nomadic cycle. Their exclusion from traditional hunting grounds, as well as the establishment of a national game park bordering the area to which they were confined, had a devastating effect on Icien society. Turnbull has since been heavily criticised for some degree of complicity in the plight of the Ik, partly on the basis of his conclusion that they were 'beyond saving as a society'.[23]

Turnbull records how drought led to severe shortages of food that became endemic. This forced Icien mothers into the practice of turning out children past the age of three to find their own sustenance. As a child could not survive alone in the Ik's environment until about the age of thirteen, the children joined what Turnbull refers to as age-bands. These bands were made up of between six and twelve children and provided some protection against other bands and also against large predators, such as the leopard. Within the bands each child formed an alliance with another close in age for defence against older children; however, these relationships were temporary and insecure, since bands realigned when new members entered or when old members were forced out. The rejection of the young child by its family undermined family ties, and the precarious nature of membership in the age-bands served to undermine other close interpersonal ties. As a consequence of this, the development of the attitude of 'basic trust' which Erik Erikson argues normally develops within the family is disturbed. The child is unable to form secure attachments or to develop a sense that the world is predictable and reliable; and as Erikson argues, this basic trust is a prerequisite for all positive attitudes towards society.[24]

In the Hobbesian world of the Ik, individuals acted in their own self-interest and to ensure their own survival and were not the focus of recrimination for doing so. Turnbull illustrated the lack of recrimination in the attitudes of the Ik with a number of examples, one in which Liza, the younger of two brothers, starved, while his elder brother survived: 'Murai would eat while his brother, starving watched. Yet he [Liza] showed no malice or hatred, no regret, nothing. As Murai said, surely it is better that one lives than that both should die.'[25]

In another example Adupa, a thirteen-year-old girl, was abandoned by her parents. Turnbull explains that Adupa was exceptionally persistent in demands that her parents provide her with food and care, so much so that members of the tribe regarded her constant demands as a sign of insanity. Her parents finally responded to her cries and took her into their compound, only to leave promising to return with food. They closed the entrance to the compound so tightly that Adupa, in her weakened condition, could not have opened it. It was about ten days before they returned, by which time she was dead. Turnbull argues that in the Ik's struggle for survival almost all relationships became exploitative. The case of Lomeja illustrates his point. On the death of his son, Lomeja argued with his wife about when to bury the body. Lomeja wanted to bury the body immediately to keep news of the death from other members of the tribe and thus avoid having to host a funeral feast. The noise of the argument alerted others and this severely depressed Lomeja, as he knew that his relations would press their entitlement to a feast that he could ill afford.[26] But this and other examples suggest that Turnbull overstates his case, since he acknowledges that some familial relationships did survive. The family was not – as he claims – a completely non-functional unit;[27] blood relationships did have some significance, even though Lomeja in this example was keen to avoid that significance.

Turnbull does acknowledge that the Ik are generous, light-hearted and affectionate when they can afford to be, and he notes that he saw evidence of this at the beginning of his two-year study of the Ik, before the famine became severe. But he records that those positive qualities became luxuries at best and liabilities at worst for the Ik. As he puts it, such qualities are 'no longer functional for the Ik; . . . they spell ruin and disaster. It seems that far from being basic human qualities, they are superficial luxuries we can afford in times of plenty, or mere mechanisms for survival and security.'[28]

In his discussion of friendship, Kant recognises that human beings will naturally look to their own wants and satisfaction and that they have every right to do so. His comments are relevant to the desperate situation of the Ik, as Turnbull portrays it. 'If I cannot secure the happiness of my neighbour otherwise than by refraining from satisfying the needs of life, no one can place upon me the obligation of looking to his happiness and showing friendship towards him.'[29] The Ik are so completely overcome by the difficulty of satisfying their own individual needs that they cannot afford displays of friendship. In the case noted above, the degree of their desperation even overcomes a sense of parental responsibility, as Adupa's parents – unable to respond to her needs – see themselves with no choice but to abandon her.

Turnbull emphasises two types of bond that persisted among the Ik despite the deprivation they suffered. One was based on shared residence in the mountains, and served to frustrate government attempts to relocate the Ik in a more hospitable environment. The second was the bond of *nyot*, which appears to bear some resemblance to Homeric guest-friendship. *Nyot* was a bond of friendship formed out of self-interest between individuals who vow to aid one another, without the right of refusal. It was established by verbal agreement and an informal exchange of gifts. Once established, the bond was indissoluble. The Ik usually established this bond with non-Ik for economic reasons. However, the disastrous economic conditions that accompanied the famine Turnbull records meant that few Ik had anything of value to trade; lack of food meant that they had little energy for work and even those who had been relatively prosperous soon found themselves in poverty. Turnbull claims that the bond of individual *nyot* friendship was the one bond that endured amid the collapse of Icien society, and he takes this as an indication that informal interpersonal relations retained some value and permanence among the Ik.[30] However, like Homeric guest-friendship, *nyot* friendship is basically a pragmatic relationship. It is engaged in as a means of achieving the mutual satisfaction of needs and has nothing to do with a notion of friendship as liking and caring for another for that person's own sake.

There is a further parallel between *nyot* friendship and relations in ancient societies. The bond of *nyot* was sometimes an avenue for affecting reconciliation in the face of disagreement at an inter-tribal level; in this sense it was not unlike *amicitia* in Roman society of the late first century BC. But like *amicitia*, it could also create ill-will, as for example in the case where two Ik found that their respective *nyot* were quarrelling and expected their support. As we have seen, Cicero's warning that *amicitia* in the public sphere can degenerate into *factio*, and thereby endanger the political stability of the state, had its genesis in his concern to minimise the degree of strife between rival Roman factions. Cicero's *De Amicitia* implies that without a certain degree of political stability, friendships between those in politics could become liabilities. Turnbull's portrayal of the Ik argues that under conditions of severe material deprivation, close interpersonal relationships such as friendship can become liabilities. These commentaries should give us pause in the face of views that idealise friendship as a complete union or a fusion

of souls, or of views that maintain that human beings have a natural inclination to form individualised bonds like those of friendship. Idealised
notions and prescriptive assessments of friendship might – at least in part –
be made possible by the relative prosperity or stability of the society in which
they are constructed; such views may underestimate the contribution of that
stability and the impact of non-ideal conditions on the formation and quality
of friendships. An Ik cannot adopt the attitude to friendship of Eudamidas
of Corinth, which Montaigne chronicles in his essay on friendship, not at
least without endangering his own life. Montaigne tells us that upon
Eudamidas' death,

> he being poor and his two friends rich, he made his will thus: 'I leave this to
> Aretheus, to feed my mother and support her in her old age; this to Charixenus,
> to see my daughter married and give her the biggest dowry he can; and in case
> one of them should chance to die, I substitute the survivor in his place'. Those
> who first saw this will laughed at it; but his heirs, having been informed of it,
> accepted it with singular satisfaction. And when one of them, Charixenus, died
> five days later, and the place of substitute was opened to Aretheus, he supported
> the mother with great care, and of five talents he had in his estate, he gave two
> and a half to his only daughter for her marriage, and two and a half for the mar-
> riage of the daughter of Eudamidas, holding their weddings on the same day.[31]

The care Aretheus shows out of friendship is predicated upon the capacity to act that his wealth allows him. This avenue of activity was not available to the Ik and such a will would have been regarded as ridiculous, rather
than comical. Aretheus' relative wealth allowed him to confirm his relationship with Eudamidas and to accord him recognition as a friend. Martin
Buber sees this kind of confirmation as typical of human beings and in fact
as definitive of our humanity: 'In all human society, at all its levels, persons
confirm one another in a practical way, to some extent or other, in their personal qualities and capacities, and a society may be termed human in the
measure to which its members confirm one another.'[32]

The most minimal degree of recognition by another at least confirms my
presence in his world, but close interpersonal ties demand more significant
confirmation. The fate that the Ik suffered provides a remarkable illustration
of the impact that poverty and starvation have on the quality of the recognition that individuals accord one another. As Turnbull portrays them, the Ik
can only afford to accord one another minimal recognition; and often that
recognition is negative and dismissive. This is destructive of the development
of interpersonal relationships and must have an impact on an individual's
sense of identity. Indeed Icien society displays in graphic fashion aspects of
human relations that have been used as imaginative illustrations in the work
of philosophers such as Sartre. Sartre explicitly endorsed the intuition, which
he ascribed to Hegel, that each human being's self-consciousness is dependent

upon the recognition of the other: 'my appearance for myself as an individual . . . is conditioned by the recognition of the Other . . . I must obtain from the Other *recognition* of my being'.[33] As noted above, his view was that conflict is the original meaning of the being-for-others of consciousness and in this his view is not dissimilar to Hegel's. But somewhat paradoxically Sartre, unlike Hegel, provided an analysis of consciousness that denied the possibility of mutual recognition. The impossibility of the kind of idealised friendship Montaigne envisages is a direct consequence of this philosophical view, whereas in the case of the Ik that impossibility is consequent upon the conflict engendered by deprived material conditions. While I argue that we have no reason to accept Sartre's view, it does throw light on the conflicts inherent in friendship, which are underplayed in more idealised accounts of friendship. A comparison of Sartre's and Hegel's approach to the analysis of consciousness will make this illumination explicit.

Self-Consciousness and its Implications for Friendship

For Sartre, as for Hegel, self-consciousness is the hallmark of human reality. Hegel saw self-consciousness as a desire for recognition formed in terms of a desire directed towards another desire. 'Self-consciousness exists in and for itself when, and by the fact that, it exists for another; that is, it exists only in being acknowledged.'[34] Hegel did not simply mean by recognition an awareness between two individuals of one another's existence. Any interaction between individuals, even violent and exploitative, implies such awareness. Rather, Hegel described a duplicated process in which each individual self-consciousness recognises the other, and then has its existence confirmed by an independent and autonomous self-consciousness. Thus self-consciousness can only be formed if at least two desires, each desiring recognition, confront one another. However, to the extent that the recognition and confirmation of the identity of each resides in the other, each one's identity is outside its own control. Consequently, Hegel maintained that each of the two beings possessed of this desire must be ready to fight to secure and control the condition of its recognition. Each must be prepared to fight to the death to subjugate the other and so secure recognition. But as Hegel states: 'This trial by death . . . does away with the truth which was supposed to issue from it, and so, too with the certainty of self generally; . . . self-consciousness learns that life is essential to it as pure self-consciousness.'[35]

As the death of either antagonist would deny the other the recognition for which he is struggling, a struggle literally to the death would be self-defeating. The more fruitful possibility is where both survive, but one is vanquished through fear of death and submits to the other. One becomes a slave and recognises the other without being recognised in return. The other becomes a master and is recognised without giving recognition. However, the victory of the master creates an impasse. He has gained recognition, but it is the recognition given by an inferior and dependent being, a slave, and thus does not constitute an objective confirmation of the master's identity. The recognition that is required for self-consciousness is that which can only be given by an equal and independent other. In a sense the experience of self-consciousness is divided between the master and the slave. The master's superiority is realised and actualised through the work of the slave, but the master is dependent on the slave, both for recognition and for his material needs. Meanwhile the slave, who is denied recognition by the master, is none the less able to transform nature through work and in doing so is able to produce objects expressive of his identity. The self-consciousness of each is inadequate.

However, Hegel envisages a resolution of the opposition between them as both desirable and possible. In fact he claims that the fight for recognition between master and slave is to be regarded historically as something that 'can only occur in the natural state, where men exist only as single, separate individuals; but it is absent in civil society and the State because here the recognition for which the combatants fought already exists'. The state recognises and treats man 'as a rational being, as free, as a person'.[36] Hegel's confidence in the possibility of mutual recognition and the dialectical nature of his master–slave struggle distinguishes it from Sartre's more unremitting version. Sartre criticised Hegel for the epistemological optimism of the claim that the opposition between master and slave can be or has been overcome:

> It seems to him [Hegel] that the *truth* of self-consciousness can appear; that is, that an objective agreement can be realized between consciousnesses – by authority of the Other's recognition of me and my recognition of the Other. This recognition can be simultaneous and reciprocal: 'I know that the other knows me as himself'. It produces actually and *in truth* the universality of self-consciousness. But the correct statement of the problem of Others renders this passage to the universal impossible. If the Other can in fact refer my 'self' to me, then at least at the end of the dialectical evolution there must be a common measure between what I am for him, what he is for me, what I am for myself, what he is for himself.[37]

Unlike Hegel, Sartre argues that this common measure cannot be established and hence that interpersonal conflict is inevitable. Unity with another is unrealisable both in theory and in fact because it would necessarily involve the disappearance of otherness in the other, on Sartre's account. For him mutual recognition or a relation between consciousnesses is by nature unthinkable, so that a relationship between two individuals can never be characterised in terms of identity or union. From the Sartrean perspective, the friend cannot be regarded as an Aristotelian second self or as sharing the same soul. Montaigne's claim that he and La Boétie were completely united, sharing everything in common – 'wills, thoughts, judgements, goods, wives, children, honour, and life'[38] – appears as a product of his imaginative desire. In reality the structure of human consciousness makes union between two individuals impossible; they must inevitably relate to one another as subject to object.[39]

Any reflective sense we imagine we have of the Other-as-subject is necessarily an abstraction for Sartre. We aim at the other's feelings, ideas, volitions and character *across* our own experiences; but the other is always out of our reach. 'The Other . . . belongs to the category of "as if". The Other is an *a priori* hypothesis with no justification save the unity which it permits to operate in our experience, an hypothesis which cannot be thought without contradiction.'[40]

As subjects we are aware of the other's feelings, desires and thoughts via our own perception of him; but only the other actually has those feelings and thoughts. In fact the nature of consciousness even makes it impossible for me to contemplate myself as subject, since as soon as I contemplate myself as subject, I have posited myself as object. I become aware of myself as an object through my positional consciousness, specifically by reflecting upon myself as an object for others. I encounter the other in the world and it is my body that provides the link between my consciousness and that of the other. My body is the necessary intermediary between myself and the other, but my body as I live it is unknown to me. I arrive at bodily self-consciousness only when I have the concept of my body as it is for others. My awareness that I am not the object of which I am conscious is given, but it is by looking at myself from the perspective of others that I recognise myself. I discover that I do not appear to myself as I do for the other, and that the world as it is for another always differs from the world as it is for me. It differs not in the sense that physical properties change, but rather in the sense that the relation of things in my universe, grouped from my point of view, disintegrates when I perceive the other as a subject. As Sartre explains, 'instead of a grouping *toward me* of the objects, there is now an orientation *which flees from me* . . . a decentralization of the world which undermines the centralization which I am simultaneously effecting'.[41]

So I discover that I have a self for others, a being-for-others, that I am unable to grasp or know. This being-for-others is the foundation of my being in that it is in my being-as-object for the other that I apprehend the other's being-as-subject; and thus become reflectively (positionally) aware of myself. The other is crucial to this awareness of myself. This realisation inevitably involves conflict, as each individual strives to remain what she is for herself and yet each is vulnerable in her relationship with the other, for neither can deny her being-for-others. If I am to maintain my autonomy, I must seek to assimilate the other as the other-looking-at-me. However, I run the risk of being assimilated in just this way by the other myself; hence Sartre's claim that conflict is the original meaning of our being-for-others. Interaction between two individuals necessarily occurs between one, as conscious subject, and the other, as object. They are inevitably separated on this basis, and are locked into struggle as each attempts to make an object of the other in order to preserve his own integrity. Although Sartre does not specifically discuss friendship, he does consider love, in a chapter on concrete relations with others; his views on love illustrate this notion of struggle:

> [T]he lover can not be satisfied with that superior form of freedom which is a free and voluntary engagement. Who would be content with a love given as pure loyalty to a sworn oath? Who would be satisfied with the words, 'I love you because I have freely engaged myself to love you and because I do not wish to go back on my word' . . . [T]he lover . . . wants to be loved by a freedom but demands that this freedom as freedom should no longer be free . . . Thus to want to be loved is to want to be placed beyond the whole system of values posited by the Other and to be the condition of all valorization and the objective foundation of all values.[42]

The lover desires absolute commitment from the beloved. To want to be loved is a paradoxical desire, since it is a desire to want to be found completely and absolutely irresistible to another, who none the less freely chooses us. Thus we face an impossible conflict in love. The desire for absolute commitment makes us vulnerable, since as lovers our being-for-the-other – our existence as lover – can be appropriated by our beloved. We can become nothing more than a tool that confirms our beloved's desirability. This is so simply because we have a being-for-others that is beyond our control.

Friends differ from Sartre's lovers in that the friend is – at least ideally – satisfied with free and voluntary engagement. A friend does not demand absolute commitment, since friendship is not generally regarded as an exclusive relationship; although Montaigne is exceptional in his opinion that 'friendship that possesses the soul and rules it with absolute sovereignty cannot possibly be double'.[43] But we generally take the view that 'the demands and degree of intimacy in friendship do not prevent one from having more than one friendship at one time', as Deutscher puts it.[44] None the less, the friend like the lover is apt to have his being-for-others surpassed towards pure objectivity. In other words, the friend also runs the risk of becoming a tool for the other's pleasure or self-esteem or of being regarded as a means to the other's ends. In any relationship between two individuals, both are metaphysically striving to determine each other as objects and are therefore locked into a struggle.

If friends are inevitably involved in a struggle for transcendence, then the notion that, as friends, each one likes and cares for the other for the other's own sake appears contradictory. Sartre's conception of interpersonal relationships requires that genuine caring for the other will be tempered by the fact that as soon as we posit the other-as-subject, we are forced to recognise our own status as objects. Consequently, if we are to maintain our own integrity we must attempt to assimilate the other as other-looking-at-me; and thus transcend the other's transcendence. To this extent, friendship is like love on Sartre's analysis. It is not impossible, but it is a contradictory effort. If I have a genuine regard for my friend, I must encounter her as subject, not as object; I must wish to encounter her subjectivity if I am to care for her for her own sake. If I relate to her as an object, the very possibility of friendship evaporates. Yet at the same time I cannot escape my responsibility to choose my own mode of being as subject. Genuine care and liking for a friend are only possible if we encounter the friend's subjectivity, but in doing so we encounter our own status as objects and are forced to attempt to recover our subjectivity. We are inevitably involved in perpetual compromise. Chapter 2's exploration of what we might mean when we say that we love a friend for her own sake illustrates the contradictory nature of this notion and reinforces the conflict that Sartre identifies. We want to be able to say that we love a friend for her own sake – or in her subjectivity. But attempts to articulate the nature of that love might be seen as objectifying the friend as the bearer of a set of qualities she instantiates, but which might easily be instantiated in another individual.

None the less, Sartre's analysis does provide a necessary condition for friendship: the ability to differentiate between one's own interests and those of the friend. There are necessary elements of identification between friends, but Sartre would see the experience of complete identification between friends, in the sense that there is no differentiation between their interests, as self-deception. His account can be interpreted as challenging and rejecting the adequacy of certain accounts of friendship – those that emphasise absolute identity. One of the values of Sartre's analysis is its recognition of an element of antagonism and perhaps even hostility in all interpersonal relationships. Our awareness of this antagonistic element sharpens our recognition of ourselves as subjects, in opposition to our recognition of ourselves as objects defined by others. To acknowledge the tension between our being-for-ourselves and our being-for-others enables us to relate to others without self-deception. In his story 'The Childhood of a Leader', Sartre describes the process by which Lucien, a young student, joins the anti-Semitic movement. Lucien accepts and embraces unquestioningly a definition of himself as an anti-Semite; a definition that is initially constructed by his friends. He embraces this definition of himself apparently for no other reason than that it relieves him of a feeling that he lacks identity:

'Oh God!' he thought, 'How I hate them! God how I hate Jews!' and he tried to draw strength from the contemplation of this immense hatred; 'I am Lucien! Somebody who can't stand Jews.' . . . Lucien's anti-semitism was . . . unrelenting and pure, it stuck out of him like a steel blade menacing other breasts. 'It's sacred,' he thought.[45]

Lucien is drawn to the camaderie of an identity shared with his friends, but Sartre portrays the relationships between them as alliances of bad faith or self-deception. Lucien recognises that the strength he tried to draw from his anti-Semitism has a tendency to 'melt away'; but he convinces himself that the real Lucien had to be sought in the eyes of others. He clings to his being-as-object for others in a vain and self-deceptive attempt to avoid his responsibility to choose his own mode of being; and to recognise that the way in which his friends define him cannot be what he is for himself. When applied to relations between friends, Sartre's analysis provides a harsh corrective to the excessive sentimentality of the more idealised conceptions of friendship. It makes the recognition of difference between friends an imperative, no matter how intimate their relationship. Complete identification becomes an example of bad faith.

In essence, however, Sartre's argument that recognition of others as subjects is impossible depends not so much on critical observation as on definition. It is his view of the nature of human consciousness that determines that consciousness is always of an object that is not a subject, and that one's-being-as-object is the only possible relation between oneself and the other-as-subject. Martin Buber provides a different and competing view of consciousness. He acknowledges that consciousness of others may collapse into consciousness of others-as-objects, but he does not make this collapse inevitable. Buber's view of consciousness both recognises the possibility of mutual recognition – which he claims constitutes the fullest expression of our humanity – and implies some qualification of idealised conceptions of friendship.

The world of relations between subject and object belongs to what Buber terms the primary word *I-It*. In saying this primary word to another, *I* relate to the other as *It*, as a thing. But this is not the only world of relations that human beings can experience. Our lives are not restricted to experiences that have some thing as their object; 'without *It* man cannot live; but he who lives with *It* alone is not a man'.[46] Human beings can also relate directly to one another, saying the primary word *I-Thou*. When *Thou* is spoken, the speaker stands in mutual relation to the other, without aim, desire or means. The *I* addresses the *Thou* with his whole person and encounters him in the full freedom of his otherness, while the *It* is encountered with only part of the person.

Buber acknowledges that we often relate to others as objects and that this is inevitable in the real world. 'Every *Thou* in the world is by its nature fated to become a thing, or continually to re-enter into the condition of things.'[47] But he insists that human beings-as-subjects can relate to one another through the suspension of the way in which the material world is generally experienced. To do so the *I* must break with the past, responding to the *Thou* in ways that are not calculated by knowledge of the past. The moment responses are calculated – for example, when the *I* begins to consider what kind of impression he is making on the other – the other becomes *It*. The *It* belongs to the world of experience and in addressing the other as *It* one manipulates, makes use of, observes. However, when one addresses another as *Thou* one relates directly, affirming the person addressed. Any kind of purpose or desire is an obstacle to the meeting that Buber suggests occurs in and creates a spaceless and timeless 'present' – a present in which everything indirect is irrelevant.

Buber is proposing a world of relation that is unthinkable from a Sartrean perspective – that of the primary word *I-Thou*. But, like Sartre, he argues that human beings are vulnerable within their interpersonal relationships. He defends the possibility of a relation between subjects that entails each individual taking a stance towards the other in which each one is completely open with the other – and is therefore vulnerable. The *I-Thou* relation involves the whole being in choosing and being chosen and as such is bound to involve risk and resemble suffering. Every *Thou* faces this risk and is in fact fated, at some point, to be once again regarded as a thing, or to re-enter the world of things continually.[48] The unity that the meeting of the *I* and *Thou* implies will inevitably be disrupted, since this kind of meeting is an ideal that cannot be maintained. Thus Buber's recognition of the vulnerability of the *I-Thou* relation implies some qualification of idealised conceptions of friendship without the rejection of those ideals implicit in Sartre's position. From the viewpoint of a commentary on relations between friends, what is of interest is Buber's accommodation of a sense of unity between human beings, despite the fact that he insists that this unity will be intermittent rather than permanently enduring. The value of his analysis is that it encompasses both ideals that characterise friendship as union or fusion and the possibility of conflict between friends.

By comparison, Sartre restricts all human interaction to encounters between a consciousness and its object, so that friendship – like all interpersonal relationship – is predicated upon an ever-present antagonism. There is necessarily a radical separation that cannot be bridged between individuals relating to one another – whether they are friends, lovers or strangers. Buber's analysis of interpersonal relations is less clearly articulated than Sartre's. The *I-Thou* relation is explained in negative terms, as a suspension of the way in which we generally experience the world, via the relation *I-*

It. Buber was aware of shortcomings in his analysis and defended his book *I and Thou* against criticism, claiming to have written the book 'under the spell of an irresistible enthusiasm', and that 'the inspiration of such enthusiasm one may not change any more, not even for the sake of exactness. For one can only estimate what one would gain, but not what would be lost.'[49] However, as Walter Kaufmann points out, this provides no justification for a poorly articulated thesis.[50] Kaufmann suggests that the central dichotomy of the book – the notion that the I of man is two-fold in that the I of the primary word *I-Thou* differs from the I of the primary word *I-It* – does not bear close examination. On his view Buber's thesis is simplistic and mistaken. It is not the case that we can only genuinely relate to another human being in brief encounters and that we inevitably relapse into states in which the other human being becomes a mere object of experience for us.[51]

Kaufmann uses the attitude of the artist engaged in painting a portrait to make the point that a genuine *I-Thou* relation is not necessarily a fleeting encounter. He argues that the artist does not lapse from the genuine *I-Thou* (*I-You*) relation

> into a deplorable attitude in which he notes the color of the hair or other qualities, reducing the You to a mere It. On the contrary, he must pay some attention to qualities and details to reveal the You on the canvas . . . Those who refuse to do this live in illusions and cultivate a relationship to an idol instead of truly confronting a You.[52]

He goes on to criticise both what he sees as Buber's Manichean denigration of the *I-It* and his unduly romantic and ecstatic notion of the *I-Thou*. To differing degrees the views of Sartre and Buber force us to make some qualification of idealised conceptions of friendship. Each provides a theoretical underpinning for our practical realisation of the way in which we are given the status of objects by others. In doing so, they underscore our separateness from others and the potential for conflict between ourselves and our friends. Despite the gulf that separates them in time, accounts of the turbulent political life of the late Roman Republic and Turnbull's portrayal of Icien society do provide dramatic practical examples of the kind of objectification Sartre and Buber identify. However, they are examples that explain alienation and conflict as a consequence of prevailing political, economic and social circumstances, rather than as a consequence of the structure of our consciousness. A Sartrean analysis of these examples might lead us to argue that the alienation imposed on human beings in these societies is a consequence of the structure of human consciousness, and that this alienation is exacerbated by the facticity that the citizens of Cicero's Rome and the Ik experience.

Whether or not we accept Sartre's ontology and its implications, or Buber's account of human relations, is immaterial to the fact that these examples indicate that the possibility of friendship is jeopardised in a society in which individuals face a pervasive threat to their existence. Whether or not the possibility of friendship is dependent on the structure of human consciousness, these examples suggest that its possibility is none the less dependent upon some minimal level of social, economic and political security or stability; and that at the very least, the attitude of trust and mutual sensitivity that friendship requires is compromised or undermined by social or political conditions that generate intense conflict between individuals. The question of the impact of the structure of human consciousness on our capacity for, and the nature of, interpersonal relations remains contentious. Buber does offer us some confirmation at the theoretical level of the possibility of genuine relationship between friends. But his argument has been criticised by Kaufmann and by Steven Katz.

Katz maintains, first, that Buber's view of the *I* of man as two-fold is arbitrary and doctrinaire; and second, that if Buber is to make the notion of *Thou* intelligible, 'some identifying skeleton of the notion of *Thou* must be given and this will require understanding the indissoluble tie between *what* the other is and *who* the other is'. Katz seems to suggest that relating to another as *Thou* cannot simply involve a suspension of the way in which we generally experience the world, or a dismissal of our past knowledge of the other. He argues that we do not have a spontaneous *Thou* relation to the other in a vacuum; rather we relate to the other as a particular *Thou* for us. The particularity of another individual is underpinned by 'philosophical, psychological, physical and social criteria which are integral to the other being as *Thou* for me'.[53] Kaufmann's criticisms of Buber have a similar flavour, particularly when he claims that Buber 'mistook intense emotion for revelation and did not realize how much rational reflection is needed if we really want to encounter the You rather than an illusion'.[54] We must reflect on the other as we find them in the world, in all their particularity and in the complex interactions in which we encounter them. Abstracting from everyday encounters suggests that we might well encounter an illusion which we have created, rather than find ourselves engaged in a direct relation with the other.

Pessimism about the possibility of enduring or close interpersonal relations is a consequence of the theoretical stances that Buber and Sartre adopt. Those stances cement alienation into the conduct of interpersonal relations, making it a structural feature of those relations – either pervasively on Buber's account or permanently on Sartre's. They act as a corrective to overly idealised views of interpersonal relations, and they indicate the importance of our recognition of our separateness from others. But the tension that emerges in the literature on friendship between union and separateness or identity and difference in relations between friends is not well captured from the perspectives of these theorists. Sartre's model simply dismisses the notion of union, while Buber's does not articulate a clear theoretical position on the possibility of union.

Unfortunately accounts that specifically address tension and alienation in friendship, such as Cicero's account of Rome in the late Republic and Turnbull's account of the Ik, do not offer an explanation in terms of anything other than human reactions under particular political, material and socio-economic conditions. Additionally, each account differs in focus with regard to relations between friends. Turnbull was providing a record of the impact of alienating circumstances on close interpersonal relations, while Cicero's critical focus was reserved for friendship in the public or civic sphere of life. Cicero continued to idealise friendship within the private sphere of life. However, as we have seen, his own death ironically illustrated the overlap between these spheres, since it was his friend Octavian who abandoned him in order to form a political alliance with Marc Antony and Lepidus.

As I have suggested above, idealised notions of friendship, such as Aristotle's primary friendship and Cicero's 'true' friendship, appear to underestimate the contribution of secure and stable material, socio-economic and political conditions to the development and maintenance of friendships. In fact Aristotle's civic ideal of the polis as a community of friends presents a special case, since the ideal was vitiated by the restriction of citizenship to a minority of the inhabitants of the state, by the practice of slavery, by the rigid sexual division of labour, and by the rejection of the family as an institutional framework of socialisation. Thus the ideal appears to have been maintained only by the exclusion of those who would threaten its cohesion. This exclusion minimises the potential for conflict between citizens with competing conceptions of the good; but it also turns a blind eye to difference within the community of friends.

As we have seen, Montaigne's account of friendship is equally restrictive in its exclusions with regard to sovereign friendship, particularly in its explicit exclusion of women from the possibility of friendship. Montaigne says of women's capacity for sovereign friendship: '[T]he ordinary capacity of women is inadequate for that communion and fellowship which is the nurse of this sacred bond; nor does their soul seem firm enough to endure the strain of so tight and durable a knot.'[55]

The world of female friendship has largely been ignored or dismissed by the philosophical tradition. Pauline Nestor refers to the extraordinary debate in Britain during the mid-nineteenth century over women's capacities for friendship and community. She quotes from a magazine article of 1870 which claimed that female friendships were notoriously shallow, and most often only a rehearsal for the serious business of relationships with men.[56] The intercession of men in women's relationships with one another was regarded as necessary if women's friendships were not to be shallow, unnatural or morbid. This prejudice is one firmly supported by Nietzsche and by Simmel, both of whom claim that women's friendships are necessarily inadequate. Simmel claimed that women were less susceptible to friendship than men, because they were the less individualised sex. He appears to have meant by this that he saw less variation among women, in general, than among men.[57] Simone de Beauvoir reinforces these challenges to women's capacity for friendship: '[F]eminine friendships . . . are very different in kind from relations between men. The latter communicate as individuals . . . while women are confined in their general feminine lot and are bound together by a kind of immanent complicity.'[58]

By contrast there are those who emphasise, and idealise, elements of compassion and sympathy within women's friendships. The suggestion is that it may be that only women can enjoy true friendship, since their socialisation makes them particularly adept at close identification with a friend. Certainly in societies in which women are responsible for the early care of children, we might expect gender differences in patterns of interaction with others and in notions of connection. Emphasis on women's capacity for identification with others recalls accounts of friendship that stress union and fusion. However, that emphasis also threatens to restrict women's friendships to interactions which are characterised by nurturance, acceptance, co-operation and support. In such relations, the expression of individuality might be discouraged or thwarted, so that women become bound within their friendships by an ethic of care and interdependence. Exclusive emphasis on identification, interdependence and support between female friends is debilitating because it does not acknowledge difference or allow for change. It immerses women in relationship and replicates between women an idealised and oppressive conception of woman-as-carer, concerned with others at the expense of herself. Both misogynistic prejudice against women's friendship and idealised notions of identification and interdependence must be dismissed if the interdependence and the expression of individuality which characterise women's friendships – as well as men's – are to be recognised.

Celebrating Difference

There are conceptions of friendship in the literature that eschew both idealisation and pessimism with regard to the possibility of friendship to focus on otherness, individual need and the toleration of difference as the key concepts underlying relations between friends. Difference is celebrated as the most crucial element in friendship. Shared activity, similarity of interest and of values and reciprocal services are seen as necessary conditions and pleasures of friendship. But within these conceptions, these necessary conditions emerge as superficial to the extent that they conceal the role of the recognition of difference in friendship, and the challenge that recognition presents to relation between friends. In the epigraph to Maurice Blanchot's book *Friendship*, the words of George Bataille indicate his insistence that the relationship is founded on a recognition of the profound separateness between self and other. He speaks of friendship, apparently contradictorily, as a state of profound detachment from others: 'friendship until that state of profound friendship where a man abandoned, abandoned by all his friends, encounters in life the one who will accompany him beyond life, himself without life, capable of free friendship, detached from all ties'.[59]

These sentiments appear curious in the context of an analysis of friendship. Bataille's reference to 'free friendship' suggests a notion that seems to have nothing to do with the familiar claim that friendship is a relationship in which we freely choose to engage; that its ties are not predicated on formal or biological ties between participants. In fact the notion of 'free friendship' flies in the face of the sense of attachment and affection that friendship is characteristically taken to imply, given Bataille's emphasis on detachment rather than attachment. 'Free friendship' is a state of profound friendship in which we glimpse ourselves beyond life and therefore beyond our connections with others. The concept of an encounter with ourselves beyond life, profoundly alone and detached from all ties, and in a sense beyond selfhood, opens us to the capacity for free and profound friendship. That encounter suggests the pervasive inevitability of separation as well as the preciousness of connection, and as such it appears to have something in common with Buber's notion of the *I-Thou* relation. The difference is that 'free friendship' is predicated upon the notion that all connection between human beings entails a recognition of their separateness.

Bataille's reference to a man encountering himself beyond life, without life, brings to mind the impact of death and perhaps the notion of an ultimate separation; but when Blanchot expands on this idea in commentary he states that 'with death all that separates disappears', so that 'death has the false virtue of appearing to return to intimacy those who have been divided by grave disagreements'.[60] Death achieves this because it erases the separation upon which relations between living individuals are predicated. Death dispels the notion of a void between individuals, a notion which is predicated on difference. Upon death we can attempt to remember the other, appealing to an absence that we imagine, but Blanchot rejects memory as a form of deceptive consolation. In speaking of the loss of friends, Seneca tells us that the thought of his dead friends is sweet and appealing: '[f]or I have had them as if I should one day lose them; I have lost them as if I have them still'.[61] Blanchot might well agree that we should have friends as if we might one day lose them, but the notion that we need not lose dead friends is self-deceptive. Our relationship was valuable when we had it and that value cannot be expunged by death, but in the other's absence we can only relate through memory and imagination, and for Blanchot this kind of relation will be deceptive. Since speech ceases with death, so does the silence in the relationship that made that speech possible. Blanchot's point is that it is what separates us that puts us authentically in relation with one another. Death dissipates that separation so that we can no longer be in authentic relation with one another. The separation on which the relation was predicated has been erased by death. The friend is lost.

On face value, the idea that what separates us puts us into authentic relation with one another might be regarded as a simply logical point: talk of relationship between entities entails that we recognise the separateness of those entities, since relation is defined as a two-or-more-place property. Two completely identical entities would share all their properties and hence be indistinguishable and not capable of relation with one another. This kind of response can be made in criticism of Aristotle's claim that the friend is another self, since from a logical point of view the friend cannot actually be another self. But both Aristotle and Blanchot use these claims to facilitate an exploration of relations between friends, to uncover the meaning we attach to those relations. For example, in his exploration of the nature of the connection between friends, Blanchot asks in reference to Bataille: '[h]ow could one agree to speak of this friend?' Blanchot is questioning what we know of a friend, the nature of the understanding we can be said to have of a friend. He argues that no one has a perspective that is capable of taking account of his proximity to a friend as well as his distance from the friend. For Blanchot there is no one who can affirm the life of a friend in any comprehensive way: 'The traits of his character, the forms of his existence, the episodes of his life, even in keeping with the search for which he felt himself responsible to the point of irresponsibility, belong to no one. There are no witnesses.'[62]

In speaking or writing of our friend what we do is to use words, writing, memory, figures or images to avoid the affirmation of a void between us – a void both insignificant and enormous. Blanchot refers to this 'insignificance' between friends as representing an enigma. But what is the nature of this enigma? What is it in the relation between friends that is puzzling or inexplicable, or that has a hidden meaning? The tension between union and separation, identity and difference, or attachment and detachment in relations between friends certainly appears to satisfy the definition of an enigma. It is puzzling and difficult to explain, if not impenetrable. In attempting to explain the enigma he identifies, Blanchot argues that it veils one affirmation: 'that everything must fade and that we can remain loyal only so long as we watch over this fading movement, to which something in us that rejects all memory already belongs'.[63] We understand at some level that all relation must fade, that death erases separation and thus relation; and that therefore our relations with friends are impermanent, vulnerable and unpredictable. This gives us cause for grief, on Blanchot's view. The lack of predictability is exacerbated by the fact that as selves we belong to no one. We are selves to whom no one can give full witness, despite our vain attempts to do so: 'Vainly do we try to maintain, with our words, with our writings, what is absent . . . We are only looking to fill a void, we cannot bear the pain: the affirmation of this void.'[64]

Two notions of the term 'void' appear to operate in Blanchot's text: that which separates friends in life and that which they face beyond life. The void we face between friends in life opens us to the recognition of the void we face in death. In recognising 'the pure interval that, from me to this other who is a friend, measures all that is between us', I recognise two things. First, I recognise the difference between my friend and myself, the interruption of being that persists between us despite our familiarity. Second, but simultaneously, in recognising the 'pure interval' between my friend and myself, I encounter myself abandoned by my friend, abandoned by all but myself. I am thrown into profound relationship with myself by this recognition; but as a consequence of this recognition I am accompanied by a self – myself – who understands the force of friendship. This self is abandoned, but not alone, since it encounters itself capable of 'free friendship'. It sees itself detached from all ties, but none the less accompanying itself. It is the power of our recognition of our separateness from the other that enables us to relate to a friend 'without dependence, without episode, . . . with all the simplicity of life'. We appreciate 'the movement of understanding in which, speaking to us, they [our friends] reserve, even on the most familiar terms, an infinite distance, the fundamental separation on the basis of which what separates becomes relation'.[65]

Sándor Márai's novel *Embers* captures some sense of the state of profound friendship to which Bataille refers. The novel represents the movement of understanding that occurs in the friendship between his two male protagonists, which is the theme of the novel. This relationship develops from a childhood friendship to a relationship in which at least one of the participants comes to recognise and appreciate what Blanchot refers to as the 'pure interval' that exists between friends. Research into the development of children's friendships by Miraca Gross and Robert Selman indicates that the development of friendships among children occurs in stages.[66] Gross explains that initially young children see friends simply as play partners who engage with them in play and will allow them to borrow playthings.

Expectations and beliefs about friendship become more sophisticated and complex with age, so that children move on to a second stage where conversations are no longer restricted to the game or activity in which the children are engaged. At the third stage, children see the friend as someone who will offer help, support and encouragement, although the child does not yet appreciate any requirement for reciprocity in this regard. It is not until the fourth stage that the child realises that in friendship the need and obligation to give comfort and support flows both ways. The giving and receiving of affection, deepening intimacy and bonding are features of this stage. Finally the child enters stage five, which Gross refers to as 'the sure shelter' stage, in which friendship is perceived as a deep and lasting relationship of trust, fidelity and unconditional acceptance. The research of Gross and Selman suggests a progression from a procedural approach to friendship in the earlier stages of development to deeper substantive notions of friendship as children begin to appreciate the perspective of the other, and to develop an appreciation of the otherness of the friend, demands for reciprocity and the potential for intimacy. Márai's novel can be seen as an exploration of the idealisation of friendship implicit in Gross's definition of the final stage of children's friendship.

Márai's main characters, Heinz and Konrad, begin their friendship with the skills typical of the later stages of childhood development, as Gross identifies them. They meet as ten-year-old boys at a military academy just outside Vienna and, as the novel's narrator explains, '[f]rom the first moment, they lived together like twins in their mother's womb'.[67] Thus Márai at least initially follows Montaigne in offering a conception of the friendship between Henrik and Konrad in their youth as an enigmatic fusion of souls. Derrida notes that the friend is regularly presented in the literature with the features of a brother, and he discusses the appeal of a notion of the friend that suggests a genetic connection of fraternity. Montaigne cherished this notion as indicative of the most sovereign of friendships, but as Derrida, commenting on Aristotle, points out: '[F]riendship does not – and above all must not – have the reliability of a natural thing or a machine; since its stability is not given by nature but is won, like constancy and "fidence", through the endurance of a virtue, primary friendship, "that which allows all the others to be named".'[68]

Derrida is discussing the way in which the question of democracy opens up in this context, since we must take account of singularities in friendship, of the question of the citizen or the subject as a countable singularity. Democracy requires respect for irreducible singularity or alterity, but at the same time 'there is no democracy without the "community of friends", without the calculation of majorities, without identifiable, stabilizable, representable subjects, all equal'. Derrida argues that these two laws are irreducible to one another, that they are 'tragically irreconcilable and forever wounding'.[69] Márai's notion of twinship or fusion between friends is an attempt to ensure both the reliability and the intimacy of the friendship. But at the same time the narrator recognises the underlying ethical problem within a relation that downplays the separateness of self and other. Márai's narrator claims that the hidden force within both friendship and love is 'the need to remove another human being from the world, body and soul, and make him uniquely theirs'. But he also says of the boys' friendship that 'like all great emotions, this one contained within itself both shame and a sense of guilt, for no one may isolate one of his fellows from the rest of human-ity with impunity'.[70] The friendship is also said to have been 'deep and wordless, as are all the emotions that will last a lifetime'.[71] The notion of a deep and wordless union contrasts – at least superficially – with Blanchot's emphasis on the separateness of friends; but the reference to the union as wordless can be taken as an intimation of the silence that Blanchot argues makes speech possible between two separate beings.

The relationship between Henrik and Konrad is portrayed as passionate and intense, as radiating 'a gentle, serious and unconditional generosity'; it is years into the relationship before they experience any sense of a rift. The rift comes as a consequence of what the narrator refers to as each one's orig-inal sin: wealth on Henrik's part and poverty on Konrad's.[72] However, Henrik's mother prefigures the novel's focus on conflict and vulnerability in friendship when Henrik's nurse expresses concern about the intensity of the relationship between the boys. Henrik's mother replies that it is our human fate to face suffering: '[o]ne day we lose the person we love. Anyone who is unable to sustain that loss fails as a human being and does not deserve our sympathy.'[73] As we saw in Chapter 2, Martha Nussbaum would agree that vulnerability to loss is an inevitable dimension of close interpersonal rela-tionships; but Márai goes further here to embrace the kind of view that Blanchot presents. Certainly we are vulnerable to loss in friendship – friend-ships can cool or collapse; but Blanchot argues that the notion of loss in friendship expands to open us to an inevitable feature of the human condi-tion in the face of death. We are necessarily watching over a fading move-ment, since everything must fade and we remain loyal to and authentic within the relationship only so long as we acknowledge this. For Henrik's mother it is not just loyalty that is at stake, but success as a human being.

We might ask whether friendship is at bottom an attempt to hide from the reality of our separation from others and hence from our own vulner-ability. The illusory comfort of another self or a brother would be a lame and contradictory good for the self-fulfilled Aristotelian man, but it might tempt those who face the challenge of recognising difference in friends and accepting its implications. Ronald Sharp argues that in fact highly idealised conceptions of friendship, such as Montaigne's, are 'not only unrealistic, but finally less idealistic than a view that acknowledges and affirms the separate identities of friends'.[74] The friend in traditional conceptions of friendship becomes an impossible idea – a reflection of oneself and perhaps even of one's own narcissism – but never a challenge or threat; that is, never a genuine other. Derrida's recognition of difference and of the separate identities of friends leads him to ask whether traditional idealised conceptions of friendship are simply another form of belief in ourselves. He suggests that the nostalgia of the sentence, attributed to Aristotle by both Diogenes Laertes and Montaigne, 'O my friends, there is no friend' reveals that 'we wish to *believe* in the other because we want, in vain, to believe in ourselves'.[75] We want to confirm a connection with another self, because it implies an affirmation of our own uncertain and enigmatic identity.

Miraca Gross's analysis of children's friendships idealises this kind of connection in the final stage of friendship, the 'sure shelter', which she characterises as a deep and lasting relationship of trust, fidelity and unconditional acceptance. Márai portrays the relationship between Konrad and Henrik as this kind of bond – a wordless union in which the boys 'made their own community' and became 'more than the sum of their two selves'. However, for Márai this bond was only relevant to '[t]he magical time of childhood'. As grown men they are described as enmeshed in 'a complicated and enigmatic relationship commonly covered by the word "friendship"'.[76] As men they must come to appreciate that friendship is not an ideal state of mind, but rather 'a duty'. The relationship between friendship and duty will be discussed in the next chapter, but what is crucial here for a discussion of friendship that focuses on the role of the recognition of difference between friends is Márai's emphasis on estrangement. The book uncovers the reason for Konrad's sudden flight from a friendship that had lasted through twenty-four years from childhood through youth and into adulthood. It then records their reunion, during which Henrik reveals something that slowly became clear to him over the forty-one years of Konrad's absence and that he had continued to deny:

> I have to acknowledge a discovery that both surprises and disturbs me: we are still, even now, friends. Evidently there is no external power that can alter human relationships. You killed something inside me, you ruined my life, but we are still friends. Friendship . . . reaches beyond personal desires and self-regard in men's hearts, its grip is greater than that of sexual desire, and it is proof against disappointment, because it asks for nothing. One can kill a friend, but death itself cannot undo a friendship that reaches back to childhood; its memory lives on like some act of silent heroism . . . the selfless human act.[77]

Márai's novel suggests that demands for fidelity in friendship are in fact evidence of an appalling vanity and egoism; and that we have no right to demand unconditional honour and loyalty from our friends.[78] Derrida would agree, since he asks what is left of a friendship that makes the virtue of the other its own condition, a friendship that demands that you 'be virtuous if you want me to love you'.[79] No doubt adopting such attitudes would serve as proofs against disappointment, but the underlying emphasis on heroism and selflessness, on asking for nothing from friends, acknowledges our profound separation from friends. It goes further, and is more explicit, than the calls of Seneca, Cicero and Emerson for self-possession to be acknowledged as a crucial trait of a good friend. In Márai's novel, Henrik's mother argues that we fail as human beings if we cannot sustain the loss of a friend, if we are not independent enough from the other to face the test that loss, disappointment and injury present to friendship. Henrik's point in the quotation above is that the friendship that he and Konrad shared cannot be undone. Its memory remains, not in the sense that the relationship continues, but in the sense that future events cannot destroy what was, despite its passing, and despite our profound isolation from a friend given our estrangement or her death. However, the case of estrangement can differ from death, and we see the significance of this difference in the narrator's comments prior to the reunion of Henrik and Konrad:

> During all these decades they had drawn strength from waiting itself, as if an entire life had been mere preparation for a single task. Konrad had known that one day he would have to come back, just as the General [Henrik] had known that someday this moment would arrive. It was what both had lived for.[80]

Henrik refers to this preparation as akin to preparation for a duel and argues that '[t]here is one duel in life, fought without sabers, that nonetheless is worth preparing for with all one's strength'.[81] On the surface, the duel appears to be between himself and Konrad, but in fact it is a duel between conceptions of friendship and within Henrik's psyche. The act for which Henrik prepares is forgiveness, but it also goes beyond forgiveness. It is an act that is a consequence of a view of friendship motivated by a concern for the relationship itself. Friendship is viewed as a relationship of duty that denies self-interested motivation, but it is a complicated and enigmatic relationship, since we are vulnerable in deeply intimate friendships. Friendship's assumption of a concern for the friend for the friend's own sake, a concern that reaches beyond personal desires and self-regard, might imply that we ask for nothing in friendship; but at the same time, if that wordless and selfless pact is broken, we are left in a kind of no-man's land. Do we ponder the poverty of our choice of friend? Do we agree with the comments attributed to Aristotle: 'O my friends, there is no friend'? Or do we – with Bataille – think of ourselves as within the arena of 'free friendship', detached from all ties but appreciative of the possibilities our experience of those ties has created? Márai's character, Henrik, appears to opt for the last alternative.

Henrik records with some bitterness his desire to understand why Konrad 'had simply bolted'. But he is equally prepared to acknowledge his own role in the events. He questions the purity of his own and Konrad's intentions within their friendship, arguing that '[e]verything turns on our intentions'.[82] However, awareness of intention requires self-knowledge, and while years of reflection have led him to an understanding of his own motivation, in his old age his desire is to understand Konrad's motivation in fleeing. He grapples with the incomprehensibility of Konrad's sin against him, given the depth of the connection that had existed between them. The characters are presented as detached and yet connected through the recognition of their own motivations. They cannot deny their friendship, but nor can they continue the friendship in the old way given the intervening events. As Blanchot might have it, their separation puts them in authentic relation with one another. They become 'free friends', despite their pain and longing for the previous twinship – that 'strange identity of impulses, sympathies, tasks, temperaments and cultural formation' – that Henrik felt had bound them together.

In the no-man's land of their present relation they do not become enemies, but the position in which Márai places them brings to mind philosophical advice on how to conduct oneself in the event that a friend should turn into an enemy. For Nietzsche, friends who become estranged 'should become more venerable for each other . . . the memory of the former friendship more sacred'.[83] In discussing this idea, Derrida argues that to be capable of this and to be able to honour and respect in the friend the enemy he can become is a sign of freedom. Freedom is seen as entailed by that respect, but that freedom is accompanied by vulnerability. Derrida explains the aggression whereby we make an enemy as a reaction to our own vulnerability; he follows Nietzsche in explaining that in making an enemy, we are in fact recognising our vulnerability and pronouncing: 'At least be my enemy!'[84]

Kant's advice is that: 'we must still reverence the old friendship and never show that we are capable of hate'.[85] To speak ill of our friends is wrong in itself, because it proves that we have no respect for friendship, that we have chosen our friends poorly and that we are ungrateful for them. Kant maintains that to speak ill of our friends is also contrary to the rule of prudence:

> We must so conduct ourselves towards a friend that there is no harm done if he should turn into an enemy. We must give him no handle against us. We ought not, of course, to assume the possibility of his becoming an enemy; any such assumption would destroy confidence between us; but it is very unwise to place ourselves in a friend's hands completely.[86]

As we saw in Chapter 2, Montaigne rejects as ridiculous the idea that we ought to acknowledge the potential for enmity to develop between friends. Like Kant, he sees this as making a genuine connection between friends impossible. But Kant's prudential view would seem to undermine genuine connection none the less. Márai challenges such prudence within the novel; since a relation that appears to satisfy the definition of 'free friendship' develops from within an idealised – but erroneous – notion of friendship as a union, a twinship and an identity of impulses. The longing for, and yet the failure of, the ideal of twinship create experiences that allow an authentic relation to develop. Derrida's discussion of Nietzsche is helpful in comprehending the view of friendship Márai explores in his novel. Derrida claims that friendship is preserved by silence, following Nietzsche's claim that:

> [I]t is error and deception regarding yourself that led them [your friends] to you; and they must have learned how to keep silent in order to remain your friend; for such human relationships almost always depend upon the fact that two or three things are never said or even so much as touched upon: if these little boulders do start to roll, however, friendship follows after them and shatters.[87]

Konrad's actions break the silence so that what Derrida refers to as 'friendship's ambiguous truth' is revealed. This truth is 'that by which friends protect themselves from the error or the illusion on which friendship is founded'. Friendship cannot resist the truth of the illusion on which it is based; in the case of Márai's novel, the illusion is the ideal of a complete union or twinship between the two friends. In fact it is their separateness rather than their sense of unity that is crucial to the relation. Yet the sense of connection and the longing for connection that friends experience over this abyss create an ambiguity they try to resist. Derrida describes dealing with this ambiguity as resisting 'the vertigo or the revolution that would have it [friendship] turning around itself'.[88]

Friendship, Illusion and Fragility

For Derrida, friendship becomes an inherently ambiguous relationship. He describes it as a relationship founded on a 'bottomless bottom', since we are forced to recognise simultaneously our ultimate separateness from our friend and yet, given that separation, our unaccountable connection with others.[89] A view of friendship as a relationship predicated on separation and difference allows for the accommodation of divergent opinion in the relationship, for openness to change and development, and for spontaneity. The intimation in Márai's novel that it also demands a preparedness to forgive anything is a curious confirmation of friendship's inherent ambiguity. Like Derrida, Henrik questions the value of a friendship in which one person loves the other for his virtue – or his loyalty or steadfastness. He argues that in an ideal friendship we see a friend's faults and accept them with all their consequences; that without such an ideal there would be no point to life. The highest things friends can offer one another are complete trust and 'blind unconditional devotion', so that in Henrik's conception of friendship the notion of reciprocity is completely abandoned. The measure of our care and concern for a friend is that we ask nothing of them for ourselves. We view the person we have chosen as a friend without any illusion; we accept the faithless friend, just as we accept the faithful one who sacrifices himself. We allow friends the expression of their difference, their spontaneity, and their development regardless of its impact on ourselves. Henrik's juxtaposition of trust in a friend, on the one hand, with acceptance of 'faithlessness and base behaviour', on the other, provides a dramatic illustration of 'the ambiguous truth' of friendship.[90] But in taking this ambiguity to its logical conclusion, friendship becomes a relationship of duty for Henrik. On the basis of our initial choice of a person as a friend, respect and loyalty are shown to the relationship, rather than to the faithless friend.

Embers raises further questions about choice, when Henrik compares the friend to the lover in his unconditional attachment and devotion. His portrayal of the relationship between the friends in their youth as a passionate and intense relationship also suggests an erotic element. This comparison and his claim that the protagonists are 'as inextricably attached as crystals in the laws of physics' bring to mind Goethe's notion of elective affinity.[91] Both the attraction and the distance between the friends seem inevitable. The attraction is predetermined if we accept the chemical analogy, and, like the illusion of twinship, it conceals distance. But the distance between the friends is given, since they are two separate individuals. Notions of choice and reciprocity take a back seat to a radical notion of duty on the one hand and a sense of inevitable, if not fatal, attraction on the other. But Márai's emphasis on duty seems to take too far the claim that it is what separates friends that puts them into authentic relation; no matter how severe the event that might be expected to precipitate a rift, the relationship does not shatter. At the same time the chemical analogy undermines the force of the recognition of the friends' separateness.

Given that the connection between friends is predicated on their separation, Derrida argues that the relationship is ambiguous and inherently fragile. Márai's novel overcomes that fragility artificially. It contrives an uneasy solution by the imposition of the notion of duty. Derrida's claim that friendship is founded on an illusion serves as a corrective to the view of friendship proffered in Márai's novel. In the long run, the connection between Henrik and Konrad does prove to be illusory, since, while Henrik argues that it survives, it does so only as a duty. It operates on a notion of duty despite difference, rather than on the presumption of action motivated by attraction, enjoyment and preference. In old age the separation between the friends is manifest; they are in authentic relation. But since the illusion of their connection is shattered and friendship is only preserved by becoming a duty, we might argue that it is in fact no longer friendship. The ideal that Márai recommends must fail on a Derridean reading, since Márai overcomes the ambiguity on which the relationship is founded. The illusion of connection between the protagonists is destroyed. However, if we are reluctant to stipulate that friendship is a duty, then the illusion of connection must persist as an impossible ideal if the friendship is to survive.

In fact we might question whether it is an illusion that we are dealing with – if we take illusion to mean something that deceives by producing a false impression. Of course there is no formal or substantial connection between friends, but friends do develop and acknowledge an understanding of the relationship between them. We might say that they imagine a connection in the sense that they create a useful fiction. As we shall see in Chapter 5, David Hume writes about the notion of self-identity as such a fiction. He argues that we have no alternative but to use the faculty of the imagination to 'feign' a principle of union among our perceptions, since there is no one constant and invariable impression which gives rise to 'what we call our SELF'.[92] Similarly, Daniel Dennett draws an analogy between the concept of self and the concept of the centre of gravity, arguing that they are both fictions. Dennett's view is that both are abstract objects which none the less serve well-defined roles within the realms in which they are used (Newtonian physics and 'people physics' respectively, as he puts it).[93] My suggestion is that the sense of connection between friends can be regarded as a similarly useful fiction, rather than an illusion.

The possibility of friendship rests on our acceptance of this tempting fiction of connection, despite its fictional status – its impossibility. While the fiction conceals our separation from the other, its power and pleasure allow us to face the abyss between us, and hence to accept and forgive some degree of faithlessness in friends. But the fiction will only take so much strain. Some events can shatter it; and Márai records such events and the revelation of the undisclosed abyss between the protagonists which those events precipitate.

Márai takes the juxtaposition of connection and commitment with acceptance of faithlessness so far that the relationship cannot survive in the present. Henrik still regards Konrad as a friend, but only in the sense that their connection still has some force. He does not feel that he has the right to rise up in protest or demand vengeance. They chose one another and that choice, evidenced over the years, must be honoured, despite the base behaviour and the failure of the individual. With the proviso that the choices we make are made once we have reached physical and intellectual maturity, Cicero takes a similar view of our duty to friendship. He tells us that if we are unfortunate in our choice of friend, then we must simply accept and put up with it. If we find we have attached ourselves to someone vicious then we must discontinue intimacy slowly, 'unlearning it' rather than sharply cutting it off, unless the wrongdoing is intolerable.[94] Intolerable wrongdoing allows us to sever a friendship, since it breaks the tension between the basis on which we identify with the friend – the fiction of connection – and our ultimate separation and difference from her. However, respect for the relationship demands that this be done slowly. Konrad's wrongdoing would seem to fit into a different and curious category. It is insufficiently intolerable to lead Henrik to deny their friendship, but not sufficiently tolerable to allow the friendship to continue. In fact it does fit into Cicero's schema, since despite Henrik's claim that they 'are still, even now, friends', the friendship is discontinued. What remains is an appreciation of the value of their past friendship and of friendship in general, rather than a friendship. If friendship becomes duty then the role of those factors regarded as integral to the modern English usage of the term 'friend' – a depth of attachment to the friend and voluntary engagement with the friend – are called into question. The next chapter goes on to explore ideas of friendship as an ethical relationship, the moral worth of friendship and the contested place of duty, inclination and choice within such a conception.

Notes

1. Cicero, 'On Friendship', pp. 102–3.
2. Hutter, *Politics as Friendship*, chapter V.
3. Dupont discusses Roman politics in *Daily life in Ancient Rome*, pp. 20–1.
4. Hutter, *Politics as Friendship*, p. 148.
5. Taylor, *Party Politics in the Age of Caesar*, pp. 175–6.
6. Ibid., p. 9.
7. Boissevain, *Friends of Friends*, p. 26.
8. Hutter, *Politics as Friendship*, p. 136.
9. Cicero, 'On Friendship', p. 92.
10. Ibid., p. 103.
11. Ibid., p. 95.
12. Hutter, p. 119.
13. Cicero, 'On Friendship', p. 99.
14. Hutter, *Politics as Friendship*, p. 168.
15. Aristotle, *Nichomachean Ethics*, 1172a6–15.
16. Tonkin, 'Right Approaches: Sources of the New Conservatism', pp. 1–14; and Oakeshott, 'On Being Conservative', p. 25.
17. Montaigne, 'Of Friendship', p. 140.
18. Nussbaum, *The Fragility of Goodness*, pp. xxix–xxx.

19. Sartre, *Being and Nothingness*, pp. 475–6.
20. Duck, *Friends, For Life*, p. 8.
21. Cicero, 'On Friendship', p. 90.
22. Turnbull, *The Mountain People*, p. 134.
23. For critiques of Turnbull see Barth, 'On responsiblity and humanity: Calling a Colleague to Account'; and Heine, 'The Mountain People: some notes on the Ik of North-Eastern Uganda'.
24. Erikson, *Childhood and Society*, pp. 247ff.
25. Turnbull, *The Mountain People*, pp. 128–9.
26. Ibid., p. 130.
27. Ibid., p. 181.
28. Ibid., p. 32.
29. Kant, 'Lecture on Friendship', p. 212.
30. Turnbull, *The Mountain People*, p. 181.
31. Montaigne, 'Of Friendship', p. 141. Montaigne has only one criticism of this example and that is of the plurality of the friends. On his view, perfect friendship is indivisible and occurs only between two. It is only common friendships that can be divided up, so that we appreciate different qualities in different friends.
32. Buber quoted in Laing, *Self and Others*, p. 98.
33. Sartre, *Being and Nothingness*, p. 320.
34. Hegel, *The Phenomenology of Spirit*, 187, p. 111.
35. Ibid., 188 and 189, pp. 114–15.
36. Hegel, *Philosophy of Mind*, 432, p. 172.
37. Sartre, *Being and Nothingness*, p. 324.
38. Montaigne, 'Of Friendship', p. 141.
39. Sartre does allow for a 'we-as-subject', but he means by this a sense of being subjects in common, or a plurality of subjects jointly aware of a particular object. He gives the audience at a theatrical performance as an example (*Being and Nothingness*, p. 535).
40. Sartre, *Being and Nothingness*, p. 310.
41. Ibid., pp. 342–3.
42. Ibid., pp. 479–80.
43. Montaigne, 'Of Friendship', p. 141.
44. Deutscher, *Subjecting and Objecting*, p. 167.
45. Sartre, *Intimacy*, pp. 153 and 156.
46. Buber, *The Writings of Martin Buber*, p. 55.
47. Ibid., p. 49.
48. Ibid., p. 45.
49. Buber quoted in Kaufmann, 'Buber's Failures and Triumph', p. 9.
50. Kaufmann, 'Buber's Failures and Triumph', p. 10.
51. In fact Kaufmann goes so far as to suggest that Buber's thesis amounts to an emotional reaction, which can be explained as the outcome of a permanent malaise Buber suffered as a consequence of his mother's abandonment of him as a small child (ibid.).
52. Ibid., pp. 9–10.
53. Katz , 'A Critical Review of Martin Buber's Epistemology of *I-Thou*', pp. 100, 104–5. I have left aside Katz's concern in this discussion that 'there *must* be, and this is a logical-ontological *must*, a necessary unifying center of consciousness

which is *not* touched by talk of *I's*, *Thou's and It's*', and that therefore Buber's ontology is unconvincing.

54. Kaufmann, 'Buber's Failures and Triumph', p. 12.
55. Montaigne, 'Of Friendship', p. 138.
56. Nestor, *Female Friendships and Communities*, p. 12.
57. Simmel, *The Sociology of Georg Simmel*, p. 138.
58. De Beauvoir, *The Second Sex*, p. 556.
59. Bataille quoted in Blanchot, *Friendship*, p. ix.
60. Blanchot, *Friendship*, p. 292.
61. Seneca, 'On Philosophy and Friendship', p. 126.
62. Blanchot, *Friendship*, p. 289.
63. Ibid.
64. Ibid.
65. Ibid., p. 291.
66. Gross, 'Gifted Children and the Gift of Friendship'; and Selman, 'The Child as Friendship Philosopher', pp. 242–72.
67. Márai, *Embers*, p. 17.
68. Derrida, *Politics of Friendship*, p. 23.
69. Ibid., p. 22.
70. Márai, *Embers*, p. 42.
71. Ibid.
72. Ibid., p. 71.
73. Ibid., p. 49.
74. Sharp, *Friendship and Literature*, p. 90.
75. Derrida, *Politics of Friendship*, p. 281.
76. Márai, *Embers*, p. 163.
77. Ibid., p. 165.
78. Ibid., pp. 128 and 220.
79. Derrida, *Politics of Friendship*, p. 23.
80. Márai, *Embers*, p. 89.
81. Ibid., p. 122.
82. Ibid., pp. 133 and 131.
83. Nietzsche, 'Star Friendship', book IV, paragraph 279, pp. 225–6.
84. Derrida, *Politics of Friendship*, p. 281. Nietzsche's recommendation that we respect in the friend the enemy he could one day become is the origin of recognition of this dimension of relations between friends (Nietzsche, 'Star Friendship', book 4, paragraph 279, pp. 225–6).
85. Kant, 'Lecture on Friendship', p. 217.
86. Ibid., p. 215.
87. Derrida, *Politics of Friendship*, p. 53.
88. Quotations in this paragraph are from Derrida, *Politics of Friendship*, p. 53.
89. Emerson's poetic and romantic advice with regard to our attitude to a friend shares this concern with separateness between friends: 'Let him [the friend] be to thee for ever a sort of beautiful enemy, untamable, devoutly revered, and not a trivial conveniency to be soon outgrown and cast aside. The hues of the opal, the light of the diamond, are not to be seen if the eye is too near' (Emerson, 'Friendship', pp. 229–30). However, he does not explicitly recognise the tension implicit in a call to regard the friend as 'a beautiful enemy'.
90. Márai, *Embers*, pp. 128–9.

91. Ibid., p. 130.
92. Hume, *A Treatise of Human Nature*, I, IV, VI, p. 251.
93. Dennett, 'Why Everyone is a Novelist', p. 1016.
94. Cicero, 'On Friendship', pp. 101, 106–7.

Part II

Friendship as an Ethical Relationship

Chapter 4

Re-Imagining the Possibility of Friendship

The Moral Significance of Friendship

The last chapter argued that the possibility of friendship rests on our acceptance of a fiction – or what Derrida argues is an illusion – of connection, despite the impossibility of any complete or sustained connection between friends. Despite the fragility of the fiction, its power and pleasure help us to accept and forgive our friends' shortcomings and to make sacrifices on our friends' behalf. Sándor Márai, in his novel *Embers,* takes the concept of - forgiveness in friendship to its limits. He presents friendship as an ethical relation founded on duty born of loyalty to the preference that initially generated the relationship. We are presented with an ideal that fully embraces the possibility of disrupting difference between friends and yet undermines that ideal via the concept of duty. By comparison, the philosophical tradition that emphasises similarity as the basis of relations between friends presents friendship as an ethical relation based on an equally problematic ideal. This latter ideal is dubious because of its denial of the possibility of disrupting difference between virtuous friends; those who find themselves in deep disagreement are presented as neither truly friends, nor truly virtuous individuals. The ideal is also challenging because its illustrious champions imply that it is achievable; in fact in Montaigne's case, that he had achieved it. On these two analyses, friends of the best kind emerge as either thoroughly dutiful or thoroughly virtuous individuals. This chapter explores the extent to which ethical epithets are relevant to relations between friends.

One of the challenges we face in discussions of friendship is how we are to think of it in terms that allow us to appreciate both the personal significance of our social engagement with our friends and the morally significant dimension of that engagement. Some commentators have suggested that recent moral philosophy makes this task difficult, since it focuses on distinctions between activity in the personal sphere of life and the impersonal demands of morality. This distinction undermines our appreciation of the significant moral dimensions of relations between friends. Lawrence Blum, for example, suggests that a focus on the conflict between personal projects and the impersonal demands of morality makes it difficult to appreciate any action or motivation which falls neither on the side of the personal and non-moral, nor on the side of the purely impersonal. He regards friendship as a case in point.[1] Blum notes that much contemporary moral theory has focused on morality understood as impersonal, impartial, universal and rational, and on the extent to which morality, so understood, constrains or ought to constrain personal projects and satisfaction. On his view, these foci undermine our capacity to appreciate friendship as a source of good to the individual. For Blum, ethical reflection need not take place within a framework defined solely by the personal–impersonal dichotomy. He argues that there are uses of the term 'impersonal' relevant to relations between friends that are not encompassed by the impersonal viewpoint characteristic of recent Kantian and utilitarian versions of moral theory in particular.

The impersonal perspective of recent moral theory requires that we show care and concern for the other on the basis of our shared humanity. The demand of Kant's ethical law of perfection and its colloquial instantiation, 'love your neighbour as yourself', illustrates this latter view, in which love for one's fellows is a duty incumbent on all human beings, whether or not one finds them worthy of love.[2] Blum recognises that individuals stand in a variety of differently structured relations with particular others (for example, teacher to student, employee to employer) as well as in unstructured relations with others (for example, stranger to stranger). But while it is clear that the impersonal or impartial perspective is appropriate to action and motivation with regard to unstructured relationships or particular structured relationships (for example, magistrate to litigants), Blum argues that adopting the impartial perspective cannot account for the value we assign to relations between friends.

Blum uses an analogy between friendship and the concept of a vocation to explain the significance of friendship without reference to a rigid personal–impersonal dichotomy. He argues that a teacher who experiences her occupation as a vocation in some way chooses or affirms the values, norms or standards of action, attitudes and sentiments of the vocation. These features of vocational agency are independent of the agent's (the particular teacher's) desires. Blum maintains that friendship is similar, in that it is characterised by values, norms, attitudes and sentiments that are also independent of the individual friend's desires. Blum recognises that many social roles that are neither vocations nor friendships share these features. But he argues that the lack of definite structure and the degree of personal variability and individuality exhibited in action within vocations and in friendship indicates that friendship is more like a vocation than a role.

A teacher who experiences her occupation as a vocation does have role obligations towards her students; and these include moral and legal constraints that can be experienced as entirely external to the agent. But Blum maintains that the moral pull associated with a vocation is distinct from the moral pull exerted by the role obligations of the occupation. The distinction lies in the particular way in which an individual agent understands the values, ideals and traditions of her vocation, and the way in which that understanding conditions her expression of those values, ideals and traditions in action. Her particular understandings may not be shared by others who also experience teaching as a vocation, since there is room for dispute and individual interpretation in these matters. However, the values, ideals and traditions constitutive of the vocation of teaching will be shared to some extent by all who experience that calling, and in that respect Blum claims that they are in one sense impersonal. They are not purely matters of personal preference unconnected with the claims of other persons; the agent does not see the reason for their pursuit as being conferred by their place in her own personal goals. As Blum puts it, '[t]he vocational agent does not take herself to be pursuing a goal simply because of its value to *her*'.[3]

Blum is alerting us to the subtlety and complexity of factors involved in action and motivation associated with a vocational calling. His point is that the concept of a vocation cannot be understood on the model of action and motivation judged from an impersonal or impartial perspective. Understanding vocational agency is not a matter of adopting either an entirely personal or an entirely impersonal perspective; and it is in this respect that friendship is analogous to a vocation. A vocation entails action and motivation that is impersonal in the sense that it is founded on principles that all who experience the vocation share to some extent. At the same time it is personal in the sense that the particular way in which the teacher understands her vocation and relates to a particular student can crucially affect the teacher's desire to act on her calling. Similarly the moral significance of motivation and action in friendship can only be explained if we recognise both the personal and the impersonal dimensions of relations between friends.

While I take Blum's point that employing such a dichotomy, by adopting either the impartial perspective or alternatively the purely personal perspective, undermines any analysis of friendship as an ethical relationship, there are disanalogies between the concepts of vocation and friendship; for example, the equality, voluntary engagement and reciprocity in terms of affection that are taken to be characteristic of friendship are not necessarily features of vocations such as teaching. None the less other theorists share his criticism of the adoption of an impartial perspective in relation to discussion of the ethical significance of friendship. In his paper 'Friendship and Duty: Some Difficult Relations', Michael Stocker argues that '[t]o treat a friend as just one person among all people may, as such, be to wrong the friend. Thus, insofar as the impartial point of view requires treating every person as just one among many, the impartial point of view can be incorrect and, indeed, immoral.'[4]

On Stocker's view we have duties of friendship, such as the duty to show special care to a friend; and the existence of conflicts between friendship and other duties does not indicate that friendship must be outside the realm of duty (much less outside the realm of morality). Stocker illustrates his point with the example of a conflict between the duty to help a friend at a particular time and the duty to fulfil work obligations at the same time. He argues that this conflict might be resolved in favour of a notion of duty that privileges duty to the employer over the duty to the friend. Such a resolution privileges the more impersonal or impartial standpoint, but it is not clear that it is necessarily the more morally commendable choice in this situation. Consequently, Stocker suggests broadening the concept of duty to include duties of friendship.[5] In doing so, he broadens the realm of morality from a focus on the impersonal standpoint to include the personal, in much the same way as Blum does. Blum's emphasis is on the intersection he identifies between the impersonal and the personal in relations between friends; but both theorists' approaches reinforce the status of friendship as an ambiguous and somewhat paradoxical relationship. Friendship is unable to be situated exclusively in the private sphere of life, given the relevance of values, norms, attitudes and sentiments that Blum emphasises are independent of the individual friends' desires. But nor is it able to be situated exclusively in the public sphere of life, given the role of desire, volition and intimacy in friendship. Thus on Stocker's view, friendship forces us to make some adjustment to the concept of duty.

Aristotelian and Kantian Heritage

Emphasis on the impersonal perspective in moral philosophy owes much to the work of Immanuel Kant, who responds to the challenge that personal relationships present for moral theorising by excluding all but *'moral friendship'* from the realm of morally significant behaviour. Kant's perfect or moral friendship is an extremely rare and highly idealised private relationship in which friends adopt an attitude to one another that they can in fact extend to the whole human race; all other friendships are amoral on

Kant's view. This appears to contrast with the Aristotelian view of friendship as a public relationship that constitutes both a political and an ethical bond between those living under the constitution of the polis and sharing a conception of the good. As Nancy Sherman notes, Kant repudiates a conception of human good as foundational to morality.[6] Aristotle does balance his treatment of friendship as a public relationship with treatment of friendship as a phenomenon of private life. However, his portrayal of the highest form of friendship – friendship of the good or primary friendship – reveals tensions between the public notion of civic friendship (presented in his ethical and political writings) and the more personal or apolitical model of friendship (evident in his ethical works). The tensions arise because Aristotle does not make an explicit distinction between the two; and it is at best unclear how the discussion of friendship as a private phenomenon is to apply to the more impersonal kinds of friendship whose organisational basis is justice. Thus as we saw in Chapter 2, Aristotle's treatment of what he refers to in the *Eudemian Ethics* and the *Nichomachean Ethics* as civic friendship sits uneasily between associations with goodness and associations with utility.[7]

However, it is possible, on my view, to use Kant's moral theory to offer an interpretation which can go some way to resolving the tensions in Aristotle's position, and to do so in a way that has relevance for contemporary views of friendship. That relevance lies in claims about the nature of the moral qualities that attach to modern friendship, despite its ambiguous and paradoxical status. This interpretation begins with a focus on Aristotle's friendship of the good, so as to make the tension between friendship as a private and a public phenomenon explicit. It then turns to Kant to consider his claims about friendship and morality and their contribution to overcoming part of the tension in Aristotle's views.

Aristotle tells us that '[f]riendship in the primary and proper sense is between good men in virtue of their goodness', and that only a good man can love his friend for the friend's own sake and not for incidental qualities associated with utility or pleasure.[8] As Chapter 2 argues, the notion of liking a friend for his own sake is problematic for modern readers. Unlike Aristotle, we do not associate loving a friend with loving him for his goodness. This association allows Aristotle to ensure that the citizens of the polis, if they are good men, will like one another, have interests in common and have a firm foundation for the communal life of the polis. But this association determines that an Aristotelian conception of love and concern for a friend for the friend's own sake cannot take account of one feature that is central to modern conceptions of friendship. I have in mind here a particular – if indistinct – notion of intentionality.

Intentionality and Inclination

Aristotle's demand for an ideal of friendship which is not based on ulterior motives can be fruitfully explored by reference to a common activity which has the reputation of transcending mere 'interest' or particularity of aim. That activity is art. Ronald Sharp has compared activity in friendship and activity in art on the grounds that both enterprises are characterised by what he calls 'indirection' – what Kant would have called 'purposiveness without purpose'.[9] Sharp does not make the analogy between friendship and art explicit, beyond suggesting that friends invent and play games that can be understood on an analogy with art, since art uses form to get closer to reality. His view is that formality, ritual, hospitality and artifice enhance intimacy between friends, rather than hindering it. Sharp is not the only commentator to draw this analogy – Seneca did the same in the first century AD.[10] Friendship might well be considered an aesthetic practice or at least a practice with a significant aesthetic dimension, where Aristotle's demand for love and care for the friend for his or her own sake can find expression. Activity within friendship requires that we sometimes dispense with the instrumental – and to some extent even the formal – employment of reason; in these situations we rely on taste and imaginative acts of identification, which work symbolically rather than through rational decision-making processes.

Kant's comments on art in the *Critique of Judgement* emphasise the indirection that artistic endeavour requires: 'Fine art . . . is a mode of representation which is intrinsically final, and which, although devoid of an end, has the effect of advancing the culture of the mental powers in the interests of social communication.'[11] Just as in the Kantian prescriptions for the aesthetic, friendship is something that has to be pursued for its own sake and not for ulterior motives; otherwise its intricate artifice, which depends on the sense of its autonomy, will collapse. But again, like aesthetic practice, the 'indirection' of friendship does not preclude criticism and continual evaluation; there is room for differences of interpretation and perhaps even an imperative to reflect on the enterprise and the possibility of differing interpretations. What 'indirection' does seem to preclude is a certain kind of intentionality. In both art and friendship, aiming at a particular outcome will not ensure the success of the enterprise and may even defeat it.[12] Thus what is transcended in friendship of the best kind is not just mere interest, personal advantage or pleasure. Friendship with any particular aim must be transcended, on the basis of this analogy, and this includes friendships based on the virtue or goodness of the friends involved. Aristotle's identification of the friend with his (the friend's) goodness does not acknowledge the call to 'indirection' of intentionality associated with relations between friends.

As Sharp's analogy between art and friendship might suggest, uncertainty is intrinsic to the intentionality and to the activity required within the aesthetic realm as well as in relations between friends. Acknowledgement of the indirection definitive of both enterprises implies openness to possibility and consequently some uncertainty. I cannot aim to make you my friend, and if I were to make such an intention explicit, I might well undermine the chance of developing a friendship with you. I simply cannot have particular intentions in friendship. Kant might explain this by pointing out that the kind of moral imperative that commands our action in relation to friends cannot be a hypothetical one. As he puts it: '[h]ypothetical imperatives declare a possible action to be practically necessary as a means to the attainment of something else that one wills (or that one may will)'.[13] A hypothetical imperative has a particular purpose and hopefully will satisfy a particular desire. Aristotle's insistence on concern for our friend for the friend's own sake is equivalent to a mental disposition in which particular or personal interest in the consequences of our actions towards friends is not our focus. The capacity of friends to relate to one another on the basis of concern for the interest and needs of the other, rather than on the basis of their own individual interests and needs, is what is crucial to friendship.

To extend the analogy with art, imaginative activity, creativity and critical evaluation may all be necessary in coming to appreciate the interests and needs of a friend. As we saw in Chapter 3, Nietzsche, Blanchot and Derrida are theorists of friendship who appreciate the place of uncertainty in relations between friends. By comparison with these modern theorists, Aristotle avoids the discomfort of uncertainty by aligning the socio-political structures of the polis with his ethical prescriptions: the free male citizens of the polis are good men united by virtue in the communal civil life of the polis. However, the nexus created between the ethical and the socio-political spheres of life determines that Aristotelian civic friendship obscures the demand for indirection in friendship as well as the recognition of difference between friends. In fact, as we have seen in Chapter 3, Aristotle's ideal of the polis as a community of virtuous friends, and its emphasis on similarity between friends, were maintained only by the exclusion of those groups and institutions that would threaten its cohesion. Bowden makes the same point when she states that 'the sharing that is characteristic of *philia* is structurally insulated against the trials of servility, poverty and oppression'.[14] Conflicts of interest, questions of identity and reciprocity between friends are less fraught if those involved hold similar places in the social structure. The values inherent in a conception of the good shared by all members of the polis constrain and thus obscure Aristotle's recognition of uncertainty and diversity in friendship, and the potential for conflict that diversity entails.

Insulation from the effects of difference is connected with a neglect of emotional intimacy between friends in Aristotle's ethics, since Aristotle associates emotional disclosure with 'womenfolk and men who are like them, [who] enjoy having others to share their moanings, and love them as friends and sympathisers'.[15] Emotional disclosure becomes a failing of women, whose exclusion from citizenship allows Aristotle to minimise the potentially disruptive role of emotion in interpersonal relations within the polis. 'A man of resolute nature takes care not to involve his friends in his own troubles . . .; and in general does not give them a chance to lament with him, because he himself does not indulge in lamentation either.'[16] As Peta Bowden comments in this regard: '[A]ctivities displaying physical, intellectual and political domination and pleasure preponderate in the domain of *philia* to the detriment of practices in emotional responsivity and expression, the communication and sharing of one's "inner life", self-revelation, and the conveying and support of personal biography and identity.'[17] Thus the resolute Aristotelian man may never come to appreciate the role of emotional disclosure in the development of close personal relationships. He is also unlikely to appreciate the role of friendship in the lives of those excluded from citizenship; or the socially disruptive possibilities of friendship to which modern commentators such as Marilyn Friedman draw attention.[18] As Badhwar argues:

> [F]riendship is able to provide refuge to those ostracised by family or neighbourhood and to challenge the status quo. Thus the socially and politically subversive potential of friendship can be an important counterweight to the power of coercive communities and especially to that of the state (which is why dictatorships universally fear and try to suppress friendship).[19]

Drawing attention to some of the shortcomings of Aristotle's analysis of *philia*, from the perspective of a modern audience, highlights the problem of the relationship between friendship as a private and as a public phenomenon in his writings. Civic friendship fails to take account of difference, of the otherness of the other, of emotional intimacy – but this is precisely because Aristotle is well aware of the difficulties which uncertainty, difference, conflict, emotional disclosure and change pose for civic friendship.[20] He recognises that the relationship and its 'intricate artifice' are vulnerable to collapse without the support of a framework of organisational justice, and he provides this framework via the rights, responsibilities, values and practices which citizenship of the polis entails – albeit at the expense of a recognition of otherness and emotion. Civic friendship is in fact 'exclusive and divisive', as Badhwar might put it.

Aristotle's exploration of friendship does include a private dimension in which he emphasises intimacy of relations, trust and reciprocity, and which indicates the value he places on the particularity of the relationship between friends. '[F]riendship is a kind of partnership' in which good men 'become better men by exercising their friendship and improving each other'; a man's consciousness of the desirability of his own existence and of the existence of his friend becomes actualised in their life together – so self-worth and self-knowledge are enhanced through friendship.[21] Friends or *philoi* are integral to living a full and happy life, and the deep affinity between them allows them to act as what we might call 'mirrors' to one another.[22]

Thus, despite Aristotle's statements of apparent contempt for emotional disclosure, to the modern reader his recognition of the depth of intimacy, concern and awareness shared by friends suggests a notion of friendship as a creative enterprise – one in which the possibilities for relationship between self and other are open to construction and to change. Aristotle's claim to reject ulterior or utilitarian motives in friendships of the good implies a demand for this openness to the other and to possibility in relationships between friends; and this is the basis of the analogy between friendship and art. Yet it is here that friendship's fragility lies. A treatment of friendship as a private phenomenon forces us to a recognition of the complex social and ethical terrain associated with relationships between friends, and hence of its vulnerability and fragility: change, difference and conflict in friendship can destabilise the relationship. Aristotle, well aware of this fragility, is keen to avoid its destructive potential and therefore avoids emphasis on intimacy via his treatment of friendship as a public relationship and his focus on goodness. His concern is to preserve the advantage he sees in the bond of civic friendship. But to do so, he must downplay the potential for disruption in relationships between friends formed on the basis of choice, dependent on reciprocity, and established on a model that supports the notion of care and concern for a friend for the friend's own sake. Consequently, a tension emerges between civic and personal friendship, since it is difficult to appreciate the value of personal friendship in the context created by Aristotle's focus on civic friendship; the lack of an explicit distinction between the two in Aristotle's writings only exacerbates this problem.

By comparison with Aristotle, Kant rejects any general claim of friendship's moral worth on the grounds that it is a relationship founded on desire and inclination. Friendship is a form of what Kant calls 'pathological love', by which he means natural affection – rather than morbid or unnatural love. He argues that human beings are naturally inclined to form preferential bonds; that '[i]t is not man's way to embrace the whole world in his good-will; he prefers to restrict it to a small circle . . . [and] is inclined to form sects, parties'.[23] However, Kant is concerned that such preference 'tends to harden the heart against and to ostracise those who stand outside the pale of the particular sect'. He fears that 'any tendency to close the heart to all but a selected few is detrimental to true spiritual goodness, which reaches out after a good-will of universal scope'.[24] Kant sees friendship as an aid in overcoming the constraint and the distrust we feel in our intercourse with others, since it allows us to reveal ourselves to others almost without reserve. But he argues that we must guard against its exclusiveness, against shutting out those not included within our charmed circle:

> Friendship is not of heaven but of the earth; the complete moral perfection of heaven must be universal; but friendship is not universal; it is a peculiar association of specific persons; it is man's refuge in this world from his distrust of his fellows, in which he can reveal his disposition to another and enter into communion with him.[25]

Thus friendship is pathological because it is necessarily a partial form of attachment to the other, and Kant compares it with 'practical love', which is morally worthwhile precisely because it is impartial and hence can be universalised. Kant wants us to conclude that a person is not morally good if he follows a standard determined by his own desires; for him the only thing that can be taken as good without qualification is a good will. The establishment of a good will is the highest practical function of reason, and one with which desire – or in Kant's terms inclination – may interfere. Because friendship involves desire or inclination, it is excluded from the range of morally significant action. All inclination – whether altruistic, self-interested or malicious – is opposed to the concept of duty, which 'includes that of a good will, exposed, however, to a certain subjective limitations and obstacles. These, so far from hiding a good will or disguising it, rather bring it out by contrast and make it shine forth more brightly.'[26] The motive of a good will is to do its duty, simply for the sake of doing so and not for any other reason. Kant explained this view, using the example of action to help those in distress:

> To help others where one can is a duty, and besides this there are many spirits of so sympathetic a temper that, without any further motive of vanity or self-interest, they find an inner pleasure in spreading happiness around them and can take delight in the contentment of others as their own work. Yet I maintain that in such a case an action of this kind, however right and however amiable it may be, has still no genuinely moral worth. It stands on the same footing as other inclinations – . . . if fortunate enough to hit on something beneficial and right and consequently honourable, [it] deserves praise and encouragement, but not esteem; for its maxim lacks moral content, namely, the performance of such actions, not from inclination, but from *duty*.[27]

Only kindness done from duty – although no inclination impels us and even if disinclination stands in our way – has moral worth. Such kindness is practical for Kant because it resides in the will, not 'in the propensions of feelings', and as a consequence it can be commanded.[28] In this respect it is akin to *agape*, the kind of love commanded by the Christian scriptures. The natural affection intrinsic to friendship cannot be commanded and so is not thought to be any great accomplishment or to be worthy of a great reward. Kant is not alone in this view. Kierkegaard also argues that love of one's neighbour is superior to friendship because friendship is preferential love; but Kierkegaard goes so far as to suggest that since friendship is preferential and hence rooted in mood and inclination, it is essentially self-love: 'Just as self-love in the strictest sense has been characterised as self-deification, so love and friendship . . . are essentially idolatry.'[29] He criticises erotic love and friendship on the basis that they are related to passion, and argues that 'all passion, whether it attacks or defends itself, fights only in one manner: either-or: [e]ither I exist and am the highest or I do not exist at all – either all or nothing'.[30] His point is that although friends are said to be equals, we cannot regard another as an equal unless we love or have regard for him in the same way as we love or regard all our fellow human beings. For him equality is 'not to make distinctions and eternal equality is not to make the slightest distinction'.[31] Christianity champions eternal love, hence love between friends is opposed to Christian love; this is the boundless and genuine love of self-renunciation. As Kierkegaard sees it:

> Christianity has thrust erotic love and friendship from the throne, the love rooted in mood and inclination, preferential love, in order to establish spiritual love in its place, love to one's neighbour, a love which in all earnestness and truth is inwardly more tender in the union of two persons than erotic love is and more faithful in the sincerity of close relationship than the most famous friendship.[32]

By contrast friendship is 'the most passionate boundlessness of preference', which excludes others to focus on the one and only. The friend is called 'remarkably and significantly enough, the *other-self*, the *other I*'. Kierkegaard concedes that passionate preference might have no selfishness in it – apart from its preference for preference, apart from the fact that it is after all preference. But he says that even so, 'it would still have this, that consciously or unconsciously there is a wilfulness about it – unconsciously insofar as it is in the power of natural predispositions, consciously insofar as it utterly surrenders itself to this power and consents to it'.[33] In addition, since friendship entails a demand that we admire our friends, it will give rise to jealous protection of our friendships and to a tendency to congratulate ourselves on our friends. Kierkegaard acknowledges that admiration is not love, but he asks whether being 'the one and only friend of this rarest object of admiration' must not cause 'this relationship to turn back in a doubtful way to the *I* from which it proceeded'.[34] It is friendship's consent to preference that Kierkegaard finds objectionable, and this leads him to agreement with Kant that love and friendship contain no ethical task; they are simply good fortune for which we should be grateful. By contrast, Christian love is morally significant, since it 'dethrones inclination and sets this *shall* in its place', recognising that we simply cannot have 'the sincerity of close relationship' with all our neighbours.[35] The implication is that friendship – despite its lack of moral worth – is at least sincere.

But despite Kant's and Kierkegaard's dismissal of the moral worth of relations between friends, both practical or Christian love and pathological or preferential love are relevant to the conduct of close interpersonal relations.[36] That relevance lies in the relationship that holds between these two forms of regard within the realm of private interpersonal relations. My argument is a two-fold one. First, it suggests that practical love and pathological love are not necessarily two opposing forms of regard. Consequently, one cannot be lauded as morally significant while the other is dismissed as morally insignificant. Rather one form of regard can be seen as underlying the other, and this structural framework becomes most apparent within close interpersonal relations such as friendship. Second, it offers a critique of practical love and its relation to duty within this framework, in the light of Kant's remarks in 'The Doctrine of Virtue'.

Resolving Tension

Aristotelian civic friendship and Kantian practical love are presented as public and impersonal phenomena. However, they share a particular feature with regard to their relation to the private as well as the public lives of individuals. From a theoretical perspective, they could be regarded as providing a basic structural framework supporting all our relations with others, whether these are personal or impersonal. Civic friendship can be seen as providing a foundation or a kind of 'bottom line' for the more personal and apolitical form of friendship, so that personal friendship can be seen as built upon the foundation of the ethical and political bond created by the relation of civic friendship. The equality that is requisite between friends finds a different expression in the public and the private spheres. Within the public sphere friends are equal as citizens, while within the private sphere they are engaged in an intimate partnership which makes life worth living: sharing 'the occupation that constitutes their existence', engaging in kindnesses and finding pleasure in one another's company. Civic friendship appears to take priority in the sense that Aristotle devotes more attention to it in his writings. But it can be given priority in a different sense and context, since it can provide a model for dealing with difference and conflict between friends.

Civic friendship can be seen as the foundation of relations within the polis, so that it conditions more intimate relations between citizens. This is not to deny the shortcomings of Aristotle's account of friendship, such as the exclusion of many of the inhabitants of the polis (women and slaves) from citizenship and hence from civic friendship. Indeed, sheer exclusion cannot fully account for the shortcomings of Aristotle's account. Exclusion does serve to repress friendship, but friendship is also repressed by a failure to account for difference and conflict in friendship. Derrida describes this repression as a failure to appreciate friendship as a place of rupture;[37] the work of Friedman and Badhwar's comments, referred to above, emphasise friendship's potential for disruption. But Aristotelian civic friendship simply conceals the possibility that citizens may have differing conceptions of what constitutes the good for the community of which they are members.

None the less, however inadequate we find Aristotelian civic friendship to be, it does provide a foundation for more personal relationships within the polis. To see Aristotle's model of personal friendship as built on a foundation of civic friendship overcomes some of the tension between these two categories of friendship. It allows us to recognise the potential for conflict and disruption in personal relationships in which the men of the polis are close enough to be able to act as 'mirrors' to one another. But it also presents that recognition as conditioned by the friends' respect for their joint citizenship of the polis and the demands of that citizenship. Cicero in *De Amicitia* draws attention to a failure of this kind of respect, which in turn led to his disdain of friendship among men engaged in politics and affairs of state.

Kant's treatment of practical and pathological love can be reinterpreted in a way that is analogous to my preceding interpretation of Aristotle's distinctions. Doing so challenges Kant's dismissal of the moral worth of friendship by providing a way of accommodating difference between friends, but one that recognises the moral significance of that accommodation. Practical love can be seen as the structural framework within which 'pathological' or intimate forms of relationship occur, so that practical love provides a foundation for 'pathological' relations, such as love and friendship. When 'pathological' love-relations fail between two individuals, then morality demands that we fall back on the concept of practical love in our interactions with those estranged from us, whether temporarily or permanently. Thus practical and so-called 'pathological' forms of love could share a closer relationship within the ethical sphere than Kant's writing might suggest.

Taking this view of the relationship between friends offers a mechanism that allows friends in conflict to accept and respect their separateness from one another, despite the pain of conflict and rupture. This is the view that Márai's protagonist Henrik takes of his friendship with Konrad in the novel *Embers*. Henrik acknowledges that he is surprised and disturbed to discover – despite Konrad having ruined his life – that he and Konrad 'are still, even now, friends'.[38] But in this case, as I have argued, the conduct of the friendship is arrested at the point of the rupture; it does not continue in the same way, so that what survives is a respect for friendship, rather than an actual friendship. Henrik makes manifest Nietzsche's suggestion that we should respect in our friend the enemy he could one day become.[39] He is unable to demonise Konrad, despite the appealing simplicity that attributing the breakdown of the relationship to Konrad might have. We find him according Konrad respect as a 'friend-become-enemy', employing imagination and intelligent judgement to try to take Konrad's perspective on events and to accept whatever causal role he had had in the events that led to the rupture. Demonising Konrad might well have allowed him to avoid what he refers to as 'the task for which it seems he had spent his entire life preparing' – that of forgiving Konrad and achieving some resolution of their estrangement.[40] Henrik argues that friendship is a law or a duty that asks for nothing, but the resolution the novel offers does ask for something. It asks Henrik to maintain respect for Konrad despite their differences, despite his wounds. Thus it seems that their intimate friendship is supported by another and broader form of regard – that between fellow beings who share an intimate history.

Conflict or disruption of some form is inevitable in close personal relationships, given the differences between individuals and the potential for disruption that difference entails. Such disruption might find expression in changes in character, misinterpretation, conflicts of interest, absence, uncertainty or deliberate deception. Aristotle and Kant both attempt to minimise these disruptions – either by excluding those who would threaten a conception of friendship as likeness and thus failing to come to terms with the otherness of the other (Aristotle), or by dismissing friendship from the realm of morally significant action (Kant). But in doing so they miss the power of intimate engagement between friends and the unique context it provides for the development of relations with others and for understanding of the self, a topic addressed in Chapter 5.

Putting aside the criticisms of Aristotelian and Kantian accounts of friendship, my argument is that both philosophers provide a theoretical structure for the maintenance of relations in the broader social context within which intimacy develops. Thus notwithstanding the shortcomings of their accounts with regard to friendship in general, close personal friendships are most coherently seen as built on the foundations of a broader and more impersonal relationship, such as Aristotelian civic friendship or Kantian practical love might constitute. It is with the breakdown of personal friendship or 'pathological' forms of love that we are able to see the foundational role of notions like civic friendship and practical love. In situations of conflict between friends or intimates, morality demands that we maintain civil relations with one another despite our differences; that we rely on notions of respect for the estranged other in our subsequent interactions. Márai's protagonist Henrik reacts to Konrad's base behaviour and abandonment of him by treating Konrad respectfully. Henrik argues that friendship is in fact and at bottom a duty, but this is a realisation that only dawns in the context of his friend's faithlessness and base behaviour. Kant would seem to have an accurate theoretical explanation of Henrik's response. Friendship for Henrik becomes the duty of respect towards the faithless friend, a duty akin to the one that Kantian practical love imposes on us, but one which is born out of the remnants of a preferential relationship.

Lawrence Blum argues that the dichotomy between the personal and the impersonal spheres of life provides an inappropriate model for discussion of the moral worth of friendship. This view of relations between friends undermines that dichotomy. It replaces it with a model that emphasises the relationship between these two spheres in individuals' lives, and between the two forms of regard generally associated with those spheres: patholog-ical love and practical love. Kant's comments in 'The Doctrine of Virtue' further destabilise the view of pathological and practical love as two oppos-ing forms of regard.[41] Writing of duties to others, Kant claims that '*[l]ove and respect* are the feelings that accompany the carrying out of these duties'; that 'one can *love* one's neighbour though he might deserve but little respect, and can show him the respect necessary for every human being regardless of the fact that he would hardly be judged worthy of love'.[42] But Kant immediately goes on to say that love and respect are basically always united by the law into one duty; so that as regards our duty to help someone poor, 'it is our duty to behave *as if* our help is either merely what is due him or but a slight service of love, so as to spare him humiliation and maintain his respect for himself'.[43] Kant's reference to behaving *as if* our help is the recipient's due seems to be an implicit recognition that in fact love and respect cannot simply be summoned up as motives or commanded. In fact to behave 'as if' we feel the requisite sentiments has affinities with action on the basis of practical love.

Practical love seems to be that attitude we adopt in behaving 'as if' we love and respect our neighbour, since practical love resides 'in the will and not in the propensions of feeling'.[44] It names an attitude, rather than what Kant refers to as an affect or an emotion and refers to principles of action. Therefore any suggestion that there is a form of love that is opposed or superior to the love we feel for those with whom we are intimate – or have a special connection – is problematic. It simply confounds love with action and interaction based on Kantian goodwill. As one commentator argues, I cannot love because I will to love and still less because I ought to love, but this does not free me of the duty to cultivate and act upon feelings of love and respect.[45] Thus I may be required to behave 'as if' I love and respect another when in fact I don't, since it may be that the other in this case (my neighbour) 'would hardly be judged worthy of love'; or it may be that the other's base behaviour and faithlessness as a friend has undermined my feelings for him – either temporarily or permanently. Alternatively, I may be required to reflect on what love and respect demands of me in a particular situation. In this last case I may well have genuine feelings of love and respect for the other who is my friend, but perhaps because I am ill, tired, confused, upset or even lazy, I may need to reflect on what love and respect would require of me. In each of these cases, I need a notion of duty relevant to the relationship I share with the other. Thus even within intimate relationships, I may need a concept of duty upon which to ground the relationship in the face of a failure of affect.

Kant's attempt to confine himself to consideration of situations that are common to all human beings makes it difficult for him to appreciate the significance of the concept of duty within the personal sphere of life. He attempts to universalise, abstracting from the range of problems that may arise given the context in which particular individuals find themselves. His focus is on the notion of a good will, on our recognition of the moral law and its relationship to problems that have universal application for human beings. He recognises difficulties that may arise given our close association with friends, the problem of difference and the possibility of conflict. But these difficulties are tangential to the concerns of the moral sphere for Kant, precisely because they are based on a relationship he regards as delicate and precarious:

> Although it is sweet to feel in possession of each other in a way that approaches fusion into one person, friendship is something so delicate (*teneritas amicitiae*) that it is never for a moment safe from interruptions if it is allowed to rest on feeling, and if this mutual sympathy and self-surrender are not subjected to principles or rules preventing excessive familiarity and limiting mutual love by requirements of respect. Such interruptions are common among uncultivated people, although they do not always result in a split (for the rabble fight and make up). Such people cannot part with each other, and yet they cannot be at one with each other since they need quarrels in order to savour the sweetness of being united in reconciliation. – But in any case the love in friendship cannot be an affect; for emotion is blind in its choice, and after a while it goes up in smoke.[46]

The only love that can be relied upon in friendship is practical love – love that turns out to be a matter of attitude, since Kant wants us to believe that it will respond to the call of duty. My suggestion that pathological love relations like friendship can be seen as based on a foundation of practical love is one way to challenge Kant's dismissal of the notion of duty in friendship.[47] But this perspective only comes into play as a way of dealing with conflict in friendship, and this is not one of Kant's concerns. Kant's real concern is with 'moral friendship', a form of friendship in which he does not anticipate conflict. Moral friendship is friendship 'considered in its perfection' as 'the union of two persons through equal mutual love and respect'. It constitutes an ideal, which exists 'here and there in its perfection' and is distinguished from pragmatic friendship, which concerns itself with the ends of others and is based on feeling and emotion. Only moral friendship has the purity and completeness requisite to duty, but this ideal of friendship appears as barely distinguishable from the regard and attention of one who takes an affective interest in the well-being of all human beings. Such a person takes to heart 'the duty of being benevolent as a friend of human beings'; that is, a friend of the whole human race.[48] The two participants in a moral friendship share a union of equal love and respect, but the relationship is not based on feeling. Their love is akin to God's love; a love bestowed equally on all, the love of saints, rather than of ordinary human beings. Only friendships that exhibit this kind of love can have any moral significance; and the rarity of this love leads Kant to warn of the dangers of friendship. But his wariness of the unreliability of feeling and the blindness of emotion is overstated. Emotion is not simply a matter of blind affect; rather it involves judgment and so is not as blind as Kant might have us believe. In fact the next chapter suggests that we may be wise to pay attention to the kind of vision it supplies to friends.

Duty, Difference and Expectation

Kant's approach to the competing demands of morality and friendship is not dissimilar from Creon's approach to the problem of the competing demands of religion and family in Sophocles' play *Antigone*. Creon recognises only one value, so that the values and virtues entailed in the maintenance of family relationships are rejected. As Martha Nussbaum puts it, his view is that 'the healthy mind just *is* the mind completely devoted to civic safety and civic well-being', so that he confines goodness and human excellence to that which is productive of civic wellbeing. The virtues of justice, honour, respect and piety are all defined in relation to civic obligation and civic wellbeing, and Creon views Antigone's attack on civil values as a sign of mental incapacity.[49] However, this kind of conflict cannot be resolved by edict, and in this respect it is similar to conflict between the demands of friendship and our duties in the public or impersonal sphere of life.

Elizabeth Telfer acknowledges the moral problems that friendship's preference can cause, but she argues that we none the less have special and specific duties to friends. She notes that friendship 'seems prima facie to involve a kind of injustice, in that it means giving preferential treatment to those who differ neither in need nor in desert – in other words that, so far from being duties, our services to friends might be construed as positively immoral'.[50] However, she adopts a rule-utilitarian position to justify the claim that we do in fact have special duties to friends. Her view is that such duties are justified because their observance is conducive to the general good; that human beings will be more effective in promoting the general good if they make the welfare of a few others their concern. Utility will be maximised if we focus our activity on the needs of a small group whose needs we know precisely, as a consequence of the special rapport and sharpened awareness we share as friends. Telfer argues that the utility of friendship is high enough to compensate for the fact that some measure of injustice is involved in it, given its uneven distribution among people with competing and equally valid claims on their fellows.[51] However, given that duties within friendship are predicated upon the special rapport and awareness that particular friends share, it will be difficult to stipulate the precise nature of those duties; since, at least in some cases, those duties will be peculiar to the particular relationship we share with a friend.

In contrast to Telfer, but still in the context of the conception of morality identified with Kant and Kierkegaard, Lawrence Blum offers a different defence of friendship and its moral worth.[52] As noted above, Blum criticises calls to impartiality in the context of friendship. He rejects the claim that impartiality is a principle and a perspective which define the moral point of view. He argues that it 'constitutes only one among other moral principles, perspectives, and virtues',[53] and that in contexts in which impartiality between the interests of all is clearly demanded of us, the demand is limited in scope. On his account it is friendship's very partiality and the intimacy of engagement it involves that enable friends to offer one another a particular kind of caring which cannot be denied moral worth. In contrast to Telfer's rule-utilitarian position, Blum's view is that since we have a special capacity to help others who are friends, we also have special duties to them. The strength and intimacy of the tie between us enable us to do for a friend what we could not do for a stranger – and hence what we could not be expected to do for a stranger.

If we accept that the personal sphere of life is included within the arena of morally relevant behaviour, then we can begin to examine those aspects of our interaction with friends that raise moral questions or moral dilemmas. Friendships cannot be so regulated by a sense of propriety and obligation that they lose their spontaneity, their accommodation of difference, their openness to change and development. Caring for a friend for that friend's own sake implies some flexibility on our part, given that such care and concern focus on the other and not on our expectations of, or plans for, the other. If we take seriously Aristotle's prescription that a good friend is one who wishes his friend well for that friend's own sake, then we recognise that friend's separateness from us, we admire his qualities and we give him room to develop them. Consequently we can expect the possibility of some degree of disagreement, conflict, competition or bad feeling between friends. As Márai's protagonist Henrik says in the novel *Embers*, friendship is not simply 'the opportunistic pleasure that two people experience in encountering each other when they think the same way about certain things at certain times in their lives, when they share the same tasks or the same needs';[54] and nor, Henrik argues, is it sympathy, since that is too hollow, empty and weak a word to express the idea that in the worst times two people will stand up for each other. Sympathy founders in a morass of vanity and egoism on Henrik's view, while camaraderie and fellowship only look like friendship.

Márai's solution – to present friendship as a duty – overcomes problems of egoism and vanity in friendship, since friendship is insulated from disappointment and hence from tension generated as a consequence of unmet expectations. But his solution also undermines the possibility that friends might encounter one another in their difference, prepared to risk disappointment, accept change and face tension, and yet be able to continue with their relationship. Disagreement or conflict in friendship need not imply that Nietzsche's 'little boulders are rolling' so that the friendship will soon follow after and shatter.[55] As the previous chapter argues, a view of friendship as a relationship that must accommodate change, difference and perhaps conflict can alert us to the fragility and ambiguity of the relationship. But it also provides us with the opportunity to consider how we might make these accommodations.

Disagreement, conflict and disappointment can have many sources in relations between friends. Emotional reactions, political differences, differences in moral values and attitudes are all potential sources of conflict. Ronald Sharp points out that 'envy is a familiar emotion, even with friends', but he goes on to argue that 'the mere presence of competition or bad feeling in friendship does not mean that the friendship is inauthentic or doomed'.[56] It is Sharp's view that in most friendships – and he includes noble friendships in his comments – aggression and competition are not absent, but tamed. Of course, some differences can lead to the disintegration of a friendship. Telfer notes that some moral defects may make a person incapable of friendship, and that hence friendship with a person we come to recognise as deeply flawed or someone we discover to be thoroughly bad will be morally problematic. But she argues that there is none the less 'no necessary incompatibility between fondness, liking, and a sense of a bond, on the one hand, and disapproval of some qualities in a person, on the other'.[57] Telfer may well be correct that those of us who share similar moral views will find it difficult to develop or maintain a friendship with someone we discover to be seriously morally deficient. However, it is important to recognise that those we might consider to be thoroughly bad characters appear capable of friendship. Such people seem to be able to preserve friendships as a sphere within their lives, isolated from the remainder of what is morally reprehensible or at least morally ambiguous to others.

It is interesting to ponder why this apparent anomaly within theories of friendship might be the case. Is it that Aristotle is mistaken about the fact that 'only good men can be friends for their own sakes'? Telfer thinks so, and thus she rejects the notion she thinks is sometimes assumed by Plato and Aristotle: that 'we need to think of our friends as good people'.[58] She explains that Aristotle holds this view because he thinks that to care for someone because of his virtue is to care for him for his own sake, while to care for him because he is useful or pleasant is not. This alerts us again to Chapter 2's discussion of the difficulties associated with establishing what we might mean by holding that friends are those who care for one another for their own sakes, if we do not associate this care with the friend's goodness. On the other hand, Aristotle's description of the friend as another self might be apposite to explaining this anomaly; we might explain that thoroughly bad characters see their friend as another self and that this allows them to maintain a friendship, despite a lack of respect for others in general. If the latter suggestion is the case, then Kant could offer an explanation; this would appear to be an illustration of the existence of pathological love without an underpinning of practical love.

Despite the difficulty of explaining friendship between thoroughly bad characters, in general our response to disapproval, disappointment and disagreement within friendship will determine how any conflict will affect the relationship. Ronald Sharp uses a personal anecdote to illustrate one mode of dealing with conflict.[59] He suggests that humour can often give vent to conflict, competition and feelings of aggression. For him humour preserves the salutary side of competition between friends – the sense in which competition serves to keep friends alert and eager to make the best of their capacities – while at the same time purging the relationship of the crude and more self-interested side of competitiveness. It might well be that interpersonal relations are inevitably marked by interpersonal conflict, as Jean-Paul Sartre's views of the structure of human consciousness led him to conclude. But what is crucial for friendship is not the question of whether we are fundamentally alienated from one another or whether we are fundamentally aggressive beings; rather, as Sharp puts it, the crucial factor is 'how we handle the aggression we have'.[60] Of course we will have to deal with aggression in other interpersonal relationships, but friendship differs from relationships predicated on formal ties. It is regarded as a relationship of choice. It flourishes in reciprocity, in free and mutual cultivation, and is dependent upon friends' liking and concern for one another for their own sakes. Its difference from relationships which are established on the basis of formal ties or obligations – whether biological, commercial, occupational or culturally determined – is undoubtedly part of its value and appeal. Within the family, blood relations, kinship and the law may determine a particular and formal connection with other family members – even though we might view particular family members as friends. But as Cicero puts it: 'relatives may lose their goodwill, friends cannot, for once goodwill has been lost, the friend is no longer a friend, but the relative is still a relative'.[61]

Friendships also differ from those relationships we might be involved in by virtue of the kind of work we do, sport we play, or interests we have – whether these are political, cultural or leisure-based. This is not to say that we might not develop lasting friendships with fellow workers, fellow team members, neighbours or people we meet at political rallies, football games, concerts or parties. In fact such relationships might be important to the lives of modern selves. As Friedman suggests, modern selves often seek involvements in communities whose norms and relationships stimulate and develop their identity and self-understanding in ways that unchosen communities of origin do not.[62] However, we are not friends in virtue of our shared occupation or employment, our social or sporting interests, or our political or religious concern. The explanation of the friendship cannot lie, for example, in satisfying a desire to play golf, since friendship precludes such a narrow instrumental focus. It might be argued that choice is significant in certain relationships structured by formal ties or shared ends; for example, we do choose to interact with fellow club members when we choose to join a sporting club. But interaction between fellow club members is conditioned by our joint club membership, the club's rules of association and our desire to play golf, rather than a concern for one another for each person's own sake. The expectations and obligations associated with structured or formal relationships provide a framework for interaction. Of course, we are free to ignore expectations or to flout obligations entailed in our formal ties with others. But this possibility only serves to emphasise the nature of the choice we make in friendship. The freedom of choice in friendship and the mutual care and liking that friends exhibit imply that the sentiments we feel carry moral significance within the relationship.

Generally in making choices we take responsibility for the morally relevant aspects of our choices and often for their consequences. We assume a connection between our choices and our actions. As Nancy Sherman notes, this is also an assumption Aristotle makes in seeing virtue as a state of character connected with choice and action,[63] and it is relevant to Aristotle's claim that friendship either implies virtue or is a kind of virtue.[64] But within friendship, the nature of our responsibility is unclear and the question of choice is complicated by our focus on our friend for that person's own sake. Thus the norms and values constitutive of the notion that we have duties towards our friends – duties of friendship – determine that friendship is characterised by a curious degree of uncertainty with regard to expectations and obligations. The question of our responsibility to friends is further complicated by recognition of the friend's separateness from us; the potential for difference and perhaps misunderstanding between us. The distance between us may make it difficult to establish what liking, care and concern for a particular friend for that person's own sake require of us. These sentiments reflect an indirect form of intentionality, one in which we act purposefully but without a purpose determined by our own self-oriented desires. This notion of intentionality was the basis of the preceding analogy between friendship and art. Both enterprises were seen as dispensing with any narrowly instrumental employment of reason, to rely on taste and imaginative acts of identification. Friendship depends on a level of communication and understanding between friends sufficient to allow taste and imaginative acts of identification to provide us with a guide to action. The notion of obligation or duty in friendship is indeterminate as a consequence of the fact that it requires indirection of intention, and also because it is dependent on the nature of communication between friends, their capacities for imaginative identification, and on questions of taste.

Michael Stocker argues that taking account of friendship provides a much-needed corrective to accounts of duty.[65] This corrective generates a synthesis of duty and friendship. It undermines the dichotomy between an ethics of care and responsibility (into which friendship falls) and a rights-based morality (into which duty falls), by revealing the possibility of a synthesis of these two schemas. Stocker draws attention to features common to both duty and friendship to explain this synthesis, noting that both can involve hierarchies and both harbour potentially problematic resolutions of conflict. Some friends – like some duties – come and should come before others. This can involve a ranking of responsibilities towards different friends, but one which cannot avoid the possibility of conflicts and dilemmas; and it may be that some conflicts are not able to be resolved in ways that allow us to escape guilt, shame and even wrongdoing. Stocker gives the example of a friendship which is undermined by a change in the values and interests of the individuals involved. The friendship has become tiresome to one of the parties so that there is no longer any pleasure in it. However, terminating the friendship is problematic since it will involve hurting the legitimate feelings of an old friend. At the same time, continuing the friendship may be worse, given the pretence it now entails. Stocker argues that the realm of ethics, including that of duties, admits of the same irresolvable conflicts and dilemmas – of dirty hands, unavoidable compunction, guilt and shame. It is Stocker's view that '[t]o operate well in regard to duties, one must be morally sensitive, and one must sensitively appreciate a wealth of details and contexts. Moral education and sensitivity, and what some see as contextualism, are as needed for duty as for friendship.'[66]

In drawing an analogy between duty and friendship, Stocker does acknowledge that friendship's value might be regarded as natural, while the notion of duty has moral value. But he argues that so far as the naturalness of friendship is concerned there is no bar to duty and friendship being inter-related, since friendship gives rise to special duties of friendship. He distin-guishes the concept of 'duties' of friendship from that of 'the duty' of friendship; his concern is with the former, the duties we have in and as a result of friendship, rather than with the latter, which suggests a duty to seek, have or maintain friendships. Stocker claims that we may well have a duty of the latter type, and perhaps he has in mind Kant's prescription in 'The Doctrine of Virtue' that '[I]t is a duty to oneself as well as to others not to *isolate* oneself but to use one's moral perfections in social inter-course . . . to cultivate a disposition of reciprocity – agreeableness, toler-ance, mutual love and respect.'[67] However, duties of friendship differ from the duty of friendship in that duties of friendship 'are at once constitutive of, and grounded by, the friendship'.[68] If we take the Aristotelian definition of a true friend as our guide – although within a modern context – then we will conclude that some acts of friendship are duties. For Aristotle, the true friend is one who desires the good of a friend for the friend's own sake, loves the other for what she is and confers benefits on the other, or at least has the disposition to do so.[69] Given this definition, love or liking, care and concern are dispositions and attitudes – expressed in action where possible – that genuine friends must exhibit towards one another.[70] Thus I have a duty to show care and concern for a friend, and my friend has a claim on my care and concern, in ways that non-friends do not.

It does seem counterintuitive to suggest that friends have a duty to feel affection towards one another or to develop an emotional bond. But, as Stocker also notes, duties of friendship cannot be regarded as duties of affection, in the sense that we are bound to feel affection towards a friend in relation to every act of friendship. We may be tired, distracted or in a bad mood, so that we don't feel any warmth of attachment at a particular time. None the less we might expect friends to act 'as if' they feel affection in sit-uations in which they are feeling emotionally depleted, but their friend is in need of their support. Indeed, the expectation that friends will exhibit certain dispositions and attitudes to one another is accompanied by further expectations: we expect that friends will take the time necessary to engage in reciprocal social intercourse so as to cultivate the relationship; that they will find opportunities for the development of affection and intimacy. But these last expectations cannot be duties, and they create a distinction between morally relevant and morally neutral choice in friendship. As

Stocker also points out, much of what is constitutive of, and valuable about, acts of friendship cannot regarded as duties. If people fulfil only their duties of friendship then their sincerity eventually comes into question. Friendship becomes a pretence if friends act 'as if' they feel the sentiment requisite to friendship when they deem it necessary, but do not choose to spend time together or interact together when they could easily do so.[71]

It must be acknowledged that any appeal to the values and norms underlying the concept of obligation or duty in friendship might appear to be paradoxical. Given the Aristotelian definition of a true friend, it is our concern for the other as friend that must motivate us, and not a concern for the values and norms of friendship. However, as I have suggested above, it is possible to argue that the notion of duty within friendship is a special indeterminate case of duty, in that it demands indirection of intention. Blum seems to adopt a similar position when he defends appeals to the norms and values of friendship by arguing that such appeals must be a way of ensuring that I am doing what needs to be done 'for, and for the sake of' a specific friend in order for my act to count as an act of friendship.[72] Thus the fact that friendship is a preferential relationship does not invalidate the notion of duty in friendship; rather it makes friendship a relationship in which the notion of duty is particularly indeterminate. The specific expression of that notion will sometimes be established within unique contexts and at the discretion of the parties to the friendship. However, as we have seen, Stocker argues that duty is not unlike friendship in this regard. In the face of a plurality of duties, establishing what duty demands will also require moral sensitivity and an appreciation of a wealth of details and contexts.

The responses of Blum and Stocker emphasise the intersection between the personal and the impersonal spheres of life in relations between friends. Acts performed for a particular friend are often material instantiations of dispositions and attitudes that are definitive of friendship in general, and they have moral significance given their role in the relationship. At the same time, they are influenced by each individual's interpretation of the duties of friendship and by different understandings of relations between self and other in friendship.

However, the admonition to act for the sake of duty is unhelpful in the event that two duties conflict. There is no a priori or clear-cut way in which to decide between a conflict of duties. Deciding which of two conflicting duties should be given the greater weight will depend upon the actual circumstances. Generally I am not prepared to lie simply for the sake of friendship, but I can imagine circumstances in which I might well be prepared to lie to protect a friend. What I decide to do in such a situation will depend on numerous factors: my understanding of my friend's situation, her background and history, her fears and concerns, her values and attitudes. I will need to achieve a kind of 'reflective equilibrium' between duties of friendship and my duty more generally from the impersonal or impartial standpoint, so as to balance one against the other in the light of the complexities of the situation.

Thus there is balance to be achieved between a focus on responsibility towards the other as friend, a focus on the self as friend, and a focus on the self as moral agent both within the context of friendship and outside that context. Difficulty in establishing what friendship requires of us becomes not only a function of the factors noted above, such as indirection of intention, our skills in communicating, our sensitivity, our capacities for imaginative identification and hence the rapport we develop with the other; it also assumes a capacity to recognise the other as separate and different from oneself. However, the recognition of difference between friends may extend to different views of what is appropriate in friendship and hence different views with regard to what is required of friends. This may take the form of conflicting interpretations of the norms and values of friendship, or conflicting views on how the norms and values of friendship relate to wider, relevant societal norms and values.

In Toni Morrison's book *Sula*, Sula runs off with the husband of her best friend, Nel. On her deathbed, Sula responds to Nel's bitterness with the following comments:

> So she [Nel] will walk on down that road, her back so straight in that old green coat, the strap of her handbag pushed back all the way to the elbow, thinking how much I have cost her and never remember the days when we were two throats and one eye and we had no price.

But any reconciliation is impossible, given their competing views of the situation. Nel, at one point, asks:

> "But what about me? What about me? Why didn't you think about me? Didn't I count? I never hurt you. What did you take him for if you didn't love him and why didn't you think about me?" And then, "I was good to you, Sula. Why don't that matter?"

And then this interchange occurs:

> "It matters, Nel, but only to you. Not to anybody else. Being good to somebody is just like being mean to somebody. Risky. You don't get nothing for it."
> "We were friends."
> "Oh, yes, good friends," said Sula.
> "And you didn't love me enough to leave him alone. To let him love me. You had to take him away."
> "What do you mean take him away? I didn't kill him, I just fucked him. If we were such good friends, how come you couldn't get over it?"

Sula's response is to ask:

> If we were such good friends, how come you couldn't get over it? [73]

The text raises the same kind of questions as Márai's novel *Embers*. Does friendship imply that we ought to be able to forgive a friend who fails to show care and concern for us? If so, does the seriousness of the failure provide a limit to the bestowal of forgiveness? Nel's view implies that the norms of friendship – if not the norms of the wider community – demanded that her husband was off-limits to Sula, while Sula's comments imply that she expects a friend to be able to forgive her act of betrayal, if they are genuinely good friends. The seriousness of Sula's failure does not appear to strike her as a reason for Nel to withhold forgiveness. The fact that Sula still sees Nel as her friend is reinforced by her final thoughts as she realises that there is not going to be any pain in her last moments. '"Well, I'll be damned," she thought, "it didn't even hurt. Wait'll I tell Nel."'[74] Her attitude brings to mind Márai's view that the idea of fidelity in friendship is an appalling egoism; that it is vanity and egoism that are the root of problems in friendship; and that we have no right to demand unconditional honour and loyalty from our friends. As Márai puts it:

> the friend expects no reward for his feelings. He does not wish the performance of any duty in return, he does not view the person he has chosen as his friend with any illusion, he sees his faults and accepts him with all their consequences . . . And if a friends fails, because he is not a true friend, is one allowed to attack his character and his weaknesses? What is the value of a friendship in which one person loves the other for his virtue, his loyalty, his steadfastness? What is the value of a love that expects loyalty? Isn't it our duty to accept the faithless friend as we do the faithful one who sacrifices himself? . . . And if a man gives someone his trust through all the years of his youth and stands ready to make sacrifices for him in manhood because of that blind, unconditional devotion, which is the highest thing any one person can offer another, only then to witness the faithlessness and base behaviour of his friend, is he permitted vengeance? And if he does rise up and demand vengeance, having been deceived and abandoned, what does that say about the validity of his friendship in the first place?[75]

Of course vanity and egoism can cause problems in friendship, but while seeing friendship purely as duty overcomes such problems, it also destroys the fiction of connection between friends. Proof against disappointment in friendship is not to expect honour and loyalty, but to be heroic and selfless, to ask for nothing. However, we might well wonder whether it is selflessness that is required in friendship, rather than a willingness to face and be prepared to maintain continually a fragile balance between care and concern for a friend and care and concern for oneself.

Our recognition of the distance that separates us as friends emphasises our profound isolation from one another, even within intimate relationships. This in turn reminds us of our status as individuals and, within the moral sphere, of our responsibilities as individual moral agents within friendship and within the wider society. The call to reciprocity and for reciprocal services in friendship is reinforced by this recognition of the self as radically separate from the other, and of friendship as a close relationship built upon a foundation of a broader and more impersonal moral relationship. Nel adopts this view. She seems to see herself as having a duty to show care and concern for Sula, and as having discharged that duty; she also recognises Sula's special claim on her care and concern. In turn she acknowledges her own needs and rights and expects that Sula should adopt the same view of relations between friends. A serious failure of love and respect for the other will undermine friendship – and Sula certainly fails on both these counts, as well as on calls to self-discipline and remorse for what Nel perceives as a gross breach of friendship. Nel's perception emphasises the gulf between her and Sula in terms of their different understandings of the requirements of friendship.

In his discussion of virtue in 'Duty and Friendship', Michael Stocker explains that what is natural, dangerous or problematic differs for different people. His view is that if people differ, for example, in ego boundaries, they will have and need different, even if related, virtues.[76] Stocker is advising us to be alive to the psychological make-up of those who embody particular doctrines about virtue. His advice is apposite to this discussion, since an awareness of the psychological make-up of friends must be applied to theories of friendship, particularly to those aspects of a theory that identify what is morally required of friends. The crucial virtue of friendship for Henrik, in Márai's novel, is forgiveness; our care and concern for a friend should extend to the point that we ask for nothing and forgive any transgression of our hopes and expectations. Nel is more equivocal; her view is that friendship is governed by certain constraints on behaviour, which may well also operate within the wider moral sphere that impinges on action within friendship. On this view, respect and propriety would have demanded that Sula forego amusing herself with Nel's husband. Sula expects Nel to forgive her behaviour, but her comment that Nel does not remember the days when they 'were two throats and one eye and had no price' implies that she expects forgiveness on the grounds that they once shared the kind of fusion that Montaigne and Cicero speak of as definitive of perfect friendship. Nel and Sula might provide Stocker with an example of people who differ with regard to their ego boundaries and who therefore differ with regard to the virtues that friendship implies.

The gulf between Nel and Sula is doubly relevant because it raises the question of the place of rational self-concern in friendship. Nel is concerned for herself; she wants to know why her care and concern for Sula were not reciprocated. Unlike Márai's Henrik, who condemns himself to a no-man's land in which he honours a collapsed friendship, Nel resents the lack of reciprocity and its effect on her happiness. But while Henrik's solution seems at least partly deceptive in that the friendship between him and Konrad does not survive, both Nel and Henrik acknowledge the distance that separates even intimate friends, while Sula does not. For all of them, sufficiently serious conflict places limitations on intimacy. Kant clearly recognises the potential for conflict between friends and saw it as inevitable. He regards friendship to be (in its perfection) 'the union of two persons through equal love and respect'. And since for him love and respect pull us in different directions, we must appreciate an inevitable tension in friendship. As Kant puts it, 'love can be regarded as an attraction and respect as repulsion, and if the principle of love bids friends draw closer, the principle of respect requires them to stay at a proper distance from each other'.[77] Morrison's Sula demands Nel's love, but is not prepared to accord Nel the respect she expects.

Kant tries to avoid this kind of conflict by stipulating that friendship cannot be a union in which we are 'chained to another's fate and encumbered with his needs'. It must be a union in which any help that each counts on from the other in case of need is only 'the outward manifestation of an inner heartfelt benevolence, which should not be put to the test since this is always dangerous'.[78] The danger lies in the fact that each friend should be generously trying to spare the other any burden, attempting to bear his burden himself and even concealing it altogether from his friend. If one does accept a favour from the other, then while he may well be able to count on equality in love, Kant claims that he will no longer be able to count on equality in respect. The help supplied will place one friend in an inferior position, being under an obligation without being able to impose obligation in return. Friendship emerges as a relationship in which there is a duty of benevolence between two people who should ensure that they are never in need of benevolence; or if they are, that the need for benevolence is shared equally between both parties. When one friend responds to the other's need for benevolence, the response places the relationship in danger.

Kant's position seems to undermine the whole idea of friendship in that it places too much emphasis on reciprocity. We act out of care and concern for a friend in need, and not for the promise of reciprocity or the equality that mutual benevolence preserves; so we need not be so concerned about equality in terms of benevolence or beneficence. Admittedly a sustained lack of reciprocity is likely to undermine a friendship, since a friend may suspect that it is an indication of a lack of heartfelt benevolence towards her. But too close an eye on maintaining equality in these matters may undermine the relationship in another way, by making us insensitive to the needs of friends. The real danger here, and the reason that Kant cannot appreciate the notion of duties of friendship, is that he is applying to close relationships principles that are more appropriate in the sphere of impersonal relationships. His approach neglects the fact that friends are others whom we can help in various ways, by virtue of the closeness of the relationship we share. Of course, from an impersonal perspective, friendship can seem to involve a kind of injustice or inequality, since it involves giving preferential treatment to those who do not necessarily differ either in need or in desert from non-friends, as Telfer has explained. As a consequence, Kant argues that feeling must be subject to principles or rules to prevent excessive familiarity and self-surrender and to limit mutual love by the requirements of respect. He is wary of the sweetness of the feeling between friends 'in possession of each other in a way that approaches fusion into one person', since relationships which are allowed to rest on feelings are never safe from interruptions.[79] Kant is right to fear that feeling can get out of hand; we can become excessively familiar, and we can take others for granted, so that our relationships are subject to the 'interruptions' Kant wants to avoid. Aristotle's call to self-sufficiency for good men serves a similar purpose. As we saw in Chapter 2, the good man flourishes in his own self-sufficiency on the basis of his capacity to exercise the intellectual virtues. Thus Aristotle's concept of the good for man is identified relatively independently of his life with his friends and in fact of his life with all others. Kant's response to the possibility that we can become overly familiar with or dependent on others is to universalise love and to recommend respect. This avoids the dilemma latent in the tension between liking and caring for a friend for that friend's own sake, while at the same time recognising that the friend is separate and different from oneself.

When Cicero dubs friendship 'a kaleidoscope and complicated thing' he recognises the depth of these tensions. But it is possible to take on board Kant's warnings about the dangers of friendship, while also recognising the value of the relationship and acknowledging the particular kind of good that is constitutive of friendship. Our relations with particular human beings are important in terms of the cultivation of our sensitivities to others, our responsiveness to others, and our ability to appreciate the significance a situation may have for particular individuals. These capacities enable us to help friends in times of need. The cultivation of our perceptual capacities involves experiencing feelings, reflecting on feelings, and being guided by others in the expression of feeling. This kind of learning occurs in close interpersonal relationships including friendships, and in turn it enables those relationships to evolve. It gives friendship part of the utilitarian value that Telfer identifies. However, the possibilities we see for intimacy and connection in friendship are influenced by competing demands for love and respect. The comfort, support, 'sweetness of feeling' and sense of affinity we find in friendship are inevitably balanced by the necessity of recognising our separation from and independence of the other. Recognition of this separation is challenging, since we are forced to recognise both what friendship demands of us in terms of duty and also our ultimate aloneness. The self in relation to others is an individual self, and part of the challenge for friends is to establish the implications for friendship of our separateness from others. Thus rational self-concern and self-assessment are as valuable in friendship as concern for the friend for her own sake. Chapter 5 turns to discuss this question and the concepts of self-constitution and self-understanding as they are relevant to relations between friends.

Notes

1. Blum, 'Vocation, Friendship, and Community', p. 174.
2. Kant, 'The Doctrine of Virtue', section 27, p. 200.
3. Blum, 'Vocation, Friendship, and Community', p. 181.
4. Stocker, 'Friendship and Duty: Some Difficult Relations', p. 228.
5. Ibid., p. 230.
6. Sherman, *Making a Necessity of Virtue*, p. 6.
7. Aristotle, *Nichomachean Ethics*, VIII, 9–12; *Eudemian Ethics*, VII, 9–10.
8. Aristotle, *Nichomachean Ethics*, 1157a10–b20.
9. Kant, *The Critique of Judgement*, book II, sections 42–6, pp. 159–69.
10. Sharp, *Friendship and Literature*, pp. 81 and 21; Seneca, 'On Philosophy and Friendship', p. 120.
11. Kant, *The Critique of Judgement*, book II, section 44, p. 166.
12. The analogy between friendship and art has been extended by Ronald Sharp in a comment that asserts that 'enjoyment, is as crucial and [as] undervalued in friendship as it is . . . in art' (Sharp, *Friendship and Literature*, p. 37). It ought to be acknowledged that indirection is a feature of all relationships of deep affection. Parents who genuinely care for their children are concerned for their child for the child's own sake; the difference between friendship and the parent-child relationship lies in the lack of equality between the young child and its parents and in the concomitant inappropriateness of expectations of reciprocity.
13. Kant, *The Moral Law*, 39, p. 78.
14. Bowden, *Caring – Gender-Sensitive Ethics*, p. 76.
15. Aristotle, *Nichomachean Ethics*, 1171a25–b16.
16. Ibid.
17. Bowden, *Caring – Gender-Sensitive Ethics*, pp. 75–6.
18. Friedman, 'Feminism and Modern Friendship: Dislocating the Community', p. 298.
19. Badhwar, 'Introduction', p. 34.
20. Aristotle, *Nichomachean Ethics*, 1165a36–1165b36, 1171a5–8.
21. Ibid., 1171b16–1172a6.
22. Ibid., 1169b11–35.
23. Kant, 'Lecture on Friendship', p. 215.
24. Ibid.
25. Ibid.
26. Kant, *The Moral Law*, pp. 8–9, p. 62.

27. Ibid., 10–11, pp. 63–4.
28. Ibid., 13, p. 65.
29. Kierkegaard, 'You Shall Love Your Neighbour', pp. 244–5.
30. Ibid., p. 236. Kierkegaard's approach to preferential love differs from Kant's in that Kierkegaard fails to acknowledge or appreciate the value of our natural tendency to form intimate relationships.
31. Ibid., p. 245.
32. Ibid., p. 235.
33. Ibid., p. 242.
34. Ibid., pp. 240 and 242.
35. Ibid., p. 235.
36. My own previous criticism of Kant also failed to recognise this relevance ('Aristotle and Derrida on Friendship').
37. Derrida, *Politics of Friendship*, p. 263.
38. Márai, *Embers*, p. 165.
39. Nietzsche, 'Star Friendship', pp. 225–6.
40. Márai, *Embers*, p. 89.
41. Kant, 'The Doctrine of Virtue'.
42. Ibid., 23, p. 198.
43. Ibid., 23, p. 198.
44. Kant, *The Moral Law*, 13, p. 65.
45. Paton, 'Kant on Friendship', p. 137.
46. Kant, 'The Doctrine of Virtue', 46, p. 216.
47. Kant does make the apparently contradictory claim that 'human beings have a duty of friendship'. However, here we seem to be dealing with the distinction Stocker makes between duties of friendship and the duty of friendship, since Kant immediately qualifies his statement, explaining that 'it is readily seen that friendship is only an idea (though a practically necessary one) and unattainable in practice, although striving for friendship . . . is a duty set by reason, and no ordinary duty but an honourable one' ('The Doctrine of Virtue', 46, p. 215).
48. Ibid., 46, p. 217.
49. Nussbaum, *The Fragility of Goodness*, pp. 56 and 54.
50. Telfer, 'Friendship', p. 261.
51. Ibid., pp. 262–3.
52. Blum, *Friendship, Altruism and Morality*.
53. Ibid., pp. 4–5.
54. Márai, *Embers*, p. 126.
55. Derrida, *Politics of Friendship*, p. 53.
56. Sharp, *Friendship and Literature*, p. 45.
57. Telfer, 'Friendship', p. 254.
58. Ibid.
59. Sharp, *Friendship and Literature*, pp. 33–4.
60. Ibid., p. 43.
61. Cicero, 'On Friendship', pp. 86–7.
62. Friedman, 'Feminism and Modern Friendship: Dislocating the Community', p. 301.
63. Sherman, *Making a Necessity of Virtue*, p. 11.
64. Aristotle, *Nichomachean Ethics*, 1155a3–24.
65. Stocker, 'Duty and Friendship', p. 59.

66. Ibid., p. 60.
67. Kant, 'The Doctrine of Virtue', p. 218.
68. Stocker, 'Duty and Friendship', pp. 59–60 and 65.
69. Aristotle, *Nichomachean Ethics*, 1157a34–1158a7.
70. Ibid., 1156b2–23 and 1157a34–b20.
71. Stocker, 'Duty and Friendship', p. 66. Other acts of friendship may not be duties, in the sense that I might go beyond what could reasonably be expected of me as a friend. Yet as Stocker points out, this does not mean that acts which go beyond the call of duty in friendship are necessarily supererogatory. On his view a supererogatory act would need a further feature of moral heroism, saintliness or some lesser form of those features (ibid., p. 68, fn. 6).
72. Blum, 'Vocation, Friendship, and Community', p. 186.
73. Morrison, *Sula*, pp. 147 and 144–5.
74. Ibid., p. 149.
75. Márai, *Embers*, pp. 128–9.
76. Stocker, 'Duty and Friendship', p. 57.
77. Kant, 'The Doctrine of Virtue', section 46, p. 215.
78. Ibid., section 46, p. 216.
79. Ibid., p. 216.

Part III

The Relationship between Friendship and Self-Understanding

Chapter 5

Seeing Oneself as Friend

Intimate engagement between friends provides a unique context for the development of relations with others and for understanding of the self. The tension between our sense of connection with a friend and our recognition of our separateness from the friend within a relationship of choice is likely to present us with dilemmas. The liking, care and concern we have for a friend, which are expressive of our connection, must be balanced by a concern for the self as a separate individual, especially in situations in which these concerns come into conflict. Kant notes in his discussion of friendship that 'if everyone cared only for himself and never troubled about any one else, there would be no friendship'.[1] He says that therefore these two motives to action in man – self-love and love of humanity (the moral motive) – must be combined, so that man cares for his own happiness and for that of others also. The problem is that there are no limits, degrees or proportions fixed to determine how these motives are to interact. Consequently tensions arise, and Kant recognises that human beings will naturally look to their own wants and satisfaction – and that they have every right to do so.

This chapter considers questions of judgement and balance in relation to the presence of tension between friends. It begins with a focus on the process of self-constitution, the role of emotion in that process, and its relation to notions of self-worth and rational self-concern. The work of David Hume is the starting point for a discussion that emphasises our dependence on others for our view of ourselves. Both Hume and Spinoza provide the theoretical substructure for a focus on the role of emotion – in interaction with imagination and reason – in assessments of self. The chapter examines the particular contribution that friends can make to this process of self-constitution, given our emotional engagement with them. It then turns to a detailed consideration of the concept of rational self-concern, and the way that concern interacts with our modern interpretation of the Aristotelian claim that a true friend is one who desires the good of a friend for that friend's own sake.

Finally it explores the contribution of that interaction to relations between friends and to the friends' understanding of themselves. Emphasis on self-understanding in friendship might appear to suggest that at bottom friendship is self-interested, that its value lies in what is to be gained from it. But as we shall see in the final chapter, an emphasis on self-understanding is akin to a focus on the finer aspects of character. That focus cannot be pursued in a narrow instrumental way within friendship; it cannot be the object of an individual's egoistic desires. If it is achieved within friendship, it is achieved indirectly as a by-product of our engagement with friends.

Friendship and the Constitution of the Self

A demand for rational self-concern suggests the need to press into service a sense of one's own self-worth. This sense develops within a social realm in interaction with others. Hence the process of the constitution of the self presumes a view of the self as part of a social world. In *A Treatise of Human Nature* David Hume initially attempts to explain 'what we call our SELF on the basis of mathematical or demonstrative reasoning'. His aim is to achieve certainty in this regard, but the enterprise turns out to be barren. He finds that such an approach makes it impossible to explain what the self is because it cannot unite consciousness over time. As he explains in the Appendix to the Treatise, his analysis of self or person reveals that it:

> is not any one impression, but that to which our several impressions and ideas are suppos'd to have reference. If any impression gives rise to the idea of self, that impression must continue invariable the same, thro' the whole course of our lives; since self is suppos'd to exist after that manner. But there is no impression constant and invariable . . . when I enter most intimately into what I call *myself*, I always stumble on some particular perception or other, of heat or cold, light or shade, love or hatred, pain or pleasure. I can never catch *myself* at any time without a perception, and never observe anything but the perception.[2]

Human consciousness appears to consist in nothing other than a bundle of perceptions. There is no evidence to support either the notion of a simple or individual substance in which our perceptions inhere, or the notion that there is any real connection between distinct perceptions. This means that we cannot explain human consciousness as anything beyond discrete episodes of perceptual awareness. Thus Hume is forced to abandon his initial approach, and he turns to the imagination as the faculty crucial to the formation of a notion of self-identity and to the process of self-constitution.

Hume claims in book I of the *Treatise* that we have no alternative but to use the imagination to 'feign' a principle of union among our many interrupted and variable perceptions of self. As a consequence of this 'feigning' activity, he claims that the notion of self-identity is a fiction. Claims of this kind are not uncommon in contemporary writing. As we saw in Chapter 3, Daniel Dennett maintains that the concept of self is a fiction, drawing an analogy between the concept of the centre of gravity of an object and the concept of self as useful fictions.[3] The view that emerges from the work of these philosophers – despite the distance in time that separates them – is one of the self as a theoretical abstraction, a fictional construction which maintains a sense of unity in the normal mind. Hume's approach to the self suggests that the notion of self is a useful, reasonable and productive fiction, and it can also demonstrate the crucial role of the passions – what the modern reader would call emotion – in the production of the self and in the development of a sense of self-worth or self-esteem.

Annette Baier points out that in book II of Hume's *Treatise*, those members of one's perceptions that are impressions of reflection – or what Hume calls passions – are important members of our perceptions. The passions 'become very important members, both for displaying the causal influence of past members and the influence of anticipation of future members, and for displaying my dependence on my fellow persons for a steady idea of myself'.[4] Passions or emotions are crucial to my recognition that past experience has influenced me, and that future experience will affect and be interpreted in the context of my emotional states. They also demonstrate that it is in taking account of my perceptions of the way in which others perceive me that I develop an idea of myself which is more or less stable and reliable.

Hume acknowledges that we live in a peopled world and that this affects the assessments we make of ourselves and of others. The possibility of stable self-assessment demands that we see ourselves in relationship to others, and the conception of self we develop depends in part on our perception of, and reactions to, the way in which we understand that others perceive us. Those others with whom we have close relationships have particularly significant roles in these processes. The credibility we give the opinions of others, especially when they are in conflict with our own; our recognition of our own motives and emotional state; our view of the motives of others and the emotional state of those others to whom we attend, will all affect our deliberations. Hume reminds us that the assessments of others affect us and have special force if they corroborate our own sentiment.[5] That force consists in the stability their corroboration helps to develop, with regard to our assessments of self; and stability is conferred despite the fact that Hume gives the faculty of the imagination a significant role in the process of assessment.

The process of self-assessment is one in which the passions and the imagination can be regarded as combining to put reason to work, albeit in a complex process of interaction. The capacity to take the point of view of others and to see ourselves as others see us is an exercise of the imagination.

This suggests that only when emotion is combined with an adequate and competent exercise of the imagination will it receive confirmation from others and consequently be deemed reasonable and appropriate to the constitution of an enduring concept of self, an enduring fiction.[6] The conceptual interplay between reason and imagination that Hume introduces in book I of the *Treatise* to explain the formation of knowledge is supplemented and complicated by his focus on passion in book II. This allows Hume to give his explanation of 'what we call our SELF'; and of course this is necessary if reason alone – isolated and disembodied – is as impotent as he suggests. If the self is to be explained as anything other than the bundle of perceptions that Hume claims it is in book I, then we need some other explanatory mechanism. The passions serve this function by including the world beyond the strictures of demonstrative reasoning – the social world – in our assessments of self. Indeed they confirm the activity of the imagination in the development of a notion of self-identity: 'our identity with regard to the passions serves to corroborate that with regard to the imagination'.[7] But despite Hume's claim that a passion is an 'original existence', the passions he introduces in book II appear in the company of reason. They are reflective passions combining impressions of reflection with ideas.[8] As Hume puts it:

> Human nature being compos'd of two principal parts, which are requisite in all its actions, the affections and the understanding; 'tis certain, that the blind motions of the former, without the direction of the latter, incapacitate men for society . . . The same liberty may be permitted to moral, which is allow'd to natural philosophers; and 'tis very usual with the latter to consider any motion as compounded and consisting of two parts separate from each other, tho' at the same time they acknowledge it to be in itself uncompounded and inseparable.[9]

Hume's view is that we may theoretically separate the understanding from the affections, or reason from passion, for the sake of enquiry and analysis; but we must acknowledge that in practice any such separation is 'as a mere fiction'. This view, which has been the focus of much philosophical debate, stands in marked contrast to Hume's more infamous suggestion of a combat between reason and passion. But as we will see in a later section, passion or emotion can be regarded as possessing an internal logic of its own. Norman Denzin draws a distinction between the reflective and pre-reflective awareness of feelings which reinforces the notion that some passions or emotions may not be amenable to reason. Denzin differentiates between two ideal forms of understanding: the cognitive and the emotional, but acknowledges that in everyday life the two forms blur together and intertwine.[10] This acknowledgement is reminiscent of Hume's claim that the two component parts of the mind, the affections and the understanding, are compounded and inseparable, despite it being theoretically 'allow'd us to consider separately' their effects. Elaborating on emotional understanding, Denzin argues that '[a]ll emotionality involves, at least on the reflective (but not the pre-reflective) level, thoughts and cognitions about the feelings one is feeling. These cognitions, however, are thought through the veil of feelings, just as feelings are felt and thought through the screens of cognition.'[11] On this view, passions which appear not to be amenable to reason can be regarded as pre-reflective emotions – that is, emotions which may well bear a relationship to thought, but one of which we are not reflectively aware.

There is a difference here between the presence of an emotion and emotional understanding. As Hume argues on the first page of book II of the *Treatise*, impressions of reflection or passions may proceed from some of our original impressions of sensation, and thereby be spontaneous; or they may proceed by the interposition of an idea, and therefore imply some reference to thought. But in neither case do we necessarily reflect or deliberate on the emotion. We need to be aware of the distinctions between spontaneous emotion; emotion as it refers to ideas; and emotional understanding. The last requires self-assessment, reflection on circumstances, on our own temperament and motives, and will involve the mechanisms we employ in taking account of the views of others. This process will engage us in reflection on the causes and objects of our emotions – reflection which emphasises the relationship between emotion and belief. It assumes an intentional account of the emotions, in which emotions are regarded as being about something, as pointing outside of themselves to something else – that is, to whatever it is that they are about. This kind of account of the emotions is sometimes referred to as the cognitive appraisal approach to emotion. It is this account which is central to the argument of this chapter.

Thinking Reasonably about Emotion

Different use is made of the terms 'feeling', 'passion', 'affect' and 'emotion' in the philosophical literature. For example, Hume uses the terms 'feeling' and 'emotion' synonymously at some points in the *Treatise*, while he argues that feelings will determine the nature of particular passions.[12] Spinoza draws a clear distinction between passion, as irrational and inadequate, and rational emotion; and he uses the term 'affect' to refer to feelings. The relationship between rational thought processes and emotion is complex on these views. It is a relationship that Kant simply rejects when he argues that emotion is a blind affect or feeling, which is not amenable to reason and hence unreliable in its choice and likely to 'go up in smoke'.[13] None the less it is one that intentional treatments of emotion take seriously. This chapter uses 'passion' and 'emotion' interchangeably in relation to discussion of Hume, but makes the distinction clear in discussion of Spinoza.

Research into spontaneous or pre-reflective emotion by neuroscientists such as Joseph Le Doux and Antonio Damasio might suggest that we should temper a commitment to an intentional account of emotion. The data Le Doux presents focuses on the physiological mechanisms – rather than the subjective experience – underlying the experience of emotions such as fear. Damasio also discusses emotion in the context of brain function, but neither Le Doux nor Damasio is reductionistic in approach; and hence they do not claim that emotions are purely non-intentional physiological processes. This leads Martha Nussbaum to argue that it would be premature to include in the definition of emotion the kind of physiological information that neuro-science has produced, especially given Le Doux's own recognition that he is not illuminating the subjective experience of fear.[14] However, analyses of the pre-reflective or spontaneous character of emotion do have something to offer those keen to understand the role of emotion in the constitution of self. Their contribution lies in the extent to which they make us responsive to the possibility that we might misdiagnose our own emotional feelings.

Hume turns to the emotions as that mechanism that brings the social world into the process of self-constitution and self-assessment. We arrive at a concept of self through an imaginatively unifying and fictive act. In order to impose a temporal unity upon our primary experience of a flood of amor-phous perceptions, we conjure up a notion of an organising 'I' – and it is this 'I' which becomes the focus of our own assessments and the assessments of others. This 'I' becomes something other than the set of mental processes that produces our bundle of perceptions. Within the temporal unity we create via our imaginative activity, there is space for the mutually reinforc-ing responses of emotion and of reason. But for Hume it is passion that motivates us; passion warms reason, while reason modifies and protects against the effects of rampant passion. Thus the role of the passions is crucial in all our interactions with others. But in close interpersonal rela-tions that are predicated on shared affection and feelings of attachment, passion or emotion comes to the fore. We bring expectations and under-standings of ourselves, of others and perhaps of friendship to our relations with friends. These generate feelings that we might identify as particular emotions and which open us to possibility, perhaps to risk or perhaps to pleasure. It is this process that is being explored in this chapter.

In his research into spontaneous emotion, Le Doux maintains that the study of emotion has been so focused on the problem of emotional con-sciousness that the basic underlying emotional mechanisms have often been given short shrift. His argument is that, contrary to what he sees as the primary supposition of cognitive appraisal theories, the core of an emotion is not an introspectively accessible conscious representation. On this view, feelings do involve conscious content, but we don't necessarily have conscious access to the processes that produce the content. And further, when we do have introspective access, we cannot be sure that the conscious content is what triggered an emotional response in the first place. Le Doux argues that we are apt to confuse or misdiagnose our emotional feelings, since our emotional responses and their conscious content are both products of specialised emotion systems that operate unconsciously.[15] Similarly, Antonio Damasio treats emotions as appraisals that are connected to particular regions of the brain and that are not necessarily or clearly made known to the self.[16] In *Looking for Spinoza*, he calls on Benedict Spinoza for theoretical endorsement of his position and for his opposition to mind–body dualism.

Damasio's interest in Spinoza is understandable, given Spinoza's view of emotions as forms of direct bodily awareness that are at the same time subjective or perspectival interpretations. As Martha Nussbaum puts it, emotions for Spinoza 'involve the appraisal of a situation for its bearing on the person's own well-being . . . [They] are not simply impulses or drives, but highly selective patterns of vision and interpretation.'[17] Spinoza offers an account of human emotion that focuses on our awareness of the body, and he challenges the notion that the body is distinct from the mind. He argues that the mind is 'the idea' of the body, so that our direct bodily awareness constitutes our mind. It is via the faculty of the imagination that we become aware of our own body and the bodies of others. But imagination is an inadequate form of knowledge, since it provides us with knowledge derived purely from our own perspective.[18] However, imaginative knowledge is an essential pre-condition for the higher kinds of knowledge: reason and intuition. It is the mind's direct awareness of body and its capacity to retain traces of bodily affections which make the inadequate knowledge of the imagination possible. But this possibility is crucial, since it also enables us to form the 'common notions' of reason, which capture what it is that things have in common and hence provide us with more adequate knowledge of ourselves and others. Feelings or 'affects' are one species of those bodily 'affections' which are constitutive of the mind. Thus reason is beholden to the deliverances of the imagination, which in turn determines that we are inevitably subject to the passions. However, reason opens us to the possibility that the passions can be transformed into rational emotions.

Thus for Spinoza the faculties of the imagination, emotion and reason interact to provide us with an understanding of ourselves and of the world. This is achieved more or less adequately, depending on the role of reason in the process of assessment. Spinoza provides us with a model of the way in which the notions that we use to make sense of the world and the feelings or affects we experience might come to be regarded as reasonable. We gain in self-esteem by coming to understand our passions. This entails understanding that the awareness of bodily modification that imagination delivers is confused; and yet that confused awareness is fundamental, since it provides us with the data that makes it possible for us to transform our passions into rational emotions. Thus rational behaviour is dependent on our capacity to understand the passions. Damasio would agree with this, given that he sees emotions as indispensable to rational decision-making.[19]

Damasio's suggestion that we may or may not have conscious awareness of physiological events that become an emotion, and Le Doux's emphasis on the possibility of misdiagnosing emotional feelings, introduce uncertainty into the attribution of emotional feelings; and Spinoza's schema also recognises this kind of uncertainty. But as Genevieve Lloyd suggests, Spinoza also offers us new ways of thinking about sociability, about the constitution of the self and about our connections with others.[20] Lloyd's explanation of the development of self-esteem from Spinoza's perspective makes these connections clear: '[Spinozistic minds] esteem themselves for the capacity this brings to understand their interdependence with other things and to strengthen their powers by collaboration with the minds of similarly structured bodies.'[21] We cannot come to understand ourselves or to develop self-esteem without recognising that our connection with others is basic, practical and embodied; that it extends to the idea that we are in fact part of wider wholes; and that imagination, affect and reason interact together in these processes. Although we will never be free of passions, we can come to understand our passions via a process in which they are transformed into rational emotion. Involvement in this process builds self-esteem.

Thus the transformation of passion into rational emotion is crucial to the development of self-esteem; but this transformation is a difficult and involved process. Since our relations with others are fundamental to this process, Spinoza's view entails a sense of our engagement with others in a joint project of self-constitution. He emphasises our dependence on one another – particularly those with whom we share rational understandings or 'common notions of reason' – for an idea of self and for a sense of self-worth. Selves simply cannot understand themselves or be understood in isolation from those relations of dependence. But, as Lloyd indicates, the connections here are novel, and they challenge us to think differently about the self, to see ourselves as part of wider wholes. The development of self-esteem is dependent upon a transformative interaction between imagination, emotion and reason as we move into the realm of more adequate ideas – both of self and of others. Our connection with others becomes substantial in the sense that we are not seen as isolated intellectual substances:[22]

to man there is nothing more useful than man – nothing, I repeat, more excellent for preserving their being can be wished for by men, than that all should so in all points agree, that the minds and bodies of all should form, as it were, one single mind and one single body, . . . [M]en who are governed by reason . . . desire for themselves nothing, which they do not also desire for the rest of mankind, and, consequently, are just, faithful and honourable in their conduct.[23]

Spinoza's view might be thought to prefigure Kant's notion of moral friendship. But in fact, while Kant's moral friendship is barely distinguishable from the friendship of an individual who takes an affective interest in the wellbeing of all human beings, Spinoza is focused on individual wellbeing.

The purpose of these comments is to acknowledge arguments for the role of spontaneous or pre-reflective emotion in understanding emotion, and therefore to recommend caution in the diagnosis and interpretation of emotion. However, the comments do not imply any criticism of intentional accounts of emotion, since the intentional accounts I address below do acknowledge spontaneous emotion. Rather my comments are intended, first, to recognise the interaction between mind and body in understanding emotion and to offer a possible way of thinking about problematic cases of analysis in intentional accounts; that is, to think of such cases as bodily devices or bodily modifications which are either automatic or confused. Second, the discussion of Spinoza is intended to highlight the interaction of imagination, emotion and reason – the same interaction to which the discussion of Hume drew attention – in coming to understand ourselves and others. Spinoza's view of ourselves and our relations with others emphasises the concept of self-esteem, a concept that I will argue is crucial to relations between friends.

Emotions, Judgements and Characterisation

Unlike Spinoza's approach to understanding the passions, modern intentional accounts of emotion do not focus on the body, or on its dependence on and connection with other bodies. However, these modern philosophical treatments of emotion are persuasive in their analysis of the influence of our connections with others, both in the way in which we interpret experience and in our understanding of self. The bodily connections and dependencies that Spinoza identifies are 'psychologised' in modern treatments of emotion. However, these theories do uncover an internal logic within emotions which might appear irrational to us on initial reflection; and like Spinoza, they do characterise emotions as 'highly selective patterns of vision and interpretation',[24] to re-use Nussbaum's description of Spinoza. Coming to understand our emotions, the repertoires of thoughts and feelings that constitute them and the use we make of those in interaction, enriches and clarifies our relations with others. For this reason, emotional understanding is significant for the kinds of interpersonal relationships we are able to establish.

Modern intentional treatments of emotion involve beliefs and focus on the connection between imaginative activity and the context within which emotions are learned. As Nussbaum puts it, they embody 'a way of seeing'.[25] They emphasise the role of emotion in mobilising our ability to imagine ourselves in the place of the other, and the interaction of that emotion with reason in making judgements about ourselves and others. Ronald de Sousa, for example, argues that all emotion emerges from within the context of our beliefs: 'On my view, emotions ask the questions which judgment answers with beliefs: . . . emotions can be said to be judgments rather in the way that scientific paradigms might be said to be "judgments": they are what we see the world "in terms of".'[26]

Robert Solomon also refers to emotions as interpretive judgements or 'constitutive interpretations of the world'. He does distinguish between spontaneous and deliberative interpretations, but argues that all 'have presupposition and entailment relationships with a large number of beliefs'.[27] Solomon goes on to argue that the intimate connection which exists between emotions, beliefs and evaluations 'allows us to explain, as traditional theories cannot, the fact that we often talk about emotions as being "warranted" or "unwarranted", "reasonable" or "unreasonable", "justified" or "unjustified"'.[28]

In elaborating on this connection between emotions and beliefs, Ronald de Sousa suggests an alternative to a theorist such as David Hume who argues that the animating principle of all passion is sympathy. De Sousa introduces concepts which seem to serve the function Hume assigns to the vivacity of the imagination in the context of emotional life – that of sensitizing us to the sentiments and interests of others. These are concepts that recognise the force of Solomon's conclusion that 'it is a person's view of his or her circumstances which is essential to emotion'.[29] De Sousa focuses on childhood experience and the genesis of emotion, arguing that '[w]e are made familiar with the vocabulary of emotion by association with paradigm scenarios, drawn first from daily life as small children, later reinforced by the stories and fairy tales to which we are exposed, and, later still, supplemented and refined by art and literature'.[30]

Within these paradigm situations we learn the characteristic objects of an emotion and a set of characteristic responses to the emotion. However, it is important to recognise that the content of this learning experience will depend in part on the nature of our parents' and care-givers' 'characteristic' objects and responses in these situations.[31] De Sousa defines emotions as 'determinate patterns of salience among objects of attention, lines of inquiry and inferential strategies'.[32] He is in substantial agreement with Hume in this regard. Just as Hume argues that it is always passion which motivates action, as reason alone can never do so, de Sousa insists that no logic can determine salience.[33] For de Sousa, emotions determine what we attend to, what we enquire about, and what we see the world in terms of. He argues that the process of coming to these determinations begins in childhood. Paradigm situations sensitise us to particular ways of interpreting experience and responding to it. The notion of salience appears to be a way of taking account of the particular beliefs, attitudes and past experience of individuals in explaining emotion, and in explaining its impact on our behaviour.

Amélie Rorty's approach to the explanation of emotion is similar to de Sousa's. Rorty emphasises the aetiology of emotions, explaining that the causal history of emotions involves three closely interwoven strands. The first of these strands includes the formative events in a person's psychological past, patterns of intentional focusing and salience, habits of thought and response. The second strand includes the social and cultural determinants of emotions; and the third includes a person's constitutional inheritance, genetically fixed patterns of sensitivity and response.[34] The third strand might prove to have much in common with Le Doux's and Damasio's positions on emotion, but it is the first of these which is the focus of this discussion. Rorty refines the notion of cause in relation to emotion by distinguishing between the immediate and the significant cause of an emotion. This allows her to explain that we often find emotions puzzling because we cannot see why the immediate cause should have such an effect. For example, we can feel anger in the face of accidental injury; as Hume puts it, 'men often fall into a violent anger for injuries, which they themselves must own to be entirely involuntary and accidental'.[35] Hume explains this by asserting that there is a natural connection between uneasiness and anger and concluding that the anger will dissipate when the violence of the impression has abated. The person will necessarily recognise the injury as accidental. If the anger does not dissipate, Hume would presumably have to regard it as unintelligible or perhaps irrational.

Rorty's distinction provides the option of acknowledging the injury as the immediate cause of the anger, while at the same time explaining the inappropriate conservation of the anger as due to an underlying significant cause. She states that the significant cause of an emotion may be an event or events long forgotten which formed a disposition or set of dispositions that are triggered by the immediate cause. So perhaps the inappropriate conservation of anger or an inappropriate response to accidental injury might be explained by a conviction developed in childhood. An individual might become inappropriately furious when he hits his thumb with a hammer (immediate cause) because his mother or father's first reaction when he injured himself as a child was often anger (significant cause). This led him to feel guilty and fearful when he hurt himself. So while the immediate target of his anger is (inappropriately) the hammer, the explanatory or significant target is his parent's reaction during childhood. In this way an emotion which appears unintelligible, irrational or inappropriately strong can be seen to exhibit what Ronald de Sousa recognises as 'minimal rationality'.[36]

For Rorty, the formation of our emotional dispositions and of our habits of thought, action and response create magnetising effects; these draw us towards and create conditions for other dispositions so that we develop magnetised dispositions. The inordinate anger upon accidental injury referred to above might reveal a magnetised disposition to avoid attributing blame to oneself, or perhaps to a grandiose feeling of responsibility to protect oneself from injury. Armed with the analysis of emotion which de Sousa and Rorty offer, we can examine a fleeting example that Hume introduces in his discussion of pride and humility in book II of the *Treatise*: that of a hypothetical feast. Hume argues that the host of a feast may feel proud of its sumptuousness, but that the guests may only feel joy. It is true, he says, that 'men sometimes boast of a great entertainment, at which they have only been present; and by so small a relation convert their pleasure into pride', but he implies that a man would be foolish to do so.[37] It does not seem unreasonable that a guest might be proud to be present at a feast, in the sense of being honoured and feeling important and valued to have been included among auspicious company. But Hume seems to imply that such a guest is proud of the occurrence and the nature of the feast in the same way as the host would be. The implication is that the guest feels undue or foolish pride in relation to a feast that he has only attended. Such a guest's undue pride provides an illustration of a failure of the imagination – an inability to imagine his situation from the point of view of the host or his fellow guests, who would presumably see no justification for his pride.

The hypothetical guest's failure of imagination is also a failure of reason – an inability to appreciate the requirements of intersubjective agreement on justified pride – a pertinent emotion in this context, given the relation it implies between the self and others. Alternatively, as a somewhat Spinozistic interpretation might suggest, the boastful guest's failure could be taken as an inability to extract from a 'general', idiosyncratic or perspectival notion of pride those aspects which commonly lead us to endorse pride as justified. The guest's representation of reality is a subjective one, which we assume has nothing in common with the representations of his fellow guests or the master of the feast. The boastful guest is excessively and undeservedly proud of himself; as such he is attempting to identify with an imaginary or idealised sense of self, which is premised on his unwillingness to accept the otherness of others and the risk which such acceptance would entail. The guest's unwillingness implies a rejection of the opinions of others, whose affirmation of the boastful guest's reaction is unlikely to be forthcoming; his peers are unlikely to sanction his pride, given the slightness of his relation to the occurrence of the feast. His subjective interpretation of reality demonstrates negatively the nexus between reason, imagination and emotion, since it is his inability to imagine how others might interpret his behaviour which in turn undermines the rationality of his grasp of the situation in which he finds himself.

The account of emotions given here suggests an explanation of this failure in terms of the foolish guest's predisposition to interpret experience in particular ways. The guest's pride in relation to the feast, despite the slightness of his connection with it, can be seen as revealing a magnetised disposition to excessive self-affirmation – perhaps the reflection of a need for affirmation not satisfied in his formative years. Thus his pride is seen as predicated upon the strength of an emotional need which prejudices the conception of self he develops. As Rorty points out, magnetising dispositions may not be sufficient to explain particular actions or reactions instantly – the guest's conjectured pride certainly appears inappropriate or irrational; but they can do so indirectly by characterising the type of beliefs, perceptions and desires a person might have.[38] The guest's pride becomes intelligible if only we know how desperate he is to make a big fellow of himself; that is, it becomes intelligible within the context of his desire for self-affirmation.

Both de Sousa and Rorty explain that our past experience and our reactions to that experience tend to predispose us to particular and often unique ways of structuring or interpreting future experience, and to particular and characteristic emotional responses. Both theorists are therefore able to account for a broad range of emotional experience and to explain inappropriate and irrational emotional responses. Their focus is on the context within which we learn to respond emotionally, and that focus enables us to include various dimensions in our assessments of self and others; for example, aspects of a person's psychological history, their past experience and the stock of their knowledge. These help us to account for tensions which emerge between a person's self-assessment and the assessments others may make of that person.

What we make of the present depends in part on how experience and habit operate upon the imagination. It is a matter of how we interpret the various facets of our experience, to what extent habit determines our expectations, how prepared we are to contemplate other possibilities, and the kinds of conclusions we have reached about the influence we can bring to bear on the present. As David Hume puts it in his discussion of the formation of ideas about the self, it is a matter of our assessment of 'our own force'.

> nothing is more laudable, than to have a value for ourselves, where we really have the qualities that are valuable . . . nothing is more useful to us in the conduct of life, than a due degree of pride, which makes us sensible of our own merit, and gives us a confidence and assurance in all our projects and enterprizes. Whatever capacity anyone may be endowed with, 'tis entirely useless to him, if he not be acquainted with it, and form not designs suitable to it. 'Tis requisite on all occasions to know our own force, and were it allowable to err on either side, 'twou'd be more advantageous to overrate our merit, than to form ideas of it, below its just standard.[39]

It is possible on the basis of experience and habit to over-rate my own merit on occasion precisely because the two principles of experience and habit do operate on the imagination. The mind employs the imagination to interpret the fruits of experience and habit and so to constitute our ideas about ourselves. This process is not a straightforward one: our predispositions – themselves at least in part the result of past experience – determine to some extent how we interpret our experience. For example, as Rorty suggests, if I have a magnetised disposition to irascibility I will have a certain specific set of low thresholds (for instance, to frustration). But I will also be more sensitive to frustrating situations, perceiving situations as frustrating; or if my self-esteem is low, then I am more likely to under-rate than over-rate my merits.

Yet, while predispositions often explain such characteristic responses and tendencies to structure experience in ways that elicit those responses, they need not determine them. I can imagine other possible responses and act to give them expression. Faced with a frustrating situation, I can choose not to express my anger as I have in the past but to develop a strategy aimed at ameliorating it: perhaps counting to ten or removing myself from the situation temporarily. It is important to emphasise that I am not arguing that emotions are matters of choice or that they are voluntary judgements. As Rorty notes, the difficulties in bringing about change in emotions make such claims seem implausible.[40] Rorty goes on to argue that an account of how people succeed in changing emotions they judge to be inappropriate or irrational is very similar to the explanation of how people change habits. To pursue her analogy, we recognise that in changing a habit people alter their behaviour, adopting new behaviours, despite an inclination to continue in their old ways. What this amounts to is a change in our reaction to an habitual inclination; a decision to go against habitual inclination and to react differently, despite the cost this extracts in energy and willpower. Correspondingly, on the basis of this analogy, emotional change will require a change in our characteristic emotional response. The emotion or feeling may persist, but we choose to express it differently, to moderate or channel its expression, when we attempt to bring about change. As Sartre has argued, this view of attempting to overcome an emotion acknowledges that 'ideas do not change men. Knowing the cause of a passion is not enough to overcome it; one must live it, one must oppose other passions to it, one must combat it tenaciously, in short one must "work oneself over".'[41]

This is not to argue that overcoming an emotion or changing a habit has nothing to do with ideas. Rather it recognises the complex and contradictory nature of the process of self-development. This point is akin to Spinoza's attitude to change when he suggests that in coming to understand the passions we transform them into rational emotions by moving from passivity to greater activity. As Lloyd interprets Spinoza, '[i]n understanding the passions we do not merely exercise an enjoyable intellectual power which leaves the passions themselves unchanged. This understanding transforms the passions into active, rational emotions.'[42] On this view, it is as a consequence of reflection upon the irrationality of a particular emotion or the undesirability of a habit that I decide to attempt to overcome an emotion or change a habit. None the less the emotion or the inclination to continue the habit will often persist, so that I find I sometimes, or even often, betray myself in my behaviour; and this may well be explained by or at least associated with physiological mechanisms of the type that Le Doux and Damasio identify.

My only option is to attempt to focus on my characteristic response to the emotion or inclination and the second-order emotions which accompany them; for example, the shame or guilt I feel before others at the apparent inappropriateness of the emotion or habit. Albert Hirschman argues that at some point in our lives we may in fact find that self-subversion becomes the principal means to self-renewal.[43] In the context of this discussion, Hirschman's claim suggests that focusing on my desire to avoid negative consequences and changing my characteristic response amounts to subversion of the problematic emotion or inclination. Le Doux and Damasio might suggest that this subversion is necessary precisely because we do not have conscious access to the processes that produced the inappropriate emotion. Consequently our only choice is to focus our awareness on the characteristic response. In this situation Le Doux would presumably argue that we should also recognise that when we do have some introspective access to such an emotion, the conscious content (Rorty's immediate cause, perhaps) is not likely to be what triggered the emotional responses in the first place.

Still, subversive change in my characteristic response to an emotion or inclination may, over time, attenuate its force. Refusing an inappropriate emotion its standard or characteristic expression disrupts its conservation.

If this disruption is accompanied by the kind of reflection on aetiology which Rorty outlines, then it might enable me to challenge the magnetising disposition which explains the emotion by attempting to form a new and contrary disposition. Relief at any reduction or attrition of the physiological concomitants of an inappropriate emotion (such as muscle tightening, redness of the face etc.), and the disappearance of the accompanying second-order emotions of shame or guilt, will also help to undermine the nexus between the significant and the immediate cause of the offending emotion. In Rorty's terminology, this is an attempt to restructure the intentional set of the associated magnetised disposition, and while that restructuring may or may not be successful, the process of altering the characteristic expression of the emotion certainly demands that, at the very least, we cautiously reflect upon the causes of the magnetised disposition.

This process is akin to the 'talking cure' of psychoanalytic therapy, which aims at emotional change. It recognises the connections between rationality and emotion, without which attempts at emotional change would make no sense. The rationality of emotion consists in the extent to which emotions involve beliefs, and it can be uncovered, as de Sousa has suggested, in the process of learning to attend to and enquire about particular features of paradigm scenarios, as well as learning to question the appropriate application of inferences suggested by paradigm scenarios. Thus understanding emotion requires that we acknowledge the development of our own repertoires of thinking and feeling, and the way in which we employ the imagination to rework and reinterpret these in the light of our present circumstances.

Reading the Other: Imaginative Transfer and the Integration of Reason and Emotion

Analysing paradigm scenarios or establishing the significant cause of an inappropriate or irrational emotion is a tricky and uncertain business, as is being able to recognise how that significant cause has disposed and continues to dispose us to behave. This is partly to be explained by the fact that the significant cause of an emotion may be an event dimly remembered or perhaps forgotten, an event of which we are no longer conscious. We must attempt – through remembering and perhaps with the help of others – a reconstruction of our past; and in doing so we are victims of what Norman Denzin calls 'our own historicizing abilities'.[44] Denzin does not define these abilities, but the nexus between imagination, emotion and reason, for which I argue, would suggest that they will depend on a number of factors. These will include the way in which we experience time – for example, in the sense of the degree to which negative emotions might perhaps lock a person into the past; our skill in linguistic construction, in drawing inferences, and in distilling consistent ideas from our perceptions; our capacity for making imaginative transfers of thought or creative leaps; the extent to which significant others in our lives might help us in these tasks of interpretation; and finally, our attitude to critical appraisal. The capacity of friends as significant others is particularly valuable in regard to the processes I am describing. My argument in this chapter is that, given the nature of their relationship, friends are uniquely positioned to help one another – either gently or provocatively – in this task of interpretation.

Close friends have a personal and emotional relationship; however, since the relationship is freely chosen, it comes without the social and legal conventions of public life or the formal obligations of kinship. Consequently friends have the potential to respond to one another in unreserved and inventive ways – if only they are prepared to face the uncertainty and risk inherent in this kind of authentic interaction. Whether friends are gentle in their appraisals of us or more provocative, being open and candid can cause offence. As Sharp explains: '[t]here are times . . . when openness is simply tactless and can end up being cruel'; however, he notes that, '[t]hough tact may often be the gentler course, there are other, more subtle games we invent in order to relate intimately without recourse to the direct assault'.[45] Sharp recognises that at least a gentle confrontation might sometimes be in order between friends, if they are to relate intimately and authentically. In the context of a relationship that has extended over more than thirty years, he goes on to describe a telephone conversation he had with his best friend at a watershed-point in both their lives:

> It was truly a conversation in which both of us were exploring, hypothesizing, testing, and validating our experiences, our values, our aspirations, and our sense of ourselves . . . We joked, we cajoled, we teased, we playacted, we confessed, we defended, and we queried. We were able to discern the shape, the status, perhaps even something of the fate of our hopes and our emerging sense of ourselves by interpreting a thousand intonations and pauses, for we had developed a language of extraordinary complexity and richness . . . One could risk exposing one's new sense of oneself in front of a friend . . . The friend is the one with whom we can play out that simultaneous perception of the value and triviality of the public. He is also the one who will somehow let us know if the new self we present is consistent with the former repertoire he knows so well. He will be able to identify and accept change but he will measure it against some sense of identity over time, and he will thus, as Robert Louis Stevenson puts it, 'keep us worthy of ourselves'.[46]

Sharp is explaining how friends might call on one another to reflect upon their dispositions, lead one another to question how past experience has shaped their behaviour, accompany one another in the process of coming to a reliable assessment of self, and serve as a catalyst to the exploration of possibilities.

The notion of imaginative transfer is crucial to this kind of activity because it draws attention to the interaction between imagination, reason and emotion in our judgements of ourselves and our judgements of others. Paul Ricoeur refers to imaginative transfer as that capacity which establishes the other as another self. In his reading of Edmund Husserl, Ricoeur argues that it is not by accident that Husserl bases his notion of analogical apperception on that of imaginative transfer. Analogy, for Ricoeur, is a critical principle which establishes the other as a self like oneself, a self with whom we share an historical relation: 'To say that you think as I do, that you experience pleasure or pain as I do, is to be able to imagine what I should think and experience if I were in your place. This transfer in the imagination of my "here" to your "there" is the root of what we call empathy (Einfühlung).'[47]

On Ricoeur's view, our capacity for imaginative transfer enables us to put ourselves in the place of the other so as to make new connections and mediations which militate against the entropy of human relations. However, Sandra Lee Bartky suggests that the notion of imagining oneself in the place of the other requires qualification. She argues that in putting myself in the place of another 'I do not think of myself at all. Nor is my imagination really mine in any but the most trivial sense'.[48] Bartky discusses the example of the Egyptian feminist Nawal El Saadawi, who describes in her book *The Hidden Face of Eve* (1980) her experience of being forced to undergo a clitoridectomy, without anaesthesia, as a child. Bartky states that:

> in reading El Saadawi's text, I must, to be sure, produce an active and vivid picturing to myself of the details of the scene, a more active and vivid picturing than is necessary to grasp the bare facts of the case. I must conjure up in my 'mind's eye' the dark bedroom, the shadowy figures of the adults. But here the idea of seeing must give way to something else: I may 'see' the utter terror of the child, her bewilderment and sense of betrayal, but I must imagine as well what it was for her to have felt this terror, this absolute incomprehension in the face of the cruelty of those she trusted. I must imagine not only the sight of the knife but what she feels as it cuts her flesh. (How unfortunate that even our term 'imagination' contains within it the idea of an 'image' – of something seen – when much of what we must learn to imagine is not something seen at all.)[49]

Of course Ricoeur is correct to point out that it is my own imagination that is engaged when I attempt to put myself in the place of the other. But Bartky's qualification is valuable, since it recognises the purpose of the imaginative transfer in achieving empathy. I am not trying to imagine what I would think and feel if I were in your place, if things were different for me. I am trying to make new connections between myself and another, to construct an avenue of mediation between us which enables me to take account of the other's perspective, relevant to making assessments both of myself and of the other. Of course, Bartky is describing a process in which self-assessment is not emphasised, and in fact her purpose here is partly ethico-political. The relevance of her comments to a discussion of friend-ship lies in her views on imaginative transfer and the establishment of one-to-one relationships. Imaginatively transferring myself into the place of a friend allows me to make connections with her, to attempt to come to understand her perspective, deepen my knowledge of her and 'feel with' her. Elizabeth Telfer stipulates that friendship is conditional on shared activity (reciprocal services, mutual contact and joint pursuits) undertaken out of friendship (out of affection, liking and the sense of bond we share); and that it also requires our acknowledgement of the fulfilment of these conditions.[50] These conditions create opportunities that make connection and mediation more penetrating between friends than between non-friends.

In my extension of Hume's example of boastful guests, I have invented a narrative in the interests of exploring reactions generally taken to be inap-propriate on the basis of misplaced pride. It may be that I am unduly cen-sorious of the boastful guest. Perhaps he feels pride by way of imaginatively transferring himself into the place of the host, who is his friend, and so his pride is a form of 'feeling with' his friend. But in the interests of argument I intend to pursue the example via an interpretation of the guest's pride as undue. In my extension of the example, we see that the boastful guest is unable to respond to the challenge of getting beyond his own self-concern. He is unable to see the hypothetical feast from the viewpoint of either the master or the other guests. The example reveals a tension between the role of the imagination and the passions. Feeling and imagination ought to come together in ways which help us to see how we are perceived by others. But the boastful guest's self-centredness prevents him from integrating feeling and imagination and therefore from making the necessary connections between self and other. An individual's ability to imagine himself in the place of others opens him to perspectives that might challenge his passions. His rational capacities are in fact founded on this ability; it is this ability that gives him some insight into the views of the other, allows him to make meaningful comparisons, and to appreciate how he is perceived by others. An inability to transfer oneself imaginatively into the place of the other will put him at odds with his fellows. Hume acknowledges that 'every particu-lar man has a peculiar position with regard to others', but goes on to point out that it would be impossible for us to converse together on reasonable terms if each of us was only to consider characters and persons as they appear from our own peculiar points of view.[51]

If we are to arrive at stable judgements of things – judgements which take a steady, general and reasonable point of view and which will be able to stand up to the criticism of others within a civilised debate – then we must undertake a reflective correction of our own peculiar sentiments. Hume argues that the first step towards this is achieved by sympathising with those who have any 'commerce' with the person about whom we may be forming a judgement, and presumably with the person herself.[52] The implication here is that we sympathise with the foolish guest's acquaintances, friends and perhaps family. These are the people who might help us to broaden our perspective in relation to the foolish guest. We can only imagine that the host of the hypothetical feast and the other guests will find it difficult to comprehend his behaviour; that is, unless they appreciate the force and the internal logic of emotion and know him well enough to understand the strength of his desire for self-affirmation.

While any person in an intimate relationship with the foolish guest might be aware of and able to understand this desire, my argument is that the understanding of a friend is particularly valuable. This is so because friendship is not predicated upon any formal tie and because ideally friends engage as individuals of equal worth within the relationship. The foolish guest's relatives or his therapist – were he to have one – might well understand this aspect of his character, but the particular nature of their relationship with him impacts upon their interaction with him. Since friends, at least generally, freely choose to engage with one another as equals in friendship, their awareness of the psychological make-up of the foolish guest, their support and understanding take on their own force or 'magic'. This force is a feature of our trust that a friend is concerned for us for our own sake, and that the friend shows this concern despite the fact that it cannot be demanded or expected. Of course this trust can be misplaced, so that friendships can fade away or even collapse under the stress of difficult circumstances. But where it is well placed, it is valuable for its endorsement of a connection between friends which is completely at their own discretion, but which is also extremely powerful, since – as Chapter Three argues – it is created by the friends and operates in the face of their recognition of their profound separation from one another.

We can imagine that a good friend of the foolish guest might find a way of alerting him to the inappropriateness of his reaction to the feast – perhaps even with humour, teasing or a jibe that pushes the foolish guest to consider his situation from the viewpoint of others, to imagine how others might interpret his behaviour – what they might think and feel about his pretensions to pride in relation to the sumptuousness of the feast. Such interventions generally startle us. We are brought up short by their provocative nature, since it is confronting to be presented with a challenge to the view of ourselves we wish to present or have carefully constructed. On the other hand it may be that we only become aware of self-assessments we have made unreflectively when the evaluations of others challenge our own unreflective assessments. Of course we can simply dismiss such challenges and we may be able to do so successfully, particularly if the challenger is a person whom we do not believe to be in a good position to make a judgement about us. However, it is more difficult to dismiss such interventions made by a good friend. If the foolish guest accepts that his good friend feels affection for him and is concerned for him for his own sake, then he has little option but to take account of his friend's point of view on his behaviour. Rational self-concern demands just this kind of accountability. It recognises that we live in a peopled world; that stable self-assessment demands that we see ourselves in relation to others; and that, in general, emotions are intentional phenomena, so that they are available for analysis. The value of friends as barometers in the process of self-assessment lies in the increased capacity their relationship gives them to transfer themselves imaginatively into one another's positions. In addition, friends' affection for and committment to one another provide a context within which critical assessment is likely to be taken seriously.

When we begin to consider why a friend might make confronting or challenging remarks about our behaviour, we are at bottom considering the question of motivation in friendship. Chapter 4 examined motivation in friendship in relation to notions of morality. It argued that friendship requires indirection in intentionality – what Kant might have referred to as 'purposiveness without purpose'. Friendship must do away with purely instrumental reasoning in the sense that friendship cannot aim at a particular outcome. Genuine care and concern for a friend for that friend's own sake demand that we are open to involvement in our friends' lives and projects. As Kant warns us, there can be no friendship if everyone cares only for himself and never troubles himself about anyone else. But this leaves friendship open to possibility and uncertainty, since the question of what constitutes care and concern for the other's own sake is open to interpretation. A friend's desires or expectations can conflict with rational self-concern. They can appear unreasonable, perhaps challenging wider moral or social values to which we are committed.

As we saw in the previous chapter, Nel, in Toni Morrison's novel *Sula*, found it impossible to disregard her own anger and bitterness and forgive Sula's seduction of her husband. She could not allow Sula the comforting memory of the depth of their friendship, even at Sula's deathbed. Care for a friend for that friend's own sake did not extend to forgiveness of this kind of behaviour, on Nel's view. Given the lack of concern Sula showed Nel when she seduced her husband, Nel's reaction is not unreasonable. In fact it illustrates a view Nussbaum takes of the significance of emotion in our lives. Nussbaum argues that emotions have value as constituent elements in a good human life. Like de Sousa, Rorty and Solomon – and as we have seen – she argues that emotions involve value judgements. On her view, they are intelligent evaluative interpretations that ascribe high importance to things outside ourselves that we do not fully control, and they render us vulnerable on account of those attachments to the external.[53] Nussbaum makes these comments in the context of an argument that as human beings we are open to chance, not least in our interpersonal relationships. Nel's intimate friendship with Sula made her vulnerable to the deep disappointment she felt, and her anger and resentment involve precisely the kind of judgements Nussbaum specifies.

Of course we must recognise, as Nancy Sherman does, that while emotions are 'modes of *registering value* (e.g., what is dangerous or beneficial, needy or attractive, disturbing or insulting) and modes of *communicating value*', they are partial and selective modes.[54] Rational self-concern might be consistent with the kind of reaction Nel displays. It might demand that Nel maintain the sense of personal integrity that commitment to particular values or norms gives her. That commitment might be revealed in the expression of anger or bitterness, or the acceptance of disagreement between friends. A friend's actions can seem unwise to us or not in her best interests. So, for example, I might be prepared to support a friend in an enterprise I consider to be foolish, but harmless. However, I might feel obliged to resist offering support or encouragement where I think the enterprise might have serious negative or untoward consequences – either for the friend or for myself; or where my involvement compromises me in some way. Thus while I will be prepared to support a friend in her projects and to assist where I can, this does not imply unqualified support or assistance.

However, I must be wary of my emotional reactions in these contexts. They can alert me to issues that have salience for me, reveal attitudes or dispositions I might not otherwise have noticed; but the decisions I make in relation to appropriate action in friendship involve a complex interplay of considerations. I can be mistaken in my judgements about what is in the best interests of a friend or of myself. I can be influenced by the kind of magnetised dispositions or patterns of salience developed in childhood that Rorty and de Sousa identify; my sense of self-worth or the level of my self-esteem may influence the decision-making process; my emotional reactions to a friend can be more or less intelligent evaluations, depending upon my awareness of these factors and the level of my maturity. These considerations draw attention to the processes of self-constitution and specifically to the view that these processes are socially mediated and uncertain in their outcomes. The discussion of the work of Spinoza and Hume was intended to emphasise the uncertainty and complexity of these processes, at least at the theoretical level. For Spinoza and Hume, self-concern becomes rational as the self comes to understand the nature and impact of its relations with others and to take account of those relations. Thus, at least ideally, friendship might be thought of as based on a rational concern for self.

Rational self-concern requires a capacity to take account of emotion, to understand our emotions as intentional phenomena, and to be alive to the possibility that our emotions might have their genesis in magnetised dispositions or patterns of salience developed in childhood. A Freudian interpretation of the unintelligible, irrational or inappropriate emotions de Sousa and Rorty identify would assign them to the realm of unconscious motivation. Although de Sousa and Rorty do not refer to psychoanalytic theory, de Sousa's notion of 'minimal rationality' does suggest a realm of motivation apart from that inhabited by human beings considered as thoroughly conscious, rational subjects. Psychoanalysis embraces the world of unconscious motivation, the division of the conscious from the unconscious mind, and the phases in development of personality. In doing so, it is able to explain familiar forms of irrationality: irrational emotional outbursts and self-deception – forms that de Sousa might attribute to minimally rational patterns of salience. These irrational or minimally rational patterns are ones that a unitary theory of consciousness, such as Descartes's or Hume's, will find it difficult to explain. Psychoanalytic explanations emerge from within an explanation of the development of human selfhood that is relevant to a discussion of friendship for the light it sheds on our capacity for rational self-concern and the level of our self-esteem.

Seeing Oneself as Friend: Self-love and Self-concern

As I have argued, the process of constituting a self is a precarious one which places us in an ambiguous relation to the other. As Donald Winnicott explains in speaking of the reality of the world in which children must live when they become adults:

> [That world] is one in which every loyalty involves something of an opposite nature which might be called a disloyalty . . . Eventually, if one goes back, one can see that these disloyalties, as I am calling them, are an essential feature of living, and they stem from the fact that it is disloyal to everything that is not oneself if one is to be oneself. The most aggressive and therefore the most dangerous words in the languages of the world are to be found in the assertion I AM. It has to be admitted, however, that only those who have reached a stage at which they can make this assertion are really qualified as adult members of society.[55]

The balance in friendship between love and care for a friend for the friend's own sake and rational self-concern involves this same tension between loyalty and disloyalty, since the two sources of concern are at least theoretically opposed. Rational self-concern can compete with care for a friend for the friend's own sake and hence be interpreted as disloyalty. If applied to friendship, Winnicott's comments might suggest that a healthy adult must straddle this tension between loyalty and disloyalty in relations with friends.

Modern theories of the constitution of the self are often strongly influenced by psychoanalytic theory, such as Winnicott's and others. For example, Pauline Chazan in *The Moral Self* refers to the work of Heinz Kohut, drawing an analogy between Aristotle's character friendship (friendship of the good or primary friendship) and Kohut's self-psychology.[56] Kohut uses the tenet of the essential unconsciousness of mental activities as the basis of an explanation of the development of a sense of identity and a sense of self-worth.[57] On his view, individuals who are capable of relating to one another on the basis of concern for the interests and needs of others in themselves, rather than relating exclusively to the other on the basis of their own individual interests and needs, are capable of 'mature self–object relations' with others. This capacity is in turn dependent upon what Kohut refers to as healthy narcissism. Chazan argues that the virtues of the good man who is capable of character friendship 'are precisely what can provide a person with the healthy narcissism that interests self psychologists'.[58]

Kohut develops the ideas of Donald Winnicott, who argues that '[i]nfants come into *being* differently according to whether conditions are favourable or unfavourable'.[59] The conditions do not determine the infant's potential, since this is inherited, but development of that potential is dependent on maternal care and consists in a process in which the infant begins the movement towards independence. As Winnicott describes the process:

> The child is beginning to separate out from the mother, and before the mother becomes objectively perceived, she is what might be called a subjective object. There is quite a jerk that the child has to experience between the use of a mother as a subjective object, that is to say an aspect of the self, and an object that is other than self and therefore outside omnipotent control; and the mother performs a most important task in adapting herself to the child's needs so that she blurs a little this terrible jerk.[60]

In the initial phases of development the child has only a limited ability to make objective perceptions, so that the main experience of relation to others – object-relating – remains relating to subjective objects, those which are in fact an aspect of self, on Winnicott's view. The developments Winnicott outlines depend on the environmental condition of 'holding'; without good enough holding these developments will be impeded. The main function of the holding environment is to reduce to a minimum impingements to which the infant must react with anxiety. The child gains confidence from the union she experiences with the mother, and she is able to reduce anxiety by relating to transitional objects (for example, cuddly toys) which stand in for the mother as a reminder of the mother's reliability. Thus the environment facilitates the maturational process in the individual. Ego-strength develops as the new individual moves further away from absolute dependence towards independence, developing a continuity of being. The establishment and development of this strength are the crucial feature indicating the psychic health of the individual.[61]

Like Winnicott, Kohut focuses on the maturational process. For Kohut the mother is a 'selfobject' for the infant, one that supports the infant's developing sense of self.[62] As Edwin Kahn explains, Kohut coined the term 'selfobject' when he discovered that many of his patients used other people as functional parts of themselves.[63] However, Kohut's view was that the infant has a natural and instinctual need to use others in this way: to idealise, and to seek strength and comfort from an omnipotent selfobject. The child's instinctual selfobject needs, such as the need for reliable care, affirmation, sensitive response, and understanding, must be satisfied if he is to develop the ego-strength that Winnicott identifies as crucial to the maturational process. Thus healthy development is facilitated by empathetic selfobjects who echo, mirror and admire the child's often grandiose and exhibitionistic display of his characteristics and abilities.

Kohut uses the metaphor of the mirror to explain the way in which a parent affirms her child's developing sense of self, responding to the child's needs for affirmation. From the perspective of an analyst concerned to establish how children develop a sense of self-worth, Kohut argues that a child's sense of self can only develop adequately if it is affirmed by the appropriate mirroring responses of parents. He argues that the child 'tries out' identities, turning to the parents for a developmentally appropriate and genuine 'mirroring' response. If the parents generally meet the child's attempts with empathetic mirroring responses, they affirm the child's sense of identity. If the parents too often fail in this regard, for example disapproving of the child's expression of anxiety or discomfort, the child begins to develop a false self. As Chazan explains 'the false self is based on compliance to the reality of the other, its function is to hide the true self in order to excite a suitable response from the other'.[64] But as Chazan goes on to point out, the consequence of this is that areas of personal experience are not responded to and remain neglected. Consequently needs go unmet, and thus they might find expression in the kind of behaviour that Hume's boastful, foolish guest exhibits.

If the parents generally respond to the child empathetically, the child is able to internalise the selfobject functions they provide and develop a cohesive self. The child develops internal structures which enable it to respond to experience with consistency and clarity; to regulate self-esteem; and to calm the self, even in the face of considerable stress – as Baker and Baker explain in their overview of Kohut's self psychology.[65] Baker and Baker apply Winnicott's tenet – that maternal care of the young child does not have to reach an ideal – to parental responses in general. In fact, contemporary treatments of Winnicott's ideas sometimes refer to the notion of the combined parent. These treatments argue that parents need only be reasonably empathetic or 'good enough' in their responses to ensure that their child's needs with regard to developing a sense of self are met. In fact, minor failures on the part of parents create the need for the development of the child's own internal structures or coping mechanisms, while basic success creates a secure enough environment to permit growth. As Winnicott would put it, the mother's gradual failures to adapt to the infant's needs are themselves adaptive, since they are related to the growing need of the child for meeting reality, for achieving separation and for the establishment of a personal identity.[66] In terms of a discussion of friendship, these failures of 'empathetic mirroring' contribute to the individual's capacity to recognise and respond maturely to the distance that separates friends, despite their intimacy.

The second aspect of self-development that Winnicott and Kohut emphasise, and which has particular relevance for a discussion of friendship, is the notion of narcissism. Both theorists challenge negative, stereotypical reactions to the notion of self-love when they take a positive attitude to narcissism and to the grandiose and exhibitionistic displays of the child. Kohut sees empathetic responses to these displays and to the child's needs as providing the kind of affirmation necessary to allow the child to move towards the development of healthy narcissism in adulthood. Part of the complexity of the process Kohut describes lies in the reciprocal nature of the interaction between parent and child: just as the parent responds to the child, so the child responds to the parent, and the responses of both are continuously modified; so that over time, the relationship between them changes and develops.

Marilyn Friedman elaborates on this complexity when she argues that social relationships and the traditions, practices and conventions of communities also impact upon identity development. Friedman points out that for the child maturing to self-consciousness in her community of origin, the community the child enters is 'found, not entered, discovered, not created'. The child finds herself in a community in which moral and other particulars of her life are given. Friedman argues that gender distinctions are also imposed upon this process and that these influence the nature of relations with others. Her view is that in a society in which early infant care is the primary responsibility of women, but not men, the processes of psychogender development 'result in a radical distinction between the genders in the extent to which the self is constituted by, and self-identifies with, its relational connection with others'. This reflects the way in which masculinity and femininity are theorised, on Friedman's view; males are theorised to seek and value ideals that seem to depend on a highly individuated conception of persons, while females by contrast are theorised to seek and value ideals of care, nurturance and connection.[67] These considerations bring a new dimension to the complexity of the processes that Kohut describes.

Kohut's self psychology also recognises the fact that the interaction between parents and children can be life-long. In discussing maturation, he notes that the mature or maturing self is not dependent on the responses of others for a sense of self-worth, but neither is it, nor should it become, immune to them.

Kohut's view was that the healthy and mature adult does not become independent of selfobjects; rather he becomes more adept at establishing mature relationships of empathetic resonance.[68] Thus in his selfobject relations the mature adult sees the other not as an aspect of himself, but as an individual in her own right. It is this healthy narcissism that provides the basis of a relationship in which genuine care for the friend for the friend's own sake is balanced by self-regard and a sense of self-worth; thus mature friends can ideally be characterised as rationally concerned with themselves. Chazan explains the mature person's relation to selfobjects well when she states that:

> the selfobject function for a person does not ever disappear, but undergoes transformation and maturation so that a person can maintain an adequate level of grandiosity. The feeling of being competent, of being 'good enough', of being able to cope well, and of being likeable or lovable are all signs of what Kohut would regard to be normal grandiosity.[69]

W. W. Meissner offers a critique and development of Kohut's self psychology that places emphasis on the role of affects or feeling in general. He sees affective expression as a core dimension of the analytic experience and takes affects – whether fear, anger or sadness – to be expressing important dimensions of the subject's relationship with objects. For him, affects can reveal something of the sense of self that underlies the subject's self-image (the way in which the individual feels about, thinks about and portrays himself).[70] In this regard, Meissner's views corroborate the views of the philosophers, discussed above, who offer intentional accounts of emotion. Meissner might say of the self-image of Hume's boastful guest that it reveals a portrayal of himself – and feelings and thoughts of himself – as duly proud of the feast he has attended. This self-image 'is highly affectively toned' and provides the guest with a principle of integration and self-organisation, as Meissner might put it. However, the affect – his pride – also leads us to suspect the sense of self that underlies the image. We suspect the inappropriateness of his pride might reflect an unmet childhood need for affirmation; that he is dependent on pride for his sense of self-worth and perhaps lacking in a normal and adequate degree of grandiosity. Appropriate affective expression is thus dependent on a certain level of self-esteem or self-regard, a stable sense of one's own worth or, as self psychologists might put it, a normal degree of grandiosity. Psychoanalysis argues that the stages in the development of self-esteem or an adequate level of grandiosity begin in childhood. Rorty and de Sousa would agree that the genesis of our predispositions towards certain emotional responses and towards structuring experience in certain ways lies in childhood. However, Rorty and de Sousa argue that these predispositions need not determine our responses; we can bring reason to bear on our pre-dispositions, imagine other responses and act to give them expression. This may be one way of describing the enterprise undertaken in psychoanalytic therapy: the patient is given the opportunity to imagine himself and his experiences anew, to restructure his experience in the context of the positive and empathetic regard of the therapist.

Healthy narcissism implies a sense of self-worth and a normal degree of grandiosity. The healthy narcissist sees herself as a competent individual; she is confident in her abilities, and feels that she is worthy of respect and appreciation. At the same time she recognises her connection with others and their status as individuals with concerns and interests analogous to her own. She can balance her own concerns against the concerns of others in a reasonable manner, rather than being overcome with concern for her own interests. This capacity for balance identifies her as rationally self-concerned, rather than narrowly self-interested. It is this capacity that makes her self-assessment stable and rational, so that it will stand up to the legitimate criticism of others within a civilised debate. The healthy narcissist might be regarded as self-sufficient or self-possessed, since such a person will not use others as functional aspects of herself. She will seek to establish relationships of reciprocal and empathetic engagement with others as persons in their own right, rather than attempt to use others to echo, mirror and admire her abilities and capacities. This characterisation of self-sufficiency assumes, as Nussbaum argues, that appropriate human self-sufficiency involves relational goods, including the pleasure and fulfilment of relations between friends.[71]

Aristotle himself did not deny the virtuous and self-sufficient man primary friendship. But, as noted in Chapter 2, there is an association between self-sufficiency and independence in the *Ethics* that creates tension in Aristotle's discussion. Perhaps we simply have to accept this tension. We might say that human beings are not (by definition) self-sufficient beings, but that the mature and healthy narcissist does not use others as aspects of himself. Thus to the extent that the individual resists using others as aspects of himself, he moves towards that self-sufficiency which is appropriate to mature human interaction. But if the healthy narcissist were to regard himself as self-sufficient then he would deceive himself; he cannot avoid the tension between independence and intimate relationship inherent in close interpersonal relationships such as friendship. An appreciation of this tension is something that literature – rather than philosophy – communicates well. Poetry and literature can capture the paradoxical – the sense in which we must aim for something, but can never be guaranteed reaching it, since to regard oneself as having reached it would undermine the sense of becoming and possibility that is inherent and valuable in the enterprise. Eugene O'Neill's comments in the Gelb's biography of him capture this idea:

> The tragedy of life is what makes it worthwhile. I think that any life which merits living lies in the effort to realize some dream, and the higher that dream is the harder it is to realize. Most decidedly we must all have our dreams, if one hasn't them, one might as well be dead. The only success is in failure. Any man who has a big enough dream must be a failure and must accept this as one of the conditions of being alive. If he ever thinks for a moment that he is a success, then he is finished.[72]

David Malouf's novel *An Imaginary Life* also reflects this sense of the role of continual struggle, of becoming and possibility in human life. If we apply his comments to the context of the life friends share, they allow us to embrace the idea that friendship is a relationship that is continually negotiated:

> Always to be pushing out like this, beyond what I know cannot be the limits – what else should a man's life be? What else should our lives be, but a continual series of beginnings, of painful settings out into the unknown, pushing off from the edges of consciousness into the mystery of what we have not yet become.[73]

My point here is similar to my argument in Chapter 3, which compared motivation in friendship to the motivation of the artist in aesthetic endeavour. The relationship between independence and dependence between friends cannot be worked out in advance. We engage wholeheartedly in interaction whose nature we cannot stipulate, just as artists engage in an enterprise whose outcome they cannot guarantee. Interaction between friends, like artistic activity, is open to possibility; its limits are not set. The particular balance achieved between dependence and independence within a friendship will be one that friends work out in interaction; their particular needs and desires, their awareness of their own motivations, and their conceptions of friendship and what it is to be a friend will all be relevant to this achievement. Just as the artist cannot determine that she will produce a masterpiece, so we cannot determine the particular nature of a friendship. In fact, making a particular intention explicit with regard to the relationship is likely to undermine rather than enhance the possibility of its achievement. Such an instrumental approach to friendship fails to recognise complex motivation, uncertainty, fragility and possibility as elements of relations between friends. Like the artist, I must dispense with instrumentality, engage in the enterprise for its own sake and be alive to the possibilities inherent in the enterprise.

Often it is our emotions that will alert us to our motivations and help us to appreciate the significance of those motivations, and the self-image which accompanies them, to our relations with friends. For example, the tensions inherent in the notions of appropriate human self-sufficiency and healthy narcissism are registered and communicated via the emotions – as Nancy Sherman's previous comments suggest. Our emotions often reveal a tension between a concern for ourselves and a concern for a friend. We can be overly concerned with ourselves to the detriment of others, but we can also be overly concerned with the welfare of others to the detriment of ourselves. It is the capacity of rationally concerned selves to recognise their motivations and preserve a balance between these concerns that interests Pauline Chazan. In the context of her argument that a certain kind of self-love is foundational for moral agency, she suggests that the capacity for rational self-concern exhibited by the healthy narcissist implies that such a person will have the virtues of the good man who is capable of Aristotelian character friendship.

Friendship, Self-Knowledge and Understanding

For Aristotle it is the good man's relation to himself that provides the foundation that makes primary friendships (character friendships) possible. This is due in part to the fact that for Aristotle 'in its extreme form friendship approximates to self-love'.[74] Thus we care for our friend in the same way as we care for ourselves. Aristotle acknowledges in this discussion that the question of whether friendship towards oneself is possible or not is dependent on taking a view of the self as two or more persons. We might be committed to a unitary view of human consciousness, or we might think that our identity with and awareness of ourselves seems to be too close to allow us to think of ourselves as two or more persons; but Aristotle none the less captures something important about self-knowledge in this discussion. We are not always transparent to ourselves. We sometimes hear ourselves say something in conversation and find the statement revealing, so that we become aware of ourselves in a new or different way. This occurs in much the same way as we might find others' statements revealing of an attitude or intention. We are able to access our own feelings in a way that we cannot access the feelings of others, and we are capable of self-reflection, but we are also revealed to ourselves in interaction with the world and with others. In the context of these considerations, Aristotle's reference to the self as two or more persons is not unintelligible. Being self-consciously aware of oneself does entail thinking of oneself as at least two kinds of entities: as both the subject and the object of reflective thought. My relation or 'aliveness' to myself, my view of the self as a site of possibility and my sensitivity to possible developments and changes enhance self-knowledge, making discoveries possible.

In another passage in book IX of the *Nichomachean Ethics*, Aristotle explains that:

> for a given person the existence of his friend is as desirable, or almost as desirable, as his own. But as we saw, what makes existence desirable is the consciousness of one's own goodness, and such consciousness is pleasant in itself. So a person ought to be conscious of his friend's existence, and this can be achieved by living together and conversing and exchanging ideas with him.[75]

Aristotle is proffering a notion of reciprocal awareness of self and other and its place in friendship of the best kind. This is not to say that he is referring to an understanding of self-awareness that a modern audience would expect. As Stern-Gillet argues, Aristotle 'was endeavouring to account for both the unity of consciousness and for the genesis of self-awareness without the benefit of what some modern philosophers would be pleased to call appropriate terminology'; her view is that Aristotle saw psychic unity as the result of a process of integration that is co-extensive with the acquisition of moral virtue.[76] None the less, Aristotle does recommend friendship for its contribution to the development of self-knowledge:

> Since, then, it is both a most difficult thing, as some of the sages have also said, to know oneself, and also a most pleasant thing (for to know oneself is pleasant) – moreover, we cannot ourselves study ourselves from ourselves, as is clear from the reproaches we bring against others without being aware that we do the same things ourselves – and this happens because of bias or passion, which in many of us obscure the accuracy of judgments; as, then, when we ourselves wish to see our own face we see it by looking into a mirror, similarly, too, when we wish to know ourselves, we would know ourselves by looking to the *philos*. For the *philos*, as we say, is another oneself.[77]

Aristotle goes on to say that since it is not possible to know oneself without having a *philos*, then the self-sufficient person will need one in order to know himself. Thus friendship enables me to take the perspective of another on myself and presumably on the world; and since this is another I trust and who trusts me, that perspective is valuable. I see myself through the eyes of my friend, and without the bias and partiality I am likely to bring to my own reflection on myself. The self is illuminated and its experience is extended in ways that would be impossible for an individual to achieve alone. In addition and by implication, in sharing my friend's life and concerns she reveals her experience to me and I gain a window on the world which I am unlikely to achieve with a stranger. Nussbaum develops this idea when she argues that, in trusting the guidance of a friend and allowing our feelings to be engaged with that other person's life and choices, we learn to see aspects of the world that we had previously missed. Our desire to share a form of life with the friend motivates this process.[78] The suggestion is that our experience in friendship provides us with data that can lead us to compare our views with those of a friend, to reflect on, re-examine and perhaps revise our views. The potential is there to learn more about ourselves and about our fellow human beings. This process is almost guaranteed in Aristotelian primary friendship, since the friend is by definition a good and virtuous man who engages in reflection, and aids his friend in contemplation and in virtuous and pleasurable activity.

For modern friends the process is complicated by the way in which our expectations and understandings of friendship interact with those of our friends. We do not generally, necessarily or exclusively identify our friends with their goodness, as Aristotle did. The goodness of friends cannot be the focus of modern friendship. If we do see goodness as integral to a friend's character, his goodness is akin to the skill of a master artist in the production of a masterpiece: necessary, but not sufficient to the enterprise. Nor do modern individuals assume that the main function or proper excellence of human beings lies in rational activity. Rather, we recognise the complex interplay between emotion, imagination and reason that underlies the process of self-constitution, and hence the relevance of that interplay to our understanding of self and others.

We are particularly cognizant of the role of emotion in galvanising and stimulating our ability to imagine ourselves in the place of the other, and the interaction of that emotion with reason in making assessments of self and others. In intimate relations with others, our attachment to and trust of those others provide a context within which affective expression is appropriate, expected and perhaps even vital to the maintenance of the relationship. As Meissner puts it, 'the communication of affects is telling us something profoundly meaningful about the quality of the individual's experience and relationships'.[79] Affective expression within friendship reinforces intimacy between friends, and at the same time it is a form of meaningful communication between friends. As such it provides friends with opportunities to understand and appreciate one another within a context that – as Stern-Gillet suggests – is not forced on us by external circumstances. We reflect on a friend's affective responses to us, on her assessments of us, and on tensions or conflicts that emerge between us. These reflections force us to consider our own motivations as well as those of our friend. This process of reflection provides us with a tentative, more-or-less successful model which we can apply – perhaps with some modification – to other relationships.

The differences between the Aristotelian view of the self and the view of the self that has been canvassed in this chapter do not negate the force of Aristotle's comments about friendship's contribution to self knowledge. Relations between friends are as valuable for the development of self-knowledge and self-understanding today as Aristotle suggests they were in the fourth century BC. Friends can reveal to us – via either subtle, provocative or even unintentional means – assessments of our character, our habits and dispositions, and our perspectives on life. These revelations provide the basis for self-criticism, self-understanding and self-assessment. Ronald Sharp neatly summarises debate on friendship's contribution to self-knowledge and self-understanding when he recognises two dimensions of friendship – a metaphysical and an ethical dimension: 'the friend not only validates and concretizes one's sense of identity and reality; he also in one way or another evaluates it'.[80] What friends reveal to us about themselves and others is also significant, since it can open us to new ways of looking at the world and new possibilities. This process of revelation in relations between friends is somewhat analogous to the way in which literature and film can impact upon us. In fact, the various aspects of our relations with friends interact with one another. A friend might recognise feelings of undue pride and act to alert us to his assessment of us by suggesting an alternative interpretation of our situation. But he can also recognise misplaced feelings of incompetence in us and attempt to bolster our self-esteem. Thus friends not only reflect aspects of our personality to us, but can challenge and perhaps act as a catalyst to modification of our own self-image.

Charles Birch in his book *Feelings* outlines a set of changes in relations among individuals who become members of a group. These changes seem relevant to the development of knowledge and understanding in relations between friends, and are not out of place in the context of Aristotle's comments in the preceding excerpt from the *Magna Moralia*. Birch lists four changes, although not in the exact order in which I am making use of them.[81] First, he refers to the way in which the 'atomic exclusiveness' of the individuals is broken so that, second, they become freely receptive and responsive to the needs and aspirations of each other. He argues that then their appreciable world expands, since they could now see through the eyes of others and feel their sensitivities. Finally he suggests that such individuals experience a greater depth and breadth of community. Birch's list of changes in sentiment and understanding outlines a highly idealised progression. But like Aristotle's treatment of primary friendship, it provides a guide to relations between friends. We are forced to modify these guides if we are to take account of the distance that often separates modern friends, or of the rival usages of the term 'friend' that the indistinct nature of the modern conception of friendship allows. But that modification does not diminish their value as ideals or general guides. The final chapter examines the nature of some of the modifications contemporary friendship demands, given the differentiation and fragmentation of contemporary life by comparison with the life of Aristotelian friends.

Notes

1. Kant, 'Lecture on Friendship', p. 212.
2. Hume, *A Treatise of Human Nature*, I, IV, VI, p. 252.
3. Dennett, 'Why Everyone is a Novelist', p. 1029.
4. Baier, *A Progress of Sentiments*, p. 130. The effects of the passions will depend on a complex of factors to be discussed in the next section.
5. Hume, *A Treatise of Human Nature*, II, I, XI, p. 322.
6. It is important to note, as Baier does (in 'Hume: The Reflective Women's Epistemologist?', p. 42), that imagining the point of view of the other ought not to be regarded as a substitute for actually listening to the points of view of others.
7. Hume, *A Treatise of Human Nature*, I, IV, VI, p. 261.
8. Berent Enç argues that Humean passions do not represent objects 'as being a certain way' and implies that therefore they are original existences, by comparison with ideas ('Hume's Unreasonable Desires', p. 241).
9. Hume, *A Treatise of Human Nature*, III, II, II, p. 493.
10. Denzin, *On Understanding Emotion*, p. 142.
11. Ibid.
12. Hume, *A Treatise of Human Nature*, II, II, IX, p. 385.
13. Kant, 'The Doctrine of Virtue', p. 216.
14. Nussbaum, *Upheavals of Thought*, pp. 115 and 118.
15. Le Doux, *The Emotional Brain*, pp. 298–9.
16. Damasio, *Looking for Spinoza*, p. 55.
17. Nussbaum, *Upheavals of Thought*, p. 501.
18. Spinoza, *The Ethics*, E1 Appendix, and EII, Note II.
19. Damasio, *Descartes' Error*, pp. xv and 245.
20. Lloyd, *Spinoza and the Ethics*, p. 88.
21. Lloyd, *Part of Nature*, p. 159.
22. Lloyd, *Spinoza and the Ethics*, p. 88.
23. Spinoza, *The Ethics*, IV, PXVIII, Note.
24. Nussbaum, *Upheavals of Thought*, p. 501.
25. Nussbaum, *Upheavals of Thought*, p. 27.
26. de Sousa, 'The Rationality of Emotions', p. 138.
27. Solomon, 'The Logic of Emotion', pp. 41–9.
28. Ibid., p. 47.
29. Ibid., p. 45.
30. de Sousa, 'The Rationality of Emotions', p. 142.
31. Amélie Rorty reminds us that it is beneficial for children to tend to absorb what she refers to as the intentional dispositions of the crucial figures around them; while this may be maladaptive in some cases, she argues that it may be advantageous for habitual responses to dominate rational considerations and only to be changed with difficulty ('Explaining Emotions', p. 120).

32. de Sousa, 'The Rationality of Emotions', p. 137.

33. Hume, *A Treatise of Human Nature*, II, III, III, p. 413.

34. Rorty, 'Explaining Emotions', p. 105. Rorty does accept that emotions are often identified without tracing their causal history, but she argues that 'a rough and unexamined but nevertheless quite specific folk psychology . . . informs such standard explanations' (ibid., p. 118). Norman Denzin suggests the same kind of historical contextualisation when he writes: 'I relive my past, emotionally, in the present. I do so in terms of the repertoires of feeling, expression, repression, distortion, and signification that were acquired in my original family situation' (*On Understanding Emotion*, p. 43).

35. Hume, *A Treatise of Human Nature*, II, II, IV, p. 350.

36. de Sousa, 'The Rationality of Emotions', pp. 129–30.

37. Hume, *A Treatise of Human Nature*, II, I, VI, p. 290.

38. Rorty, 'Explaining Emotions', p. 106.

39. Hume, *A Treatise of Human Nature*, III, III, II, pp. 596–7.

40. Rorty, 'Explaining Emotions', p. 119.

41. Sartre, *Search for a Method*, pp. 12–13.

42. Lloyd, *Spinoza and the Ethics*, p. 72.

43. Hirschman, *A Propensity to Self-Subversion*, ch. 1.

44. Denzin, *On Understanding Emotion*, p. 43.

45. Sharp, *Friendship and Literature*, pp. 29–30.

46. Sharp, *Friendship and Literature*, pp. 34–5.

47. Ricoeur, 'Imagination in Discourse and Action', p. 128.

48. Bartky, 'Sympathy and Solidarity', p. 192.

49. Ibid.

50. The shared activity condition does not imply that friendship cannot be maintained at a distance, since, as Ronald Sharp points out, 'there is a physical distance and there is a psychic or spiritual distance' (*Friendship and Literature*, pp. 32–3). Telfer's conditions of friendship are discussed in Chapter 2 of this book.

51. Hume, *A Treatise of Human Nature*, III, III, I, p. 581.

52. Ibid., pp. 582–3.

53. Nussbaum, *The Fragility of Goodness*, pp. xxvii and xxix.

54. Sherman, *Making a Necessity of Virtue*, p. 28.

55. Winnicott, *Home Is Where We Start From*, pp. 140–1.

56. Chazan, *The Moral Self*, ch. IV.

57. Kohut and Seitz, 'Concepts and Theories of Psychoanalysis', p. 339.

58. Ibid., p. 81.

59. Winnicott, *The Maturational Processes and the Facilitating Environment*, p. 43.

60. Winnicott, *Home Is Where We Start From*, p. 131.

61. For the various elements of this discussion see Winnicott, *Home Is Where We Start From*, pp. 72–3 and 133, and Winnicott, *The Maturational Processes and the Facilitating Environment*, pp. 47, 50 and 52.

62. Kohut, *How Does Analysis Cure?*, p. 49.

63. Kahn, 'Heinz Kohut and Carl Rogers', pp. 894 and 897.

64. Chazan, *The Moral Self*, p. 84.

65. Baker and Baker, 'Heinz Kohut's Self Psychology: An Overview', especially p. 4.

66. Winnicott, *The Maturational Processes and the Facilitating Environment*, p. 97.
67. Friedman, 'Feminism and Modern Friendship: Dislocating the Community', pp. 285, 289–90 and 295.
68. Kohut, *How does analysis cure?*, p. 185.
69. Chazan, *The Moral Self*, p. 80.
70. Meissner, 'Phenomenology of the Self', pp. 69, 71–2.
71. Nussbaum, *The Fragility of Goodness*, p. xxx. Self-sufficiency is discussed in more detail in Chapter 2 of this book.
72. O'Neill quoted in Gelb and Gelb, *O'Neill*, p. 337.
73. Malouf, *An Imaginary Life*, p. 135.
74. Aristotle, *Nichomachean Ethics*, 166a16–b4.
75. Ibid., 1170a24–b15.
76. Stern-Gillet, *Aristotle's Philosophy of Friendship*, pp. 24–6.
77. Aristotle, *Magna Moralia*, in *The Complete Works of Aristotle*, 1213a10–26.
78. Nussbaum, *Love's Knowledge*, p. 238.
79. Meissner, 'Phenomenology of the Self', p. 68.
80. Sharp, *Friendship and Literature*, p. 35.
81. Birch, *Feelings*, p. 31.

Chapter 6

Friendship in Contemporary Life

Chapter 5 argued that the ability to take account of the perceptions and expectations of others is crucial to the development of a coherent or stable conception of self, and that this ability is affected by the kinds of dispositions and attitudes we develop as a result of experience: the formative events in our psychological past; the patterns of salience and habits of thought and response we develop. Our emotions are important conduits for registering and communicating value in this regard. They are intelligent evaluative interpretations, which reveal particular dispositions, attitudes and thoughts to others and to ourselves. The previous chapter also argued that those with whom we are intimate have crucial roles in these processes, and that the uniqueness of our relationship with friends makes them particularly significant in the process. This chapter revisits psychoanalytic perspectives on the formation of identity and the constitution of the self, focusing on the role of language, discourse and imagination in these processes. It does so to emphasise the creativity that is implicit in relations between friends. Friendship emerges as a creative and uncertain synthesis of the play of forces that create identity and difference between friends. That creativity is illustrated by the use of an analogy between narrative discourse and friendship. The chapter begins with a comparison between ancient and modern conceptions of friendship, to draw attention to the particular and peculiar forces that generate difference between modern friends.

Friendship, Fragmentation and Creativity

Aristotle located friendship within the public sphere, as a bond that constituted and sustained the polis. But the public sphere for him was one in which, ideally, all citizens as good men shared a conception and a pursuit of the good. Thus, as we have seen, Aristotle emphasised sameness among friends. Modern friends may have a common conception of the good life, but they share only particular aspects of life, rather than a total common sphere of life as the citizens of the polis had done. The modern person does not necessarily define his good in terms of a good which he shares with others. As Georg Simmel held, modern culture, society and personality are by nature fragmented. There is a plurality of claims made upon modern persons and they are caught in the intersection of cross-cutting interests and expectations. While this encourages the expression of individuality and a greater differentiation between persons, it makes for discontinuity in personal relations; such discontinuity was not characteristic of the polis, at least not in Aristotle's version of it. As a consequence, modern individuals simply cannot sustain a friendship in the Aristotelian sense. As Simmel remarked of modern friendship:

> [T]he modern way of feeling tends more heavily toward differentiated friendships, which cover only one aspect of the personality, without playing into other aspects of it . . . These differentiated friendships which connect us with one individual in terms of affection, with another in terms of common intellectual aspects, with a third, in terms of religious impulses, and with a fourth, in terms of common experiences – all these friendships present a very peculiar synthesis in regard to questions of discretion, of reciprocal revelation and concealment. They require that the friends do not look into those mutual spheres of interest and feeling which, after all, are not included in the relation and which, if touched upon, would make them feel painfully the limits of their mutual understanding.[1]

The access modern friends have to one another's experience, expectations and motivations is constrained by the degree of differentiation that characterises their relationships. Urban dislocation and the time constraints imposed by the degree of mobility and the complexity typical of the lives of modern individuals exacerbate the tendency Simmel identifies. The phenomenon of the 'urban tribe', referred to in Chapter 1, is a creative attempt to overcome some of the effects of the dislocation and fragmentation of contemporary city life. The 'urban tribe' can be seen as providing a new and broader category of modern friendship, as its members provide the support, affection, company and sense of connection that might once have been found within the family or within marital relations. But it does not overcome the fragmentation and differentiation that is a feature of modern friendships, since the members of such tribes generally share the local and domestic spheres of their lives, rather than all spheres of life.

Simmel explains that complete intimacy becomes more difficult as differentiation among human beings increases, arguing that for modern individuals '[p]ersonalities are perhaps too uniquely individualized to allow full reciprocity of understanding and receptivity, which always, after all, requires much creative imagination and much divination which is oriented only toward the other'.[2] On Simmel's view, modern friendship is a relation based entirely on the individualities of the personalities involved; and he draws attention to a correlation between the most pointed individualisation and the restriction of the relationship to only two participants.[3] The implication is that the degree of individualisation that is typical of modern persons determines that they have less in common. Consequently, we can conclude that they should not expect to find the reciprocity of understanding that Aristotle suggests was typical of relations between the good men of the polis. Since mutual understanding is more difficult to achieve, then it is perhaps more likely that modern friendships will be restricted to two participants. The small size of the polis no doubt impacted upon the homogeneity of relations within the polis, and more populous and heterogeneous modern societies undoubtedly encourage greater differentiation and individualisation among their members. However, the increase in the number of people engaged in interaction within modern societies might modify some of the effects Simmel identifies. Given that some modern individuals will have greatly increased opportunities for interaction with a large number of others, differentiation might be less devastating to the development of mutual understanding than Simmel envisages. Indeed, as we have seen, Aristotelian civic friendship is an exclusive and divisive form of relation, if relations between the entire population of the polis are taken into account. Modern friendship is highly differentiated and difficult to define in part because of its inclusiveness – a feature that we have reason to commend. It is the exclusivity of Aristotelian civic friendship that contributes to its homogeneity.

While it is clear that modern friendship does strain under conditions and within contexts that did not assail ancient conceptions of friendship, something of significance in Aristotle's analysis of friendship does carry over to modern conceptions. His claim that a friend loves and cares for his friend for that friend's own sake appears to be compatible with a more modern notion of friendship – one in which the friend is valued for what he is, for himself, rather than as a fellow citizen. However, as we have seen, Aristotle associates the good man's essential nature with his rational capacities and with the practice of the virtues; more specifically, he identifies the good and truly wise man with the practice of the intellectual virtues and with contemplative activity. Thus for the Aristotelian good man, to be concerned with a friend in himself is to be concerned with his goodness, with the cultivation of his intellect, with aiding him in virtuous and contemplative activity and in the achievement of wisdom. Chapter 2 draws attention to the difficulty modern friends face when we try to articulate what we might mean when we refer to the friend in herself or himself. The value that modern friends place on what Stern-Gillet refers to as the unicity and individual irreplaceability of friends suggests that it is what radically differentiates a friend from others that is significant for us.[4]

Of course valuing a friend for his own sake, even in the case of Aristotelian primary friends, must allow for some sense of difference, in that the friends are not identical; they must be distinguishable from one another in some way. But friendship in the modern world is characterised by a more substantive sense of difference. A dialectic between sameness and difference is imposed upon modern friendship by the context in which many modern individuals live. The emphasis that Aristotle, Cicero and especially Montaigne place on similarity between true or virtuous friends downplays the possibility of such a dialectic. As a consequence, their analyses can only be cautiously applied to modern friendship, which – given the differentiation and fragmentation that Simmel describes – must take account of this dialectic.

Friendship requires more than a recognition of the similarities upon which a friendship might initially have developed, and more than a recognition of the shared activity, reciprocal services and mutual liking upon which it might be cultivated. Recognition and tolerance of difference are also required if relationships are not to falter at the first sign of disagreement or in the face of any unmet expectations. Friends – particularly modern friends – cannot be expected to be in sympathy on all matters. The spheres of life they have in common may well be opposed by spheres of life in which they participate separately, but which are at odds with the values, interests and possibilities of their shared spheres. Henrik and Konrad in Márai's novel *Embers* are uncomfortable with one another in the context of a visit to Konrad's family in his home town – despite the intimacy of the relationship they share. As Simmel's views would lead us to expect, their experiences in that context make them feel their differences sharply. They are unable to bridge the gap that opens between them in the face of their differences, and it is left unarticulated and unexplored. As the narrator comments of this visit: 'They stayed in the town for four days. As they left, for the first time in their lives, they felt that something had come between them. As if one of them were in the other's debt. It could not be put into words.'[5]

It is only in retrospect that Henrik can comment that he could feel 'the profound loneliness' that Konrad felt in the face of their difference and regardless of their close friendship; only in retrospect could he grasp that Konrad had lived among, and yet never belonged with, Henrik, his family and his peers.[6] The forces that create difference for modern friends can be social and economic in nature – as they are for Henrik and Konrad; disparities in social status, political influence and wealth interact with temperament to make Márai's protagonists aware of the distance that separates them. Those forces might as easily be cultural or religious influences that inhibit friends' capacity to understand and interact with one another in particular contexts.

In fact, as Chapter 5 suggests, differences between friends may extend to differences in their conceptions of themselves and of one another. These differences might be explained by magnetised dispositions which lead them to interpret experience in particular and differing ways. Hume's hypothetical foolish guest is likely to experience some tension in his relations with friends, given what I have suggested is his magnetised disposition for excessive self-affirmation. This tension might be expressed explicitly: his friends might make fun of his undue pride; or it might be expressed in the form of his friends' reacting by distancing themselves from him, given their conflicting interpretation of the events that generate the foolish guest's pride. A view of relations between friends that takes account of this kind of magnetised disposition regards the self as a socially generated and mediated construct. Emphasis on social mediation in turn draws attention to the role of language in the process of self-constitution and to the self as a linguistically structured construct. The role of language in this process is discussed in further detail below, along with the special connection which some commentators recognise between narrative and friendship.

Of course the kinds of differences that arise between friends may not necessarily be a source of friction, disappointment or misunderstanding between them. Friends might value difference, rather than feeling it painfully. However, to come to value difference requires some recognition of and reflection upon that difference. David Malouf's book *An Imaginary Life*, although set in ancient times, provides a striking example of a friendship in which the recognition of difference opens a character – that of Ovid – to dramatic and welcome change. Ovid, in exile in a village distant from Rome, befriends and attempts to enculturate a wild Child. The Child in fact becomes Ovid's teacher, as Ovid becomes aware of the depth and wisdom of his view of the world: 'And where is he leading me, since I know at last that it is he who is the leader, he now who is inducting me into the mysteries of a world I have never for a moment understood.'[7] The Child opens Ovid to new possibilities in a process in which Ovid's view of the world is unsettled and challenged by that of the Child.

Relations between modern friends may not provide examples of the kind of dramatic difference and equally dramatic change that Malouf describes. However, the recognition of difference between friends is crucial to an authentic relationship, as Blanchot and Derrida make clear when they emphasise the separateness, rather than the similarity and connection, between friends. For them the relation between friends is predicated on their separateness; it is separation that in fact creates the relation between friends. Thus, as Chapter 3 argues, our conception of our friends and their identities must take account of difference, as well as acknowledging similarity in terms of what friends share. This implies that we ought to expect some tension or disagreement between friends and be prepared to accept some degree of change in a friend. We may need to adjust our conception of the identity of the friend in response to that acceptance – just as we ought to be alive to the changes friends might stimulate in us. If aspects of a friend's nature change – particularly those we had come to think of as characteristic of the person – then one's conception both of the friend and of the friendship may undergo re-evaluation. Of course, it is possible that one's conception of a friend might be questioned or altered to such an extent that the friendship cannot survive, and Márai's novel *Embers* provides an illustration of such a case.

Despite their emphasis on similarity between friends, the ancients did allow for the possibility of some change in friends, at least in the more inferior kinds of friendship. Cicero argues that the wise avoid the difficulties associated with change in a friend by being cautious in bestowing their affections, and not bestowing them on unworthy men. Worthy men are unlikely to change in terms of their character and interests. But in the friendships of ordinary folk, where changes in character or interests do take place, or in which friends do fall into disagreement about politics, he recommends that:

> we shall have to take care lest people think that we are not just terminating a friendship, but rather becoming active enemies. For there is nothing more unseemly than openly to enter the lists against someone with whom you have lived on terms of intimacy . . . Our first task . . . must be to see that no break in our friendship occurs, or, if it does, that our friendships should seem to fade away rather than be stamped out. We must be extremely careful not to let friendship turn into serious personal enmity, for this is what causes hard feelings, harsh words, even insult and abuse . . . There is a degree of respect which we must pay to a friendship that has been.[8]

Cicero did allow that there was room in friendship for some degree of indulgence or tolerance of the less honourable wishes of friends. However, tolerance could only go so far. As we saw in Chapter 4, Toni Morrison's novel *Sula* provides a modern example of the limits of tolerance in a friendship in which the friends had shared a high degree of intimacy. Nel and Sula disagree over the demands of friendship, and their subsequent disappointment with one another leads to a re-evaluation of one another and of their friendship. As a consequence of this, reconciliation between them becomes impossible.

The significance that change in a friend has for a friendship is a matter of judgement. There are inconsequential ways in which friends can change. Changes in style of dress or hair colour, for example, are unlikely to be perceived as essential or fundamental changes and are unlikely to threaten one's conception of a friend's identity. Rather our view of consequential change in a friend – change that is dramatic enough to demand re-evaluation of the friendship – will be related to a view of the friend's identity that, as Alisdair MacIntyre suggests, 'is just that identity presupposed by the unity of the character which the unity of a narrative requires. Without such unity there would not be subjects of whom stories could be told.'[9]

Within this narrative concept of selfhood, it is the coherence of the story that establishes the identity of its subject. The notion of intelligibility provides the conceptual link between a person's actions and the narrative that those actions constitute. Others have a significant role in this process. They too can provide an account of an individual's story; their set of memories can be called upon to corroborate a friend's presence, memories and the story a friend tells on the basis of these. And as Chapter 5 argues, others also have a significant role in the construction of our self-narratives, since they are crucial to the process of self-consitution and hence to the conception of self that an individual develops. As psychoanalytic and psychological scholarship indicates, the nature of our relations with and dependence on others is related to processes of self-constitution that have their genesis in childhood. Thus a contemporary treatment of relations between friends must be seen as related to the outcome of earlier processes of development. An explanation of the breakdown of relations between Nel and Sula in Morrison's *Sula* has as much to do with the impact of their own conceptions of self on their interaction as it does with expectations and notions of duty in friendship. For example, Sula's inability to accept the legitimacy of Nel's distress may well be exacerbated by what Kohut would refer to as an inappropriate level of grandiosity. Each friend's capacity to balance her own concerns with the concerns of others will have been affected by a variety of factors. The fragmentation and differentiation of modern friendships only serve to complicate this process, since modern friends may share less of one another's lives and hence may need to be more sensitive to the extent of their differences.

As we saw in Chapter 5, Kohut makes metaphorical use of the term 'mirroring' in his self psychology to explain the complexity of the interaction in which we all engage as selves constituting ourselves in relation to others. In the context of relations between friends, psychoanalytic notions of mirroring are relevant in the sense that they help to explain the kind of magnetised dispositions, patterns of salience and response developed in childhood, which can impact upon interactions between friends. The psychoanalyst Jacques Lacan also draws attention to the role of the mirror in the process of developing an identity, as the child recognises via the specular image both its separation from and identity with the other. The notion of 'mirroring' in the context of identity formation can also be used to draw attention to the creative dimensions of our interactions with friends. This third notion of mirroring, specific to relations between friends, is addressed below; it includes the use of an analogy that is drawn between friendship and narrative discourse.

But first, examining Lacan's use of the notion will help to draw out the significance of this analogy. Lacan's work is relevant for the connections it develops between the notions of mirroring in social interaction, language and self-constitution, and for the similarities evident between his approach and Ricoeur's views on the role of discourse in creating meaning. My emphasis in this discussion is on the creativity evident in these processes, and on the impact of the recognition of that creativity on self-understanding within the context of our relations with those others who are our friends.

Lacan argues that it is only by means of an identification with others that the ego can constitute itself as a subject. He regards the formation of personal identity as a process of dialectic identification with the other; thus he shares an emphasis on social mediation with the theorists discussed in Chapter 5. But he brings the role of language and imaginative activity in the process of identification to the fore. For Lacan the self is an imaginative entity that is constituted or constructed through the Other, via linguistic and symbolic representation. Thus the self is a work of the order of the imaginary – an imaginary identification with the Other. Through the agency of what Lacan refers to as 'the order of the symbolic' – that is, through language – this imaginary identification orients us to the world in which we find ourselves. However, this construction of self always and necessarily fails, since to become my own subject I must identify with the Other – an identification which for Lacan is always *méconnaisance* (a misrecognition or misidentification). Lacan uses the concept of the mirror stage to offer an explanation of the genesis of the construction of this imaginary self in childhood. He says of the child before his image in the mirror: 'he experiences in play the relation between the movements assumed in the image and the reflected environment, and between this virtual complex and the reality it reduplicates – the child's own body, and the persons and things, around him.'[10]

The function of the mirror stage is to move the child whose initial experience is of a fragmented body to a promised form of totality and mastery, and lastly to what Lacan refers to as 'the assumption of the armour of an alienating identity'.[11] However, this process creates a predicament: the child recognises both its separateness and its identity with others; it sees itself as separate from its environment, from others, from its mother, and yet at the same time the child sees itself as others see it – to some extent as an other and therefore to some extent as alienated from itself. Its image is, as Lacan puts it, 'the trap of imaginary capture', and he describes it as an abyss formed 'in the mortifying gap of the mirror-stage'.[12] Lacan's reference to this abyss is reminiscent of Chapter 3's discussion of the abyss between friends whose unaccountable connection is predicated upon their separation. The abyss between friends mirrors the abyss which Lacan maintains all selves must face in the process of their imaginary identification with the

Other. Of course the child faces this predicament of identification unconsciously. Friends face a similar tension between separateness from and identity with one another – with more or less awareness. Conflict between
friends may bring this tension into conscious awareness; although, as I
suggest below, a conception of friendship predicated on similarity may
undermine any recognition of the tension. However, we might well expect
that the processes of identity formation and self-constitution that occur in
childhood will condition the possibilities that are open to us in our later
relations with friends, since they will impact upon the conception of self we
develop and on our capacity for what Kohut calls 'mature selfobject relations' with others.

Language is crucial in this process of recognising both the self's separation from others and its identity with them. Lacan argues that it is via language – which generates discourse within culturally and historically
variable social contexts – that the child attempts to disguise its status as
'gap' or 'lack' and to acquire an identity of its own. The subject posits itself
in language despite the lack of a stable identity. To this extent its sense of
self is fictional and the process by which it achieves that sense of self is a
creative enterprise. From the Lacanian perspective, the self can be seen as a
product of interaction between imaginary signification and language. The
representation of self which the child sees in the mirror is one that is imbued
with familial and cultural significance – significance which is continually
communicated to the child through language and within discourse.[13]

Hermeneutic approaches to the constitution of the self also emphasise
language and discourse. However different in his orientation from Lacan,
Ricoeur's emphasis on discourse complements Lacan's claim that the self's
history is constituted in the communication which discourse represents.
Ricoeur argues that: '[W]hile language is only a prior condition of communication, for which it provides the codes, it is in discourse that all messages
are exchanged. So discourse not only has a world, but it has an other,
another person, an interlocutor to whom it is addressed.'[14]

For Ricoeur, language is actualised in discourse. Language is akin to a set
of encoded instructions which become meaningful only by being put to use
in the world, while discourse is realised as an event in which something
happens when someone speaks.[15] Consequently discourse differs from language for Ricoeur, in that it is understood as meaning. It is an expression of
culture, or, as he puts it, a 'projection of the world'.[16] On Ricoeur's view,
the meaning we – as speakers – give that world and our own existence
within it emerges through the elements of our discourse – that is, through
the signs, symbols and texts of our culture. Thus the meaning we give our
own existence as friends and the concept of friendship are created within
discourse. Ricoeur's treatment of the text illustrates this process.

Ricoeur defines the text as any discourse fixed by writing, and argues that a text 'is much more than a particular case of intersubjective communication: . . . it displays a fundamental characteristic of the very historicity of human experience, namely that it is communication in and through distance'.[17] As such, it should be recognised for its potential to extend the possibilities of human experience through imaginative activity. Ricoeur's focus on discourse as communication emphasises that the self is engaged in a dialogue in its search for identity – a dialogue which develops as our capacity for language develops. So for both Lacan and Ricoeur, the child – like all speakers – finds itself embedded within discourse, within a world of interlocutors and a culture of signs, symbols and texts. All selves are engaged in a dialogue with others on whom they are in some sense dependent, and yet from whom they are attempting to differentiate themselves. When Ricoeur argues that all texts can extend the possibilities of human experience through imaginative activity, he privileges one form of text. For him, fictional narrative is best able to address the difficulties associated with communicating our experience of time and of redescribing reality. Thus fictional narrative has a prized position in relation to our search for identity. In fact autobiographical narrative seems to me to be a particularly good example of the kind of communication Ricoeur is explaining. It responds to our perception of the 'discordance' of time, our experience of contingency and fragmentation, and opens up new possibilities of being-in-the-world.

It is my view that these features of autobiographical narrative allow such texts to serve a role in our lives analogous to the role that others can take in our lives, particularly those others who are our friends. Autobiographical texts can serve as mirrors in the sense that they can create possibilities that allow readers exposed to these texts to see themselves differently. This potential for 'mirroring' implicit in the work of autobiographers complements Lacan's use of the actual mirror image and Kohut's metaphorical usage of the term 'mirroring' in explaining the process of self-constitution. It brings together the discussion of self-constitution and the role of discourse as the vehicle by which speakers create meaning. In doing so, this third example of the notion of mirroring allows us to draw an analogy between narrative texts and friendship, since both narrative and our relations with friends open us to the possibility of self-development and increased self-understanding. This suggests a view of the literary text as a metaphorical mirror, but also as a metaphorical friend. This latter comparison is one that Elizabeth Telfer, Wayne Booth and Martha Nussbaum also make. For example, Telfer argues that friendship enlarges our knowledge and that in this sense it can be compared to our reading of works of literature:

> Through friendship we can know what it is like to feel or think or do certain things which we do not feel, think or do ourselves. And our knowledge is not

merely knowledge by description, but knowledge by acquaintance, derived from our sympathetic sharing of [a friend's] experience.

We might compare this effect of friendship with that of reading a great work of literature. C. S. Lewis, trying to answer the question 'What is the good of Literature?' says 'We want to be more than ourselves . . . we want to see with other eyes, to imagine with other imaginations, to feel with other hearts, as well as with our own.'

'It is not a question of knowing [in the sense of gratifying our rational curiosity about other people's psychology] at all. It is *connaître* not *savoir*; it is *erleben*: we become these other selves.'[18]

An excerpt from John Stuart Mill's autobiography illustrates the idea of the text as both mirror and friend. Mill, reading Marmontel's *Memoirs*, writes of the effect a particular passage had on him. He tells us that he

> came to the passage which relates to his [Marmontel's] father's death, the distressed position of the family and the sudden inspiration by which he, then a mere boy, felt, and made them feel, that he would be everything to them – would supply the place of all that they had lost. A vivid conception of the scene and its feelings came over me, and I was moved to tears. From this moment my burden grew lighter. The oppression of the thought that all feeling was dead within me, was gone. I was no longer hopeless.[19]

Mill's reaction to the images which Marmontel created in recounting his experience is to attempt to imitate creatively the action the narrative describes. Mill interprets the passage as mirroring or reflecting something of himself. He recognises a possibility for himself and acts on that recognition, engaging in a process of self-discovery through his interaction with the text. Marmontel's narrative opens up a new dimension for Mill as he imaginatively adopts Marmontel's project, putting himself to some extent in Marmontel's place. The narrative presents him with a possible way of being at a time when he is overcome by intense melancholy, and in this context it leads him, as he puts it, 'to adopt a theory of life' – one which he found appealing. Mill states that he still holds that happiness is the end of life, but he now concludes that it cannot be attained by making it a direct end. He cannot directly aim for contentment or a sense of self-worth. Those who are happy 'have their minds fixed on some object other than their own happiness; on the happiness of others, on the improvement of mankind, even on some art or pursuit, followed not as a means, but as itself an ideal end'.[20]

Marmontel's text acts upon Mill as interaction with a friend might. The text exposes him to principles, vicarious experience and advice that allow him to produce judgements and to revise his opinions. It becomes 'friendly' by virtue of the possibilities it uncovers and Mill's response to those possibilities. Wayne Booth considers this interaction to be a form of practical reasoning or argument, a mode of reflection and evaluation, which he refers to as 'coduction': a co-operative argument between human beings via a text.[21] This kind of practical reasoning between human beings is a form of interaction in which actual friends are well placed to take part. Unlike texts, which might serendipitously resonate with our experience and just as serendipitously give us hope and perhaps resolve for the future, friends are those who have shared experience and who know one another. In the best friendships, friends are those we trust, those who have our interests at heart, those who know us well and whom we know well. They are likely to have a good capacity to imagine our situation and to represent in their imaginations our sentiments. Consequently their advice, consultation and evaluations will have force with us, and the degree of credibility we give their opinions is likely to outweigh the credibility we assign to the opinions of others in general.

Ricoeur's claim that literary texts reveal possibilities for being is made within the context of his conviction that 'there is no self-understanding which is not mediated by signs, symbols and texts'.[22] We come to understand ourselves, to find meaning for ourselves through the medium of language as discourse. This implies that self-understanding is achieved only indirectly, through the spoken and written word and within interaction with other speakers, writers and readers.[23] Mill's 'cloud of melancholy gradually drew off' after his textual interaction with Marmontel; that interaction brought him, as Ricoeur would contend, to a new level of self-understanding.

My purpose in referring to the theoretical work of Lacan, Ricoeur and Kohut in this chapter has been to emphasise first their recognition of the self's essential and inevitable relation to others, and second the crucial role of language and discourse in that relation. The emphasis on alterity, interaction and communication in their work is complemented by the illustration in Mill's autobiography of the significance of the self's relation to others. Mill demonstrates the way in which discursive interaction mediates his self-understanding and contributes to the creative process by which he constitutes his self. The self is clearly portrayed as a self constructed in relation to others. The analogy between literary texts and friends is developed as an illustration of the way in which those others who are our friends open us to the benefits of a broader range of experience than we can hope to have alone. Imagining how a situation is experienced by a friend, and comparing our experience with that of the friend, also provide us with opportunities for reflection and evaluation, which otherwise are unlikely to be available to us. The process of reflection and evaluation we undertake enhances our capacity to take the point of view of our friend.

This is an exercise of the imagination – one that engages the emotions. David Marshall's comments in *The Surprising Effects of Sympathy* make it clear that imagining oneself in the place of the other cannot be divorced from some kind of representation of the other's emotional state: 'since we cannot know the experience or sentiments of another person, we must represent in our imagination copies of the sentiments that we ourselves feel as we imagine ourselves in someone else's place and person'.[24] To imagine myself in the place of the other is to imagine how that person might feel and think. Doing so is easier for those others who are friends and intimates, since they are likely to be aware of specific circumstances of one another's lives that might affect the nature of their experience. They combine a particularly well-informed and hence reliable exercise of the imagination with emotion in taking the perspective of the other. Consequently, they are in a better position than many others to appreciate the possibilities for redescribing reality that imaginative transfer presents. They are also in a better position to provide feedback to one another as regards the development of a reliable and enduring concept of self.

Balance in an Unstable Enterprise

It may appear paradoxical that the capacity to put oneself imaginatively in the place of another, to imagine how a situation is experienced from the perspective of the other, aids in the development of one's own capacity for rational self-assessment, since, of course, we cannot know the experience or sentiments of another person. R. D. Laing and Alfred Schutz recognise the impossibility of being able to experience someone else's experience. Schutz acknowledges that the everyday world is from its outset a social, cultural world in which we interrelate in manifold ways of interaction with fellow human beings known to us in varying degrees of intimacy and anonymity. Consequently we can only understand others' experience, their motives and goals, fragmentarily and briefly – in particular situations. Schutz goes on to argue that we experience others' motives and goals in their typicality and that these typified patterns of others' behaviour become in turn motives of our own action.[25] The subjective meaning which others bestow upon their actions is only fragmentarily available to us, but for both Schutz and Laing, we do experience them as best we can – in their typicality or as they appear to us. Schutz's view is that our own behaviour is affected by the assessments we make of the typical patterns of the motives and ends of other agents. And certainly we imitate others, and this impetus to imitate is advantageous, since it ensures the survival and transmission of codes of behaviour that guarantee the identity and cohesion of society.[26] This kind of view emphasises not only that we do in fact put ourselves in the place of others, but that doing so is a commonplace of the process of socialisation. As I have argued, in friendship and in relation to the degree of the intimacy we share with friends, we have greater access to the subjective meaning friends bestow on their actions, greater understanding of their experience, and an appreciation of how and why their patterns of behaviour might differ from what we take to be typical. However, as Simmel points out above, the differentiated nature of modern friendship places limitations on the access that modern friends have to one another's lives. Our conception of the identity of a friend and our understanding of the friend can only be built upon those spheres of life that we have in common, and hence may be fragmentary.

From Ricoeur's point of view, it is the imagination which provides the milieu within which we compare and contrast motives,[27] and which therefore would enable us to develop both the typified patterns of others' behaviour for which Schutz argues, and the particular patterns that might be exhibited by friends. In imagining ourselves in the place of others we gain access to their perceptions and experiences, and these provide us with the basis for our understanding and assessment of the subjective meaning others impose upon their experience. Of course, we could try to establish this by simply asking the other about her perceptions, experience and feelings, provided that we are assured of an honest reply; and between friends this kind of enquiry is facilitated by the degree of the trust and intimacy they share. But, even within friendship, it is not always appropriate or possible to do so.

In cases where I suspect a friend's perceptions of me to be negative or perhaps to be unfair, I might be reluctant to ask my friend about his perceptions or feelings. Rather I might first try to imagine myself in his place, to consider whether his apparent assessment of me might seem justifiable from his perspective. A complex process of balancing and counterbalancing of perceptions and assessments occurs as I try to interpret the other's behaviour and to establish its significance for me and for our friendship. This involves me in rational assessment of the import of the perspectives of the other; but it also demands some acknowledgement of the value and also the shortcomings of imagination and of the nexus between imagination and emotion in attributing meaning. The decision as to whether the opinions and assessments of others are just or credible is not straightforward. We must bring a tempered scepticism to our deliberations on these matters – to be somewhat sceptical of the regard of others without being dismissive of it; to take it seriously but not unquestioningly. The acts of balance and judgement involved in this process cannot be determined ahead of our interactions with others and our participation in social and cultural discourse. The uncertainty and indeterminacy that accompany them are part of what it is to be a self.

The complexity of this process of balance and judgement is increased as we recognise that we must learn to assign weight or significance to the views of others, who, as Gregory Bateson argues, are often as complexly motivated as we are ourselves. Bateson makes these comments in the context of an explanation of human verbal communication. He argues that our verbal communication can and always does operate at many contrasting levels of abstraction, and he gives examples of metalinguistic and metacommunicative messages implicit in discourse. For him, an important stage in the evolution of communication occurs when we cease to respond 'automatically' to the mood-signs of another and become able to recognise communicative signs as signals. As he puts it, each one of us must learn 'to recognise that the other individual's and its own signals are only signals, which can be trusted, distrusted, falsified, denied, amplified, corrected and so forth'.[28]

Given the trust implicit between friends, we might expect that these difficulties are minimised in friendship and close interpersonal relationships. However, Bateson is right to remind us that we are complexly motivated creatures. We are not always transparent to ourselves, and our motivations often reveal themselves to us – and to others – within our interactions with those close to us. Thus a tempered scepticism is as critical to reflection upon our own opinions and perceptions as it is to those of others, since each of us is prone to misrepresentation, misidentification, error and deception.

As I have argued in the previous chapter, the ability to imagine oneself in the place of the other is important to the development of a stable conception of self. This is in turn crucial to the capacity for mature engagement with friends. The healthily narcissistic self is able to balance rational self-concern with liking, care and concern for a friend for that friend's own sake. But since the ability to take imaginatively the perspective of the other does not give us direct access to the thoughts and feelings of others, it involves us in a delicate process of interpretation. Bateson's emphasis on human communication as an evolutionary process that occurs at different levels of abstraction, and on our natures as complexly motivated beings, reminds us of the difficulties inherent in our interpretive activity. Chapter 5 makes reference to this activity, noting that our skills in linguistic construction and in making imaginative transfers of thought and feeling are supplemented by skills in drawing inferences and in distilling consistent ideas from our perceptions. Given that these are features of social interaction in general, we must acknowledge them as foundational to our relations with friends.

The fragmentation and differentiation of modern friendship, to which Simmel draws attention, underscore the notion that – despite our intimacy – a friend's experience, perceptions, motives and goals are none the less only fragmentarily available to us; and this is often on the basis of analogy with our own experience. Despite the intimacy of our relationship with friends, our interpretative activity must remain to some extent creative and exploratory; as a consequence it is uncertain and ought to be open to revision. Traditional philosophical emphases on similarity, shared activity and mutual liking between friends disguise the relevance to friendship of the kind of interpretive activity identified here. What we share with friends and our similarities must be balanced by a recognition of our difference and a consideration of the degree of access we have to one another's experience. These considerations imply that friendship is potentially a fragile and unstable enterprise. But they are two factors among a variety of factors that impact upon the stability of friendship and the nature and quality of our engagement with friends. One of the most important of these factors is the role of choice in friendship.

The fact that relations between friends are predicated on freedom of choice determines that the relationship is less stable than more formal relationships in which we engage. Questions about commitment between friends, what can be expected of a friend, about the notion of duty in friendship and about what to do in the face of conflict with friends are open-ended. As Chapter 4 argues, friendship is characterised by a curious degree of uncertainty with regard to expectations and obligations. Formal ties might oblige us to remain in contact with others despite disappointment or disagreement. They might bring with them moral or legal responsibilities which demand that we put aside feelings of animosity to fulfil those responsibilities. In the face of conflict or disappointment in friendship, we can choose to abandon the relationship, rather than deal with the source of the conflict. Of course we can abandon our relationship with relatives too, but as Cicero reminds us, they still remain our relatives, while a lost or abandoned friend is no longer a friend.

The lost or abandoned friendship leaves its trace on us, in terms of its impact upon our conception of friendship. It might close us to possibility, perhaps cementing a view of friendship as a relationship based on similarity in which any expression of difference or failure to meet the other's expectations is a fatal challenge to the relationship. It might lead us to question our view of the value of friendship, to make it less central or important to our lives. Conflict can, however, provide an opportunity to consider and respond to the challenge that the discovery of difference presents to friendship and to the recognition of distance that difference implies. Some difference can be devastating to friendship – as the conflict between Nel and Sula in Toni Morrison's novel *Sula* indicates. But conflict can also lead to a revision of one's view of friendship. Henrik undergoes precisely this kind of revision of his relationship with Konrad in Márai's novel *Embers*, when, as we saw in Chapter 3, he comes to the view that friendship is a duty. Conflict can also revitalise a friendship if the friends are able to tolerate any disappointment or hurt that the conflict causes, and can use the experience to come to a better understanding of one another, of themselves and of relations with friends in general.

The stability of friendship, as well as the nature and quality of our engagement with friends, can also be affected by social and economic factors, since these can impact on our ability to engage in relations with friends. Colin Turnbull in his book *The Mountain People* presents an extreme example of the effect of severe and prolonged material deprivation on the development and maintenance of friendships among the Ik.[29] His work suggests that some minimal level of security with regard to the provision of material resources is necessary to the cultivation of friendship relations. Some of Turnbull's critics insist that he has overstated his case. But among the ancients, Cicero certainly recognised that friendships may be unable to withstand the pressure of fierce competition – in Cicero's case, for power and political influence, rather than for material resources. However, as the story of the friendship of Pylades and Orestes or of Patroclus and Achilles indicates, some friends will be prepared to sacrifice their own interests in favour of the interests of a friend, even at extreme cost to themselves.

As we saw, Kant and Kierkegaard attempt to insulate human social relationships from instability by eschewing the notion of preference. For them, the crucial feature of concern for the other for that other's own sake is our recognition of the other's value as a fellow human being – a value the other shares with all others. But this approach leads Kierkegaard to dismiss friendship and love altogether, as essentially forms of idolatry or self-love.[30] Although Kant also rejects the moral worth of relations founded on preference, he does acknowledge that where we care for the happiness of others and where this care is reciprocated, the happiness of each is promoted by the generosity of the other. For Kant, '[t]his is the Idea of friendship, in which self-love is superseded by a generous reciprocity of love'.[31] So for Kant friendship becomes an ethical Idea, derived from the understanding rather than from experience. It enables us to measure the extent to which actual friendships are defective. Actual friendships are suspect to the extent that they focus on our regard for the friend as a particular individual, rather than on that generous reciprocity of love that we can extend to all our fellow human beings. Chapter 4 suggests an interpretation of Kant's views that might allow the moral worth of friendship to be appreciated despite its exclusivity and preference. Friendship might be seen as underpinned by or founded upon Kantian practical love. However, an explicit recognition by friends that they are valued for their status as fellow human beings rather than for themselves, while it might promote stability in interpersonal relationships, is likely to undermine friendship. As Stern-Gillet so clearly points out, modern friendship gives pride of place to the unicity or uniqueness of friends and to their individual irreplaceability.[32]

This focus on unicity and irreplaceability along with the differentiated nature of modern friendship once again draws attention to difference among individual friends. If we were to attempt to explain what it is that is unique about an individual friend, we might try to articulate what it is that distinguishes her from others: her qualities and talents, the values that give her life meaning, her place in the society in which she lives and perhaps her view of that society. These considerations will impact on the formation of that individual's friendships. If, for example, what is crucial to me as an individual living in a modern Western society is how my status might be measured in terms of my wealth and material possessions, then the accumulation of wealth will be a major focus of my life. I am likely to admire and enjoy the company of those who are wealthy. I may envy such people. These sentiments may act as further incentives in my quest to accumulate wealth, but they are also likely to determine that I seek out the company of those who are wealthy, that I attempt to develop relationships with such people. Where I discover companions I like and who share my perspective on life, I am likely to look for opportunities to engage in interaction with them in the hope of developing friendships. Our shared interest in wealth and its accumulation will provide the basis of these relationships. Those qualities or features that distinguish me from certain others become the basis of my identification or 'feeling-with' my wealthy friends.

My quest to accumulate wealth will influence the nature of my engagement with friends. However, my quest will also inevitably involve me in activities that have consequences for others. I shall have to make decisions about the conduct of my business, the nature of my investments, the prices at which commodities are sold, the salaries paid to employees, the time I devote to other spheres of my life. I may have to face conflict among my values; ethical values may be found to compete with economic considerations. I shall have to make choices and these may well be uncomfortable. However, the discomfort of these choices might be alleviated if I make them in a social milieu within which economic considerations are generally given priority over ethical ones. If my friends and companions share my perspective on life, and are perhaps like-minded business associates, then they will share my inclination to give priority to economic considerations or to justify ethical failures in terms of positive economic consequences.

Aristotle would tell me that I am engaged in a relationship that can only be regarded as a qualified friendship. It is friendship only incidentally, on the basis of its analogy with primary friendship in which the friends are friends 'for each other's sake, because their bond is goodness'.[33] Aristotle may well be right to characterise my relationship in this way. My friendship is at bottom instrumental in focus; my friends serve to stimulate, enhance and provide approbation of the major goal of my life: the accumulation of wealth. But I am unlikely to appreciate an Aristotelian characterisation of my relationships. Like the so-called 'friends' Boissevain discusses in his study of friendship among the members of the mafiosi, I am likely to be perplexed by an Aristotelian characterisation of my relationships. The mafioso is immersed in a culture that is indifferent or hostile to legal restraint. What we take to be the skewed or distorted moral framework of the Mafia's members would presumably make it difficult for them to recognise the value Aristotle sees in primary friendship, or the inferiority of friendships of utility. This is a dramatic example of the way in which cultural understandings can influence the nature and quality of our relationships with friends. Despite Aristotle's qualification of friendships of utility and pleasure as inferior kinds of friendship, he none the less still describes these relationships as friendships; and I argue that we would not want to deny that such relationships are friendships. Regardless of their inferiority, the friendships of utility I imagine myself engaged in above must, after all, be distinguishable from purely commercial relationships or alliances with business colleagues.

Aristotle argues in the *Nichomachean Ethics* that friends of utility do not spend much time together and may not even like one another.[34] This suggests that utility friendships might not be distinguishable from business or commercial relationships. Within modern societies in which friends participate in only certain spheres of one another's lives, relations between friends are equally ambiguous. We may have colleagues who share in our lives by virtue of our common employment or commercial interests, but whom we regard as friends. The distinction between these friendships and friendships that Aristotle might identify as primary friendships is not as clear as an anachronistic application of his taxonomy to modern friendship might suggest. The distinction is complicated by the fact that friendships with fellow employees or business associates share aspects with features constitutive of Aristotle's primary friendship: the friends engage in shared activity, they are like-minded, they profess to like each other and are useful to one another. Aristotle himself acknowledges this overlap in his discussion of primary friendship. Thus a modern friendship between fellow employees might be established on the basis of utility, and it might well be inherently unstable, given that the utility of the relationship to its participants might evaporate for any number of reasons. But the relationship cannot be regarded as a friendship at all if its utility to the friends becomes its explicit objective.

The demand for indirection of intention that Chapter 4 argues is requisite to friendship is a crucial factor in the designation of these relationships as friendships. Friends must show some concern for one another in themselves, rather than simply for the advantage they gain from their relationship. John Cooper argues that Aristotle, in the *Politics*, emphasises that mere mutual commerce does not involve the participants in any interest in one another as persons, any concern for the kind of people they are, while civic friendship – which is a form of utility friendship – does.[35] The implication is that at least in one example of utility friendship there is some indirection of intention present. Aristotle may mean to imply that some concern for friends in themselves is present in all friendships of utility, so that he may agree with my claim that some indirection of intention is necessary in all friendships. However, I hope to show that the tension in utility friendships between the enjoyment of mutual advantage and the participants' concern for one another in themselves is only apparent, and only worked out, in retrospect. This is one explanation of the ambiguous nature of modern friendship.

The Ambiguity of Friendship

My claim is that modern participants in relationships that Aristotle might describe as friendships of utility or pleasure must demonstrate some regard for one another as individuals in themselves or for their own sake. The qualification of these kinds of friendships that Aristotle might make on the basis of utility or pleasure must remain unarticulated and unexplored. This makes such relationships ambiguous, since the utilitarian focus in a friendship of utility is not explicit and may not be clearly apparent to the participants; in fact it is unlikely to become apparent unless the utility is disturbed in some way. If my wealthy friend loses his fortune, the importance of his wealth to me as his friend might become apparent to me and to others. I might find myself with ambivalent feelings about him, feel uncomfortable in his presence or find myself avoiding his company. I could justify this to myself as an indication of my view that friendship is a relationship that is predicated on similarity and that the change in his circumstances makes it difficult for us to relate in the way we once did. My view of friendship is one that coincides with common assumptions about friendship and hence it provides me with an easy justification. And certainly, changes in circumstances, which might have any number of causes – a move to a different city or country, changes in one's domestic or family circumstances, illness, conversion to a particular religion – can sometimes make it difficult to continue relationships with friends. In modern societies the demands of employment often dictate high levels of mobility among the population, and this impacts upon our engagement with friends.

I might elaborate on the cooling of my friendship by arguing that what I enjoy in friendship is the idea or experience of intimate relations with friends who can provide me with a sense of accompaniment in life, and hence that I find it impossible to continue with the friendship, given my friend's change of fortunes. This might well be indicative of flaws in my character: of excessive self-concern or an inability to care for another for that person's own sake. But however jaundiced, inauthentic or superficial my analysis of the collapse of my friendship might appear to others, I might not go beyond this to question myself or my conception of friendship. My view of friendship as predicated on similarity and enjoyment might explain my inability to continue a friendship in the face of changes in my friend's fortunes, and it might also reinforce my reluctance to accept the challenge that change, unmet expectations or feelings of discomfort present to my conception of friendship.

However, rather than attempting to offer a justification, I might be forced to a recognition that the ground of our relationship was in fact its utility to me. This recognition presents me with a challenge. It might be a catalyst to reflection, both on myself and on the nature of my connection with others in friendship. I might be forced to recognise that I have little or no concern for the other in himself and to question my status as friend. My self-interest might be more apparent in a situation in which my friendship comes under stress because my business interests are directly affected. For example, my friend's commercial interests might come to intersect with mine, so that we are in competition with regard to a particular business venture. My success in this venture calls for ruthless behaviour with regard to the interests of my friend. Aristotle argues that friendships of utility will collapse under this kind of pressure: '[w]ith the disappearance of the ground for the friendship, the friendship breaks up, because that is what kept it alive'.[36] If I choose to act ruthlessly in this situation, utility will appear to be my over-riding concern within the relationship. Utility will be made explicit as the ground of the relationship, whereas up until this point the relationship between the utility of the relationship to the participants and their regard for one another in themselves has not been revealed. But this relationship must now be worked out.

Ruthless behaviour on my part may well lead to the collapse of the relationship. However, the reaction of my friend and business associate to my behaviour might determine what happens in the relationship. My friend might be prepared to tolerate this kind of behaviour, at least to some extent or within limits. When we try to explain this kind of reaction within the context of a conception of friendship, we might argue that my friend regards my behaviour as just what one ought to expect in these circumstances. Consequently my behaviour is not disturbing enough to outweigh the value of our relationship to him. This latter explanation brings to mind Chapter 1's discussion of Kant's attempt to provide a unified account of friendship. Kant argues that a friendship of need is presupposed in every friendship. He has in mind not crude material need, but the need for trust or confidence in the goodwill of others. Admittedly, the goodwill I extend to my friend in the above example is qualified, since I do not allow it to interfere with my commercial interests. However, my friend may accept this qualification as a fact of life in the business world and remain confident of my goodwill towards him in other spheres of life we happen to share. Alternatively he may be able to look beyond my apparent shortcomings to maintain the relationship none the less. My point in introducing these examples is to suggest that modern friendship is not neatly or easily accommodated within Aristotle's taxonomy, and to suggest that an individual's expectations of friendship will affect the nature of their engagement with friends. Different individuals will tolerate or expect different levels of commitment within friendship, and the same individuals may expect differing levels of commitment from friends depending upon the particular sphere of life they have in common with those friends. Our expectations of friendship in general may differ from the expectation of identity or fusion – which Montaigne's essay on friendship might lead us to expect – to the conviction that in fact 'there is no friend' – as the famous quotation attributed to Aristotle suggests.

The view of friendship explored in Chapter 3 presents a model of friendship predicated on difference, rather than similarity. Blanchot emphasises the fact that it is what separates us that puts us into authentic relation with one another as friends, while Nietzsche and Derrida point to the illusion of connection between friends, their recognition of their ultimate separation from one another, and yet given that separation, their unaccountable connection.[37] On this kind of view, friendship is inherently ambiguous. Here the ambiguity is not explained by the indirection of intention that I argue is requisite even to Aristotle's inferior kinds of friendship, if they are to be regarded as friendship. Rather the ambiguity is inherent in a conception of friendship that recognises both similarity and difference. This is a conception that acknowledges the impossibility of any complete and sustained connection between friends, but one which sees the value of what Derrida argues is the illusion of connection – or what I have referred to as the fiction of connection. Such a conception is open to divergence between friends – at least to some extent. It allows for and expects the expression of divergent opinion, divergent motivations, and is open to change and development.

Derrida suggests that given the illusory – or perhaps fictional – nature of the connection between friends, it is best that we keep silent about our unaccountable connection. Stern-Gillet's comments that modern friendships are fundamentally non-rational and perhaps not fit matters for close analytical scrutiny would seem to confirm Derrida's view. There does appear to be something unaccountable about the connection between friends.[38] As we saw in Chapter 2, Goethe in his novella *Elective Affinities* attempts to give our connection with others a substantial basis via an analogy between the affinity we feel with others and the notion of chemical attraction. The notion of a chemical affinity between friends undermines the Derridean view of the connection between friends as illusory. But even if Goethe's suggestion is correct, the claim that friendship is a voluntary relationship implies that we are responsible for the choices we make in friendship. Thus, either the notion of volition in friendship and the notion of 'chemical affinity' contradict one another, or any 'chemical affinity' that exists between friends is not decisive. As Chapter 2 argues, the attempt to provide a substantial foundation for the connection and liking between friends proves to be fraught with difficulty. If we instead try to explain our connection and liking for a friend by enumerating the various traits and qualities our friend possesses, we must none the less acknowledge that we do not narrowly identify the friend with those characteristics. We are left with a tension between liking our friend for his traits and qualities and liking him uniquely – as in some way a unique and irreplaceable instantiation of those traits and qualities. As we saw, Elizabeth Telfer uses the analogy between artistic endeavour and friendship that so often provides what seems the only way to explain motivation, attraction and activity in friendship. She argues that liking in friendship is difficult to analyse since it is 'a quasi-aesthetic attitude', akin to 'finding a person to one's taste'.[39] She suggests that our reaction to friends is similar to our reaction to works of art in that what we appreciate is the whole personality as a unified thing.

The connection between friends is clearly difficult to explain, but we can only see it as founded on an error or an illusion if we take the illusion to be a commitment to the idea that friendship consists in a complete union. Derrida appears to take this view when he writes that the error or illusion on which friendship is founded resists its own abyss.[40] Friendship appears to be seen as founded on a fantasy of twinship and an identity of impulses between friends, which resists the truth of the abyss it faces. However, the connection between friends can be seen as one that is intersubjectively created and nurtured. On this view, it is a fictional connection in the sense that it is imagined by the parties to the friendship, who none the less recognise the impossibility of complete union. The connection is supported and cultivated by shared activity, reciprocal services, mutual enjoyment and understanding, indications of respect and trust, and expressions of affection. But it is a fragile connection, given the variety of factors that affect our inclination and our capacity to form friendships, and given its dependence upon cultivation.

A model of friendship predicated on difference alerts us to the illusion of the ideal of complete union or twinship between friends, and emphasises instead the inherent ambiguity of a relationship in which we are forced to recognise simultaneously our ultimate separateness from our friends and yet, given that separation, our unaccountable connection with them. It is the shock of difference that Márai's novel uncovers which leads Henrik to argue that life is only bearable when we know who we are; that is, when we come to terms – without illusion – with the person we are in our own eyes and in the eyes of our friends. Derrida quotes Nietzsche to suggest that we may not want friends who actually know about us, and that those friends who do know about one another had best keep silent if they are to remain friends. But Nietzsche none the less advises that recognising the 'inextricable interweaving of character, occupation, talent and environment' that occurs in relations between friends might free us from the bitterness of disappointment in friendship.[41] The implication is that the recognition of difference is crucial to authentic relations between friends, and that it may ameliorate our pain or disappointment in the face of conflict or injury. Márai's protagonist Henrik illustrates the force of this view when he comments that solitude – imposed by his recognition of the gulf between himself and Konrad – has brought him knowledge.[42] Thus in the face of injury we can come to appreciate the nature of our connection with friends as an intersubjectively created and cultivated synthesis. This is a synthesis that must accommodate – and is therefore complicated by – an interweaving of different factors, and not least among these is the complex nature of our motivations.

Concluding Remarks

Models of friendship based on similarity seek to identify criteria upon which our union or affinity with others is established. However, the difficulty of explaining our connection with friends is only complicated by claims that the relationship is non-rational; that any sense of complete union or fusion is based on an illusory ideal; and that the modern concept of friendship is indistinct. By comparison, a conception of friendship which takes account of difference changes the focus of our attention. It provides a context within which change, disagreement and conflict are more likely to act as catalysts to reflection on the nature of our connection with others, on our own behaviour and on that of our friends. Within that context our motives in friendship and the motives of others are more likely to be apparent to us.

Aristotle, Cicero and Emerson all see the difficulty of a failure to recognise our separateness from the other in friendship. They call for self-sufficiency and self-possession to avoid a clawing dependence on friends. But in fact such calls suggest that the emphasis in the philosophical tradition on union, affinity and similarity among friends is founded on an insufficient acknowledgement of difference in friendship. The emphasis on union simply maintains the illusion that Derrida identifies as a tempting but impossible ideal of fusion. Derrida, in discussing the work of Blanchot, suggests that 'there is no longer a friend in the sense of what the entire tradition has taught us'; that the Greeks have provided us with a model of what is excellent in human relations, but that it is 'blurred, complicated, neutralized' by the enigmatic character it receives from opposite imperatives with the model – 'at once pure reciprocity and unrequited generosity'.[43] The fragmented and differentiated nature of modern friendships and the indistinctness of the concept in general make the demands of the philosophical tradition difficult to apply to modern friendship.

My argument is that friendship is best understood as a 'family resemblance' concept. Aspects of that concept can be enriched by 'what the tradition has taught us', but that concept is – to adapt Cicero's terminology – a kaleidoscopic and complicated thing. Wittgenstein's comments about 'family resemblance' concepts state that 'a complicated network of similarities overlapping and criss-crossing' is revealed in analysis of the various senses of such terms.[44] The analysis of the various uses of the term reveals no one sense as ideal or definitive of its usage. To understand the term we must consider how it is used within various contexts. In contemporary literature, the term 'friendship' is often used to refer to relationships that are freely chosen; that are characterised by mutual liking, affection and enjoyment; and that flourish in shared and reciprocal activity and in steady, free and mutual cultivation. Friendship is taken to be a relationship in which the participants like and show concern for one another for their own sakes, rather than out of any narrow self-interest or ulterior motive. This last criterion is one that Aristotle takes to be definitive of relations between friends of the best kind, and modern friendships in which the friends exhibit this attitude are highly esteemed. It is a criterion that must have some application to forms of friendship that Aristotle would have described as inferior. If friendships which Aristotle would have regarded as friendships of utility are able to be distinguished from thoroughly instrumental relationships – such as purely commercial relationships, business alliances, or relationships between individuals who find themselves as joint members of a team – then friends of utility must demonstrate some degree of liking, care and concern for one another for the others' own sakes; at least within the limits of their capacity to do so.

It is possible to find relationships in which the participants are referred to as friends, but in which some of the typical criteria or assumptions are absent. Within ancient Greek conceptions of friendship, guest-friendships fall into this category. Guest-friends might have a relationship by virtue of an obligation inherited as a result of family history. Affective considerations and the concept of choice in friendship are not applicable to these relationships, since the guest-friends might not even know one another. The relationships can be imposed upon individuals as duties and may be maintained purely out of self-interest. These friends may not even like one another.

Within a contemporary context we encounter similar relationships. Individuals referred to as 'family friends' may in fact be people with whom we have little in common and may not particularly like. The relationship we share with them has perhaps been inherited from another family member or is a function of being a member of a particular family. Consequently we acknowledge and participate – at least to some degree – in a relationship we refer to as friendship, despite the qualifications that apply to it.

With regard to the development of our notions of friendship, we refer to the relationships in which young children engage as friendships. This is despite our recognition that young children initially take a procedural approach to friendship, in which they engage in some of the outward manifestations of friendship. As they mature they move into the later stages of development and to more substantive notions of friendship; they begin to appreciate the perspective of the other, to develop an appreciation of the otherness of the friend, and to recognise demands for reciprocity and the potential for intimacy.[45] Thus children move from a view of friendship as a relationship focused on self, which is perhaps pleasant and advantageous to the self, to gradually less self-centred conceptions. However, the early stages are none the less referred to as friendships. We might argue that they are friendships on the basis of two interrelated conditions: they are identified as friendships by those close to the children and perhaps by the children themselves; and they satisfy some of the criteria we identify as typical of friendship, such as joint activity and spending time together. If we recognise friendship as a family resemblance concept, this identification will be acceptable, since there will be no one relationship between individuals that can be identified as an archetypical example of friendship.

The preceding examples illustrate variety in the usage of the term 'friendship', but are peripheral uses of the term. However, we do engage with others whom we are not hesitant to describe as friends, despite certain misgivings about the nature of our relationship; friendships in which we have misgivings about the quality or degree of mutual affection or the quality of reciprocity are examples. I might be disturbed by what appears to be an imbalance of affection or wonder about the level of my friend's commitment to our relationship. I might be puzzled to find that a friendship which appeared to be fading is suddenly reignited, or upset to find that my friend appears to have lost interest in our friendship. As a consequence of a change in circumstance or of conflict, I might suspect that my friend and I differ in our understanding of the ground of our friendship. Simmel would argue that these kinds of difficulties are likely to emerge in modern society, given the nature of the differentiated friendships that are typical of modern life. Such friendships might connect us with others on the basis of a variety of shared features: our common intellectual interests, common religious impulses, shared place of employment, similar social roles, or joint participation in sport. There is much that is not revealed to us – and as Simmel suggests, perhaps even concealed from us – in differentiated friendships. Pressures from spheres of life that friends do not share can undermine a relationship; changes in employment, social role or place of residence can also affect such friendships. From an Aristotelian perspective, these could well prove to be relationships that would fit into the category of friendships of utility or pleasure and hence be regarded as qualified friendships. But modern friendships in which the friends regard their liking and care for one another in themselves as the focus of the relationship can also be undermined or attenuated by changes in the circumstances of the friends, such as the imposition of distance.

In enumerating a variety of usages of the term 'friendship', I do not mean to imply that some of the constitutive criteria of the concept are not more common or more appealing than others. If we take the concept of family resemblance literally, we recognise that within a family, resemblance between family members might be predicated on a certain feature or features: most members of a family might share a particular physical trait or traits, such as particularly short stature and red hair. For the casual observer, these physical features might be identified as the best indicators of membership in a particular family – appearance being a relatively reliable indicator of family resemblance. By analogy with family resemblance, there are features that might appear more commonly than others in relationships identified as friendships, and Telfer's conditions of friendship embody these. Other features might be more appealing in terms of their ethical or social value. The notion that friendship entails liking, care and concern for a friend for the friend's own sake falls into this category. Liking and care for a friend for her own sake are facilitated by the indirection of intention that Chapter 4 argues is necessary to friendship of the best kind. Indirection of intention rejects any narrow instrumental focus on a particular project or outcome that we wish to undertake in relation to the friend; rather it places our focus on the friend herself and her concerns. The value of a model of friendship predicated on difference rather than similarity is clear here. The recognition of difference encourages a view of the other as separate from ourselves; it alerts us to the possibility that the friend's desires, motives and concerns might conflict with our own and that we might need to tolerate some friction, or accept difference and perhaps some disappointment. At the same time, a model of friendship predicated on difference alerts us to the force of the view expressed in Chapter 5, that is, the need to balance our concern for the friend in herself with a rational self-concern.

Modern friends might regard certain of their friendships as primary friendships by analogy with Aristotelian friendships of the best kind. Examples of friendship that we admire and to which we may aspire are provided by relationships that are relatively permanent, and in which friends appear to exhibit liking, care and concern for one another in themselves, notwithstanding the difficulty of establishing what this kind of motivation entails; by relationships in which the friends are not self-interested, and in which they prove themselves to be trustworthy and commendable characters. The appeal of such forms of friendship lies not in any sense that these are archetypical cases of friendship, but in their ethical implications and in the value of their achievements. What we appreciate in the best kinds of friendship might be the pleasure of genuine engagement, but we also appreciate achievements in terms of the development of our more commendable qualities or in our dispositions: we might regard ourselves as better persons, develop a deeper understanding of ourselves and of others, or find that we are happier as a consequence of the friendship. These achievements are by-products of our genuine engagement, and hence these friendships differ from those in which self-interest plays a more obvious role; where gains in terms of wealth, power and influence, or perhaps employment opportunities, are important motivating factors of engagement in the relationship.

Stern-Gillet points out that one of the important differences between these two kinds of relationship is that those friendships which approximate to Aristotelian primary friendship bring with them achievements that cannot be the focus of competition between friends. Fine character and self-knowledge are not benefits achieved by one person at the expense of another; they are non-material and non-tangible benefits. In fact, as Aristotle himself argues, we are likely to be able to accelerate these kinds of achievements by assisting one another in their development.[46] What friendships of the best kind and friendships of utility have in common from an ethical perspective is the fact that the benefits which accrue to the participants cannot be the sole objective of the friendships. If social advantage or financial benefits become explicit as the ground upon which a friendship is predicated, then those objectives will frustrate and destroy the enterprise. Similarly, if the development of a fine character or self-understanding were to become the explicit focus of a friendship, it would also flounder. A benefit can be seen as a by-product of the nature of our engagement with friends, or as the ground of the friendship. However, in practice, the distinction between the statuses of the benefit in these two cases is likely to be vague. That distinction is best appreciated from within particular friendships, to which friends bring differing needs, understandings and expectations. The demand that some element of liking and concern for a friend in himself or herself be present in all relationships between friends might only be minimally satisfied in some relationships; and individual friends will have their own responses to the degree of commitment evident in circumstances in which a friend's less honourable motives are revealed. But however superficially the demand for concern for a friend in himself or herself is satisfied, its satisfaction undermines the force of Aristotle's taxonomy. The three kinds of friendship Aristotle identifies are not absolutely distinguishable from one another on the basis of this demand; and, as we saw in Chapter 2, Aristotle himself appears to acknowledge this.

The differentiated nature of modern friendship only exacerbates the difficulty of satisfying this demand, since we may not be aware of aspects of a friend's character that are crucial to the capacity to care for the friend for that friend's own sake. Further, since modern friends do not necessarily relate to one another in terms of their moral goodness, they do not expect their friends to be paragons of virtue. By comparison, Aristotle argues that friends of the best kind are good men similar in their goodness. Their concern for one another is mediated by a set of impersonal values. Thus the Aristotelian good man identifies his friend with the friend's goodnesss, wisdom and fine character. From the perspective of modern readers of Aristotle, this identification is problematic. It suggests that the participants in an Aristotelian primary friendship are no better placed in terms of the requirement to love and care for a friend for the friend's own sake than are friends of utility or pleasure. Aristotelian friends of the good are forced to associate one another with Aristotle's normative view of selfhood. As Stern-Gillet argues:

> Aristotle sets out to identify the conditions which individuals must meet in order actually to become what they have it in them to become. While Aristotle's modern successors focus on the unicity of individuals, he is concerned with specific essences. Unsurprisingly therefore, their theories of the identity of persons are descriptive in intent while his notion of self, following from prior claims of proper human function (*ergon*), is primarily normative.[47]

We might agree that many of the characteristics Aristotle gives the good man are admirable. In fact – as Stern-Gillet also points out – as modern friends we might 'generally want to be loved for qualities which are both commendable and central to our personality'; and hence our intuitions about the best kinds of friendship are perhaps not so different from Aristotle's.[48] But modern friendships do not focus on the impersonal values of goodness or contemplation. Part of the explanation of this lies in the fact that modern friendships emphasise unicity or uniqueness, so that to be concerned for a friend for that friend's own sake is to be concerned with him as a unique individual – rather than to be concerned with his goodness. However, this leaves modern friends with the dilemma referred to repeatedly within this book: we want to be able to explain our attraction to a friend on the basis of her uniqueness, but when we try to encapsulate or articulate that uniqueness we are forced to focus on the appeal of a set of qualities or traits possessed by the friend, but not necessarily unique to her. Telfer's suggestion that we explain our reaction to a friend by analogy with our reaction to a work of art gives us a new framework for reflection, but the dilemma none the less remains. We have no alternative but to accept it and to recognise that what Derrida describes as our unaccountable connection with friends is in fact the result of a creative enterprise. This is an enterprise in which individuals engage imaginatively and practically to develop and cultivate a synthesis of their understandings and expectations of friendship. This synthesis is most authentically achieved by those who are alive to their own motivations in interacting with friends. Friendships are always under negotiation in action and in response to the various constraints and limitations imposed on them. The idea of complete union between friends is tempting, but its impossibility alerts us to the ambiguity and fragility of a relationship of connection that is predicated upon difference.

A turn to focus on the difference underlying the connection beween friends provides us with an indirect means of attempting to ensure that our concern is focused on the other for his or her own sake, since it emphasises the other's separation from us. It encourages us to appreciate what Blanchot refers to as 'the movement of understanding in which, speaking to us, they [our friends] reserve, even on the most familiar terms, an infinite distance, the fundamental separation on the basis of which what separates becomes relation'.[49] This appreciation reminds us that the connection to the world with which friends provide one another is one that is not forced on us or determined by circumstance. A model of friendship which emphasises difference, rather than similarity, opens the relationship to possibility, and of course to the vulnerability inherent in possibility, since the relationship may not survive the strain that difference can impose on it. However, the experience of intimate relations with friends can provide us with a sense of accompaniment in life, with different perspectives on life, and hence it can broaden our own experience vicariously and widen our moral horizons. It may challenge us to think differently about life and about ourselves, and perhaps to act differently in the world. Our interactions with friends open us to the hope that these possibilities might be uncovered, to the degree that we are ready and able to embrace them; and we might be only minimally prepared to embrace the possibilities that friendship offers. However, it is a curious feature of friendship that these possibilities – which we might think of as benefits or rewards – will not be revealed to us and will not materialise, if our purpose in engaging in friendship is to achieve and enjoy them. The benefits are by-products of engagement in friendship with a friend for that friend's own sake.

Notes

1. Simmel, *The Sociology of Georg Simmel*, p. 326.
2. Ibid., p. 326.
3. Ibid., pp. 137–8.
4. Stern-Gillet, *Aristotle's Philosophy of Friendship*, p. 75.
5. Márai, *Embers*, p. 54.
6. Ibid., pp. 138–9.
7. Malouf, *An Imaginary Life*, p. 145.
8. Cicero, 'On Friendship', XXI, 77–8, p. 107.
9. MacIntyre, *After Virtue*, p. 203.
10. Lacan, *Écrits*, p. 1.
11. Ibid., p. 4.
12. Ibid., p. 211.
13. Ibid., pp. 43 and 49–55. This is a process which is importantly repeated in the 'interlocution' between the psychoanalyst and her subject – that is, in 'the inter-subjective continuity of the discourse in which the subject's history is consti-tuted'. For Lacan the unconscious is part of that discourse, 'in so far as it is transindividual, that is not at the disposal of the subject in re-establishing the continuity of his conscious discourse' (p. 43).
14. Ricoeur, 'The Hermeneutical Function of Distanciation', in *Hermeneutics and the Human Sciences*, p. 133.
15. Ibid., p. 133. Ricoeur draws on the work of Ferdinand de Saussure and Louis Hjelmslev to make these distinctions.
16. Ibid., p. 132.
17. Ricoeur, 'Imagination in Discourse and Action', p. 131; and 'What Is a Text? Explanation and Understanding', in *Hermeneutics and the Human Sciences*, p. 145. Ricoeur's argument is that the objective meaning of a text is open to inter-pretation; it is not something which can be explained simply by reference to the author's intentions.
18. Telfer, 'Friendship', pp. 266–7.
19. Mill, *Autobiography*, p. 91.
20. Ibid., p. 92.
21. Booth, *The Company We Keep*, pp. 70–5.
22. Ricoeur, 'On Interpretation', p. 191.
23. However, for Ricoeur there is no possibility of total mediation, no chance that the subject can become transparent to itself, precisely because of the possibil-ities which texts unfold, discover and reveal; '[t]o understand oneself is to understand oneself as one confronts the text and to receive from it the condi-tions for a self other than that which first undertakes the reading' (ibid., p. 193). In 'The Hermeneutical Function of Distanciation' (in *Hermeneutics and the Human Sciences*, p. 144), Ricoeur elaborates on the role of the reader: '[a]s reader, I find myself only by losing myself. Reading introduces me into the imag-inative variations of the *ego*', emphasising the sense in which the text is a site of potentiality for the reader, and not least for the reader who is also writer.
24. Marshall, *The Surprising Effects of Sympathy*, especially, p. 5.
25. Schutz, *Collected Papers. I: The Problem of Social Reality*, p. 61. As Laing puts this point: '"[m]y experience of you" is just another form of words for "you-as-I-experience-you"' (*Politics of Experience*, p. 16).

26. This is a view of imitation expressed by Elena Russo, 'The Self, Real and Imaginary: Social Sentiment in Marivaux and Hume', p. 128.
27. Ricoeur, 'Imagination in Discourse and Action', p. 126.
28. Bateson, *Steps to an Ecology of Mind*, p. 151.
29. See Chapter 2's discussion of Turnbull.
30. Kierkegaard, 'You Shall Love Your Neighbour', pp. 244–5.
31. Kant, 'Lecture on Friendship', pp. 210–11. This discussion of Kant focuses on pp. 210–12 of his 'Lecture on Friendship'.
32. Stern-Gillet, *Aristotle's Philosophy of Friendship*, pp. 8 and 75.
33. Aristotle, *Nichomachean Ethics*, 1157a34–b20.
34. Ibid., 1156a16–b2.
35. Cooper, 'Political Animals and Civic Friendship', p. 319.
36. Aristotle, *Nichomachean Ethics*, 1156a16–b2.
37. Derrida, *Politics of Friendship*, pp. 52–3.
38. Stern-Gillet, *Aristotle's Philosophy of Friendship*, p. 8.
39. Telfer, 'Friendship', p. 253.
40. Derrida, *Politics of Friendship*, p. 53.
41. Ibid.
42. Márai, *Embers*, p. 159.
43. Derrida, *Politics of Friendship*, pp. 299–300. Derrida is discussing *Michel Foucault as I Imagine Him* by Blanchot, Foucault and others.
44. Wittgenstein, *Philosophical Investigations*, S.66.
45. The research of Miraca Gross and Robert Selman into the development of children's friendships is discussed in Chapter 3.
46. Aristotle, *Nichomachean Ethics*, 1177a25–b13.
47. Stern-Gillet, *Aristotle's Philosophy of Friendship*, pp. 172–3.
48. Ibid., p. 177.
49. Blanchot, *Friendship*, p. 291.

Bibliography

Adkins, A. W. H. (1963), 'Friendship and "Self-Sufficiency" in Homer and Aristotle', *Classical Quarterly*, Vol. XIII, No. 1.

Aeschines [1919] (1968), *The Speeches of Aeschines*, C. D. Adams (ed.), London: William Heinemann.

Annas, Julia (1977), 'Plato and Aristotle on Friendship and Altruism', *Mind*, Vol. 86.

Aquinas, Thomas [1269–72] (1991), 'Questions on Love and Charity', in Michael Pakaluk (ed.), *Other Selves: Philosophers on Friendship*, Indianapolis: Hackett.

Aristotle [pre-335 BC] (1915), *The Eudemian Ethics*, W. D. Ross (ed.), *The Works of Aristotle*, Oxford: Oxford University Press.

Aristotle [335? BC] (1981), *The Politics*, trans. T. A. Sinclair, London: Penguin.

Aristotle [335? BC] (1983), *The Ethics of Aristotle: The Nichomachean Ethics*, trans. J. A. K. Thomson, Harmondsworth: Penguin.

Aristotle [335? BC] (1984), *The Complete Works of Aristotle*, Bollingen Series LXXI: 2, Jonathan Barnes (ed.), Princeton, NJ: Princeton University Press.

Badhwar, Neera Kapur (1993), 'Introduction', in Neera Kapur Badhwar (ed.), *Friendship – A Philosophical Reader*, Ithaca, NY: Cornell University Press.

Baier, Annette (1993), 'Hume: The Reflective Women's Epistemologist?', in Louise Antony and Charlotte Witt (eds), *A Mind Of One's Own*, Boulder, CO: Westview Press.

Baier, Annette (1994), *A Progress of Sentiments*, Cambridge, MA: Harvard University Press.

Baker, Howard and Margaret Baker (1987), 'Heinz Kohut's Self Psychology: An Overview', *American Journal of Psychiatry*, Vol. 144, No. 1, January.

Barth, Fredrik (1974), 'On Responsibility and Humanity: Calling a Colleague to Account', *Current Anthropology*, March.

Bartky, Sandra Lee (1997), 'Sympathy and Solidarity', in Diana Tietjens Meyer (ed.), *Feminists Rethink the Self*, Boulder, CO: Westview.

Bateson, Gregory (1973), *Steps to an Ecology of Mind*, London: Paladin.

Birch, Charles (1996), *Feelings*, Kensington, NSW: University of New South Wales Press.

Blanchot, Maurice (1977), *Friendship*, trans. Elizabeth Rottenberg, Stanford, CA: Stanford University Press.

Blum, Lawrence (1980), *Friendship, Altruism and Morality*, London: Routledge and Kegan Paul.

Blum, Lawrence (1990), 'Vocation, Friendship, and Community', in Owen Flanagan and Amélie Rorty (eds), *Identity, Character, and Morality – Essays in Moral Psychology*, Cambridge, MA: MIT Press.

Boissevain, Jeremy (1974), *Friends of Friends: Networks, Manipulations and Coalitions*, Oxford: Blackwell.

Booth, Wayne C. (1988), *The Company We Keep: An Ethics of Fiction*, Berkeley, CA: University of California Press.

Bowden, Peta (1997), *Caring – Gender-Sensitive Ethics*, London: Routledge.

Buber, Martin (1956), *The Writings of Martin Buber*, W. Herberg (ed.), New York: Meridian.

Chazan, Pauline (1998), *The Moral Self*, London and New York: Routledge.

Cicero [44 BC] (1991), 'On Friendship' (*De Amicitia*), in Michael Pakaluk (ed.), *Other Selves: Philosophers on Friendship*, Indianapolis: Hackett.

Cooper, John M. (1993), 'Political Animals and Civic Friendship', in Neera Kapur Badhwar (ed.), *Friendship – A Philosophical Reader*, Ithaca, NY: Cornell University Press.

Damasio, Antonio R. (1996), *Descartes' Error*, London: Macmillan.

Damasio, Antonio R. (2003), *Looking for Spinoza*, Orlando, FL: Harcourt.

Davis, John (2002), 'A Marxist Influence on Wittgenstein via Sraffa', in Gavin Kitching and Nigel Pleasants (eds), *Marx and Wittgenstein*, London and New York: Routledge.

De Beauvoir, Simone [1949] (1972), *The Second Sex*, Harmondsworth: Penguin.

Dennett, Daniel C. (1988), 'Why Everyone is a Novelist', *Times Literary Supplement*, September 16–22.

Denzin, Norman K. (1984), *On Understanding Emotion*, San Francisco: Jossey-Bass.

Derrida, Jacques (1997), *Politics of Friendship*, trans. George Collins, London: Verso.

de Sousa, Ronald (1980), 'The Rationality of Emotions', in Amélie O. Rorty (ed.), *Explaining Emotions*, Berkeley, CA: University of California Press.

Deutscher, Max (1983), *Subjecting and Objecting*, St Lucia: University of Queensland Press.

Dodds, E. R. (1973), *The Greeks and the Irrational*, Berkeley, CA: University of California Press.

Duck, Steve (1983), *Friends, For Life: The Psychology of Close Relationships*, Brighton: Harvester.

Dupont, Florence (1992), *Daily Life in Ancient Rome*, trans. Christopher Woodall, Oxford: Blackwell.

Emerson, Ralph Waldo [1840–1] (1991), 'Friendship', in Michael Pakaluk (ed.), *Other Selves: Philosophers on Friendship*, Indianapolis: Hackett.

Enç, Berent (1996), 'Hume's Unreasonable Desires', *History of Philosophy Quarterly*, Vol. 13, No. 2, April.

Erikson, Erik [1950] (1993), *Childhood and Society*, New York: W. W. Norton.

Foucault, Michel (1985), *The Uses of Pleasure: The History of Sexuality*, trans. Robert Hurley, Vol. 2, New York: Vintage.

Friedman, Marilyn (1993), 'Feminism and Modern Friendship: Dislocating the Community', in Neera Kapur Badhwar (ed.), *Friendship – A Philosophical Reader*, Ithaca, NY: Cornell University Press.

Gatens, Moira and Genevieve Lloyd (1999), *Collective Imaginings: Spinoza, Past and Present*, London and New York: Routledge.

Gelb, Arthur and Barbara Gelb (1962), *O'Neill*, London: Jonathan Cape.

Goethe, Johann Wolfgang von [1806] (1971), *Elective Affinities*, trans. R. J. Hollingdale, Harmondsworth: Penguin.

Gross, Miraca (2002), 'Gifted Children and the Gift of Friendship', *Understanding Our Gifted*, Vol. 15, No. 3, Spring.

Hegel, G. F. W. [1830] (1971), *Philosophy of Mind*, trans. W. Wallace, London: Clarendon Press.

Hegel, G. F. W. [1807] (1977), *The Phenomenology of Spirit*, trans. A. V. Miller, Oxford: Oxford University Press.

Heine, Bernd (1985), 'The Mountain People: Some Notes on the Ik of North-Eastern Uganda', *Africa*, Vol. 55, No. 1.

Heller, Agnes (1988) 'The Beauty of Friendship', in *Friendship*, special issue of *South Atlantic Quarterly*, Vol. 97, No.1.

Hirschman, Albert (1996), *A Propensity to Self-Subversion*, Cambridge, MA: Harvard University Press.

Homer [*c*. tenth century BC] (1891), *The Iliad of Homer*, trans. John Purves, London: Percival.

Hume, David [1888] (1978), *A Treatise of Human Nature*, L. A. Selby-Bigge (ed.), 2nd edn, Oxford: Clarendon Press.

Hutter, Horst (1978), *Politics as Friendship*, Waterloo, Ont.: Wilfrid Laurier University Press.

Jackson, Peter (1981), 'Relativism and the Character of Subjectivity in Homer's *Iliad*', unpublished masters thesis, Macquarie University, NSW.

Kahn, Edwin (1985), 'Heinz Kohut and Carl Rogers', *American Psychologist*, Vol. 40, No. 8, August.

Kant, Immanuel [1790] (1952), *The Critique of Judgement*, trans. James Creed Meredith, Oxford: Clarendon Press.

Kant, Immanuel [1775–80] (1991a), 'Lecture on Friendship', in Michael Pakaluk (ed.), *Other Selves: Philosophers on Friendship*, Indianapolis: Hackett.

Kant, Immanuel [1785] (1991b), *The Moral Law – Groundwork of the Metaphysic of Morals*, trans. H. J. Paton, London and New York: Routledge.

Kant, Immanuel [1785] (1996), 'Metaphysical First Principles of the Doctrine of Virtue', in *The Metaphysics of Morals*, trans. and ed. Mary Gregor, Cambridge: Cambridge University Press.

Katz, Stephen (1984), 'A Critical Review of Martin Buber's Epistemology of I-Thou', in *Martin Buber: A Centenary Volume*, Haim Gordon and Jochanan Bloch (eds), Jersey City: KTAV.

Kaufmann, Walter (1984), 'Buber's Failures and Triumph', in *Martin Buber: A Centenary Volume*, Haim Gordon and Jochanan Bloch (eds), Jersey City: KTAV.

Kierkegaard, Søren [1846–7] (1991), 'You Shall Love Your Neighbour', in Michael Pakaluk (ed.), *Other Selves: Philosophers on Friendship*, Indianapolis: Hackett.

Kohut, Heinz (1984), *How Does Analysis Cure?*, Arnold Goldberg and Paul Stepansky (eds), Chicago: Chicago University Press.

Kohut, Heinz and Philip F. D. Seitz (1978), 'Concepts and Theories of Psychoanalysis', in Paul H. Ornstein (ed.), *The Search for the Self*, Vol. I, New York: International Universities Press.

Korsgaard, Christine M. (1996), *Creating the Kingdom of Ends*, Cambridge: Cambridge University Press.

Lacan, Jacques (1977), *Écrits: A Selection*, trans. Alan Sheridan, New York: W. W. Norton.

Laing, R. D. (1967), *The Politics of Experience*, Harmondsworth: Penguin.

Laing, R. D. [1961] (1971), *Self and Others*, 2nd edn, Harmondsworth: Penguin.

Le Doux, Joseph (1998), *The Emotional Brain*, New York: Touchstone.

Lloyd, Genevieve (1994), *Part of Nature – Self-Knowledge in Spinoza's Ethics*, Ithaca, NY, and London: Cornell University Press.

Lloyd, Genevieve (1996), *Spinoza and the Ethics*, London: Routledge.

Lynch, Sandra (2002), 'Aristotle and Derrida on Friendship', *Contretemps 3: The Online Journal of Philosophy*, University of Sydney, July.

MacIntyre, Alasdair (1981), *After Virtue: A Study in Moral Theory*, Notre Dame: University of Notre Dame Press.

Malouf, David (1980), *An Imaginary Life*, Sydney: Pan.

Márai, Sándor [1942] (2001), *Embers*, trans. Carol Brown Janeway, London: Penguin.

Marshall, David (1988), *The Surprising Effects of Sympathy*, Chicago: University of Chicago Press.

Meissner, W. W. (1983), 'Phenomenology of the Self', in Arnold Goldberg (ed.), *The Future of Psychoanalysis*, New York: International Universities Press.

Mill, John Stuart (1957), *Autobiography*, New York: Liberal Arts Press.

Montaigne [1572–6, 1578–80] (1965), 'Of Friendship', in *The Complete Essays of Montaigne*, trans. Donald M. Frame, Stanford, CA: Stanford University Press.

Morrison, Toni (1973), *Sula*, New York: Plume Books.

Mulgan, Richard (2000), 'The Role of Friendship in Aristotle's Political Theory', in P. King and H. Devere (eds), *The Challenge to Friendship in Modernity*, London: Frank Cass.

Nagel, Thomas (1979), 'Moral Luck', in *Mortal Questions*, New York: Cambridge University Press.

Nestor, Pauline (1985), *Female Friendships and Communities*, Oxford: Clarendon Press.

Nietzsche, Friedrich [1887] (1974), 'Star Friendship', in *The Gay Science*, trans. Walter Kaufmann, New York: Vintage Books.

Nussbaum, Martha (1986), *The Fragility of Goodness*, 2nd edn, Cambridge: Cambridge University Press.

Nussbaum, Martha (1990), *Love's Knowledge: Essays on Philosophy and Literature*, New York: Oxford University Press.

Nussbaum, Martha (2001), *Upheavals of Thought – The Intelligence of Emotions*, Cambridge: Cambridge University Press.

Oakeshott, Michael (1972), 'On Being Conservative', in Oakeshott, *Rationalism in Politics: And Other Essays*, London: Methuen.

Pakaluk, Michael (ed.), *Other Selves: Philosophers on Friendship*, Indianopolis: Hackett.

Paton, H. J. (1993), 'Kant on Friendship', in Neera Kapur Badhurar (ed.), *Friendship – A Philosophical Reader*, Ithaca, NY: Cornell University Press.

Plato [388 BC?] (1973), *The Collected Dialogues*, Bollingen Series LXXI, Edith Hamilton and Huntington Cairns (eds), Princeton, NJ: Princeton University Press.

Price, A. W. (1990), *Love and Friendship in Plato and Aristotle*, Oxford: Clarendon Press.

Ricoeur, Paul (1981), *Hermeneutics and the Human Sciences – Essays on Language, Action and Interpretation*, John B. Thompson (ed.), New York: Cambridge University Press.

Ricoeur, Paul (1983), 'On Interpretation', in Alan Montefiore (ed.), *Philosophy in France Today*, Cambridge: Cambridge University Press.

Ricoeur, Paul (1994), 'Imagination in Discourse and Action', in Gillian Robinson and John Rundell (eds), *Rethinking Imagination*, London: Routledge.

Rorty, Amélie O. (1980), 'Explaining Emotions', in Amélie Rorty (ed.), *Explaining Emotions*, Berkeley, CA: University of California Press.

Russo, Elena (1997), 'The Self, Real and Imaginary: Social Sentiment in Marivaux and Hume', in Elena Russo (ed.), *Yale French Studies*, No. 92: *Exploring the Conversible World*, New Haven, CT: Yale University Press.

Sartre, Jean-Paul (1956), *Being and Nothingness*, trans. Hazel Barnes, New York: Washington Square Press.

Sartre, Jean-Paul [1948] (1960), *Intimacy*, trans. L. Alexander, New York: Berkley.

Sartre, Jean-Paul (1968), *Search for a Method*, New York: Vintage Books.

Schutz, Alfred (1973), *Collected Papers. I: The Problem of Social Reality*, Maurice Natanson (ed.), The Hague: Martinus Nijhoff.

Selman, Robert (1981), 'The Child as Friendship Philosopher', in S. R. Asher and J. M. Gottman (eds), *The Development of Children's Friendship*, Cambridge: Cambridge University Press.

Seneca [AD 63–5] (1991), 'On Philosophy and Friendship – Epistle IX', in Michael Pakaluk (ed.), *Other Selves: Philosophers on Friendship*, Indianapolis: Hackett.

Sharp, Ronald (1968), *Friendship and Literature: Spirit and Form*, Durham, NC: Duke University Press.

Sherman, Nancy (1997), *Making a Necessity of Virtue*, Cambridge: Cambridge University Press.

Simmel, Georg (1950), *The Sociology of Georg Simmel*, trans. K. H. Wolff, New York: Free Press.

Solomon, Robert C. (1977), 'The Logic of Emotion', *Noûs*, Vol. 11.

Spinoza, Benedict [1677] (1955), *The Ethics*, trans. R. H. M. Elwes, New York: Dover.

Steer, A. G. (1990), *Goethe's Elective Affinities – The Robe of Nessus*, Heidelberg: Carl Winter, Universitätsverlag.

Stern-Gillet, Suzanne (1995), *Aristotle's Philosophy of Friendship*, Albany, NY: State University of New York Press.

Stocker, Michael (1987), 'Duty and Friendship: Toward a Synthesis of Gilligan's Contrastive Moral Concepts', in Eva Feder Kittay and Diana T. Meyers (eds), *Women and Moral Theory*, Totowa, NJ: Rowan & Littlefield.

Stocker, Michael (1990), 'Friendship and Duty: Some Difficult Relations', in Owen Flanagan and Amélie Rorty (eds), *Identity, Character, and Morality – Essays in Moral Psychology*, Cambridge, MA: MIT Press.

Taylor, L. R. (1968), *Party Politics in the Age of Caesar*, Los Angeles: University of California Press.

Telfer, Elizabeth (1991), 'Friendship', in Michael Pakaluk (ed.), *Other Selves: Philosophers on Friendship*, Indianapolis: Hackett.

Tonkin, Boyd (1983), 'Right Approaches: Sources of the New Conservatism', *Proceedings of the Conference Confronting the Crisis: War, Politics and Culture in the Eighties*, Essex, July.

Turnbull, Colin M. (1973), *The Mountain People*, New York: Simon & Schuster.

Winnicott, D. W. (1966), *The Maturational Processes and the Facilitating Environment*, New York: International Universities Press.

Winnicott, D. W. [1986] (1990), *Home Is Where We Start From*, Clare Winnicott, Ray Shepherd and Madeleine Davis (eds), London: Penguin.

Wittgenstein, Ludwig [1953] (1978), *Philosophical Investigations*, Part I, trans. G. E. M. Anscombe, 3rd edn, New York: Macmillan.

Index